Government Paternalism

Government Paternalism

Nanny State or Helpful Friend?

Julian Le Grand and Bill New

Princeton University Press
Princeton & Oxford

Contents

Preface

A few years ago, one of us (Julian Le Grand) had the privilege of being seconded to No. 10 Downing Street to work as the health policy adviser to the then prime minister, Tony Blair. On the second day of his appointment, he got into an argument with the secretary of state for health, John Reid. The previous day Le Grand had been discussing with the prime minister the possibility of banning smoking in public places, a policy that had been successfully implemented in California and was coming into force in Ireland. Tony Blair was interested in the idea, although he indicated that, as in the United States, it might be better left to local, rather than central, governments to decide.

In contrast, the secretary of state was unhappy with the idea of a ban on smoking in pubs and restaurants. He was on public record as having pointed out that smoking was one of the few pleasures left to poor and disadvantaged people in our society, and he was reluctant to add to their burdens. However, he did accept that there was a problem of passive smoking—of damage to people's health from the inadvertent inhaling of others' cigarette smoke—and had some suggestions for dealing with it. For instance, why not set aside a room in every pub or restaurant reserved entirely for smokers? They would have to carry in their own drink and food—no bar or restaurant staff (the chief victims of passive smoking) could enter. But, once in the room, smokers could smoke to their hearts' content, being able to enjoy the activity without disturbing anyone else and, crucially, only putting themselves at risk of harm.

Le Grand found this suggestion difficult to counter. He felt instinctively that the health dangers associated with smoking are so great that all smokers should be discouraged from smoking, and that anything putting significant barriers in their way—and there was little doubt that banning smoking in the principal public areas for social activities for all would indeed be a significant barrier—was desirable. On the other hand, he recognized that we do live in a society that values individual autonomy and freedom. The secretary of state was far from alone in disliking the paternalism implicit in the smoking ban proposal. Those advocating the ban, including Le Grand, had received voluminous correspondence decrying the "nanny state" and pointing to the dangers of infantilizing the population by treating them as children incapable of making their own decisions. The critics argued that, if people knew about the risks of smoking but nonetheless judged that the pleasure they got from the activity outweighed those risks, then, if no one else were harmed, why should they not indulge in the activity? Did the government really have a right to intervene to save people from themselves? Was government paternalism justified? Or was John Stuart Mill right when he argued in his famous book *On Liberty* that the only legitimate reason for governments to intervene in an individual's behavior was to prevent harm to others, and that to promote the individual's own good was "not sufficient warrant" to justify such intervention?

The policy of banning smoking in public places in England was eventually implemented, though not until several years later, after Le Grand had stepped down as policy adviser and there was a different secretary of state. But since then issues involving questions about paternalistic government similar to those raised by the smoking ban have moved up the policy agenda. Obesity, apparently driven by individuals' eating too much and exercising too little, is on the rise. Life expectancy has increased dramatically, but people are not saving enough for their pensions during their working lives; too many of them look as though they are going to have a long old age but a miserable one mired in poverty. And there have been a number of well-publicized cases where terminally ill patients were denied the right to die, or to be helped to die, at the time and place of their own choosing—despite often impassioned pleas from themselves and their caregivers. In each of these cases, as with the smoking ban, the key question was: what should be the role of the state or, more precisely, the role of the government of the state? Is it part of the role of the government to try to restrict the amount or type of food that people eat? Should it compel people to save for their pensions? Should it prosecute friends and relatives who help the terminally ill kill themselves?

Bill New wrote his PhD thesis on the general topic of state paternalism and published a seminal article based on the thesis in the highly ranked journal *Economics and Philosophy* (New 1999). In discussion it seemed to both New and Le Grand that the time was right for a development of their ideas to see if they could successfully meet what might be thought of as the John Stuart Mill challenge: are there circumstances in which the individual's own good *is* sufficient warrant to justify a paternalistic intervention? If so, what are those circumstances, and how best might the government intervene?

This book is the result of that collaboration. We should assure the impatient reader that we do not duck the challenge. In fact, we argue that Mill was wrong. There are circumstances when it is legitimate for a government to act paternalistically; moreover, there are ways of doing so that do not suffer, or suffer only minimally, from the erosion of autonomy that many associate with the nanny state. However, the route to that conclusion goes through some dense forest, and we ask for the reader's indulgence in allowing us to try to clear out a good deal of undergrowth on the way.

In writing this book we have incurred too many debts fully to list here. But we must particularly thank Jonathan Roberts, who has read and edited the whole manuscript and made invaluable suggestions for improvement. We are also most grateful to Albert Weale, David Owen, and two anonymous referees who also read the whole manuscript and made extremely helpful suggestions, almost all of which we have taken on board. We have had useful discussions with many people on the topics that form the central thesis of the book, among whom we should mention particularly Robert Goodin, Tony Hockley, Adam Oliver, and Matthew Rabin. And we do appreciate the patience of our editors at Princeton University Press, who have waited an unconscionably long time for the final manuscript to emerge.

Government Paternalism

Government Patent Policy

1 Introduction

Should smoking be banned? Is it right for governments to prosecute those who help the terminally ill to kill themselves? Should individuals be compelled to save for their old age? Why do most countries require their citizens to wear seat belts in a car? Why do they also require motorcycle riders to wear helmets? Should sadomasochistic sexual practices between consenting adults be made illegal? Is it appropriate for government to regulate the content of popular foods so as to tackle the growth in obesity in the population?

All these are examples of what is becoming one of the major social questions of the twenty-first century: should the government save people from themselves? More specifically, are there circumstances when the state, or the government of the state, should intervene to protect individuals from the possibly damaging consequences of their own decisions, even if those decisions affect only themselves, and even if the individuals concerned made the decisions while in full possession of their faculties and of all the relevant information? In other words, can government paternalism be justified?

The debate does not stop there. Even if it could be demonstrated that there is a case for saving people from themselves, are there not serious risks involved in allowing the government to be the agent of paternalism? Does this not create a "nanny state," invading the autonomy of the individuals concerned and potentially infantilizing them? Or, yet worse, by legitimizing a paternalistic government, are we actually creating a potentially tyrannical state, justifying its intervention in every aspect of our lives?

Finally, even if all these risks were accepted and it was agreed that a paternalistic intervention was called for, what form should that intervention take? There are a variety of ways the government can affect individual behavior: banning or otherwise legally restricting potentially damaging behavior; taxing it; or the currently fashionable idea of "nudging" or reframing the choices that individuals face. Do all these have an equal impact on individual freedom and autonomy—or are some less dangerous than others?

This book is an attempt to answer some of these questions. It begins with issues of definition. Before discussing possible justifications for paternalism, it is necessary to specify what is meant by the term. How should it be defined? What different kinds of paternalism can be identified? The book then considers the extent of paternalism, examining some current forms of government policy to see the extent to which their rationale or consequences may be described as wholly or partly paternalistic. Following these preliminaries, the book then addresses the central question as to whether government paternalism can be justified, and, if so, in what circumstances. In light of those justifications, we then examine some aspects of paternalism in practice, or what might be termed the policy and politics of paternalism.

More specifically, chapter 2 discusses the strengths and weaknesses of the various definitions of paternalism and paternalistic policies that political philosophers and others have put forward. These definitions usually have three components: there is interference in the individual's freedom; the intention of such interference is the promotion of the individual's own good; and there is an absence of individual consent. We argue that all these components present conceptual difficulties, but the major problem is with the first. Some forms of policies that seem undeniably paternalistic, such as opera subsidies or the newly fashionable nudge ideas derived from so-called libertarian paternalism, do not obviously interfere with individual freedom. In fact in such cases, as indeed in all cases of government paternalism, the essential characteristic is the government mistrusting the individual's judgment. It does not believe that, without the intervention, the individual will make the "right" decision—"right" in terms of promoting the individual's own good, at least as the government perceives it. Without this intervention, the individual's judgment, and the behavior resulting from that judgment, will fail to promote her own good, or at least not as much as that good would be promoted through the intervention. It therefore seems preferable to define paternalism, not in terms of the intervention itself or of its consequences, but in terms of (a failure of) individual judgment; and so we propose a definition of our own that does not refer to coercion but instead incorporates this view of the government's intention. In brief, we conclude that government intervention is paternalistic with respect to an individual if it is intended (a) to address a failure of judgment by that individual and (b) to further the individual's own good.

Chapter 3 discusses some of the confusions in the literature over the different terminologies used to describe various kinds of paternalism. We distinguish between a number of different types. Of these the most important is between *ends*- and *means*-related paternalism: that is, between paternalistic interventions whose intention is to replace the individual's judgment because the government does not approve of the individual's *ends*—the aims or outcomes that he seeks to achieve—and paternalistic interventions that arise because the government perceives problems with the judgment that the individual has made concerning the *means* that are appropriate for achieving those ends and intervenes to assist the individual to overcome these problems and thus better to achieve his own ends. This distinction is important because later in the book (chapter 5) we argue that only means-related paternalism can be justified, and that ends-related paternalism has no place in a liberal democracy.

Chapter 4 discusses the prevalence of paternalistic elements in existing government policies. It argues that many of the justifications conventionally put forward for such policies—whether derived from the economic theory of market failure that identify interventions to achieve social efficiency or from various theories of equity or social justice—seem insufficient to justify both the scale of the government intervention and the form that the intervention takes. Hence it is not unreasonable to suppose that in these cases a strong element of paternalistic motivation is involved.

The book then moves into normative territory. It examines whether paternalism can ever be justified, and, if so, in what form and in what circumstances. Chapter 5 discusses arguments over paternalism derived from considerations of individual well-being. It points to an increasing volume of evidence from behavioral economics and psychology of what we term "reasoning failure": the fact that individuals, in trying to achieve the end of improving their well-being, often make mistakes and do so in a systematic way. It considers four possible sources for such failure: limited technical ability, limited experience or imagination, limited willpower, and limited objectivity. The existence of these forms of reasoning failure means that there is an opening for *means-related* paternalism; that is, for paternalistic interventions that improve or replace the means by which individuals obtain their ends.

However, there is no similar accumulation of evidence that individuals make mistakes over their ends; that is, over the factors that contribute to their well-being. Indeed, since such ends are essentially value-driven, it is hard to see what form such evidence might take. Hence chapter 5 concludes by rejecting *ends-related* paternalism—that is, paternalistic interventions designed to change or to replace individuals' ends or aims—but accepting the well-being case for *means-related* paternalism—that is, paternalistic interventions designed to help the individual to achieve her own ends when she does not have the means to do so as effectively herself.

Chapter 6 considers what is perhaps the major objection to all forms of paternalism, including means-related: that it harms or inappropriately restricts individual autonomy. This is often characterized in terms of the "nanny state": the state is seen to treat its citizens as a nanny treats her charges, instead of as autonomous adults. If a paternalistic policy has a deleterious impact on an individual's autonomy, then this adversely affects her citizenship rights. In addition, psychological theory suggests that it may also damage her well-being and her intrinsic motivation to change her behavior in the areas affected. At the extreme, the argument asserts that treating people like children turns them into children.

The chapter assesses the arguments of the "soft paternalists" who endeavor to overcome these challenges by arguing that the individuals affected in fact have little autonomy to be violated. We demonstrate that, in almost all cases of paternalistic interventions, there is indeed an impact on autonomy, actual or perceived, and the nanny state challenge cannot be avoided in this fashion. However, unless an individual's autonomy is regarded as an absolute right never to be violated, that is not the end of the argument. Rather, we need to trade off how much we are willing to allow the government to intervene in people's autonomy against the amount of good (in terms of well-being) that can be promoted or harm prevented as a result of an intervention. This judgment in turn rests on the extent to which we believe that people actually fail to make adequate judgments in their own interests. This will inevitably result in the need to trade off the value of well-being against the value of autonomy in different situations. If a specific means-related paternalistic intervention delivers a large gain in an individual's well-being with only a minor infringement of the individual's autonomy, then the intervention is probably justified; but one involving a small gain in well-being but a severe diminution of autonomy is likely to be unacceptable.

Chapter 7 focuses on a significant recent development that relates directly to the trade-off between well-being and paternalism: that of so-called libertarian or asymmetric paternalism and the associated nudge policies. These are government interventions that seek to change the context in which people make choices—the "choice architecture," in the term of their principal proponents, Richard Thaler and Cass Sunstein (2008, 3)—so as to nudge them to make decisions in the direction that the government wants. Examples include the automatic enrollment of employees in pension plans, so that individuals who do not wish to participate in these plans have to make a conscious decision to opt out of them; an opt-out organ donation scheme where, instead of people having to carry a card to indicate their willingness to donate their organs in the event of a fatal accident, they have to carry a card to signal that they are *un*willing; and the positioning of healthy foods in a cafeteria so that they are the first item that customers encounter, not the last. All these can lead to substantial changes in individual behavior, with far more employees saving appropriately for their old age, with many more organs becoming available for donation, and with people eating more healthfully. Yet they appear to achieve these changes without affecting autonomy or freedom, since they leave the actual choices that people face untouched.

Critics of nudge policies have disputed the contention that they have no impact on autonomy, claiming that they work best when they are unperceived, and hence that they involve a degree of trickery or deception that inevitably reduces autonomy. We address these criticisms in the chapter, arguing that they can be partly resolved by introducing various transparency mechanisms. We conclude that at least some nudge policies can indeed significantly raise well-being and can do so with only minor infringements of autonomy.

Ultimately, the usefulness of all these arguments (as indeed of any philosophical argument) will depend on how they "cash out" in practice. Chapter 8 assesses actual paternalistic policies, some of which are already in place, some of which are proposed, against the criteria we have put forward to assess: the impact on well-being and on autonomy. We examine three areas where paternalistic interventions could be (and/or have been) considered: smoking, pensions, and assisted suicide. In the cases of pensions and smoking, we argue that there is evidence of significant reasoning failure and that therefore some form of intervention is justified, provided that the impact on autonomy can be minimized. Of the possible forms of intervention in those areas, we consider legally restrictive interventions, financial incentives, and libertarian paternalistic proposals. We conclude that restrictions tend to score badly overall, but that financial incentives and the opt-in/opt-out plans score well. With respect to assisted suicide, we argue that there is relatively little evidence of reasoning failure for the individuals concerned, and hence that paternalistic intervention to prevent assistance is not justified.

Chapter 9 considers what might be termed the politics of paternalism. In previous chapters we demonstrate that there is a case for paternalistic intervention by the government to address individual reasoning failure, and we describe ways in which this may be done to maximize the benefits of intervention in terms of improving individual well-being while minimizing the cost in terms of the impact on individual autonomy. However, these contributions on their own are not enough to provide an unanswerable case for paternalistic interventions in every situation of individual reasoning failure. For that would require demonstrating that, in the relevant circumstances, the government *can* make better decisions than the individual, and also that it *will* do so. Neither of these is obviously correct. The government, after all, is not some abstract benevolent entity but is itself a collection of individuals—politicians, civil servants, and advisers—who interact with one another in a variety of ways. These individuals are likely to be subject to the kinds of reasoning failure that we have previously ascribed to some of the people engaging in self-damaging behavior. Even if they are not subject to such failures, they may have their own agenda, being rather more concerned with maximizing their own well-being than with the well-being of the citizens whose interests they are supposed to be serving. In terms of a metaphor that one of us has used elsewhere, some may be self-interested knaves, not public-spirited knights (Le Grand 2006).

Chapter 9 argues that the government can indeed raise the well-being of individuals who suffer from reasoning failure, even when allowance is made for possible reasoning failure among those individuals who constitute the government. However, democratic mechanisms must be put in place to ensure that the latter do not pursue their own agenda and turn the paternalistic state into an instrument of authoritarianism. In particular, we argue for a retrospective endorsement of the policy concerned, with either a vote taken in the representative assembly or a referendum.

The final chapter summarizes the book's arguments and uses them to address what might be viewed as the central questions with which we have been grappling: Is a paternalistic government necessarily a nanny state that infantilizes its citizens and illegitimately erodes their autonomy? Or could it be a helpful friend that promotes their well-being at minimal, if any, cost to autonomy? For the answers to these questions, read on.

2 What Is Paternalism?

A simple definition of paternalism is the interference by some outside agent in a person's freedom for the latter's own good. It describes an action deemed impermissible by John Stuart Mill's classic statement of the liberal position in *On Liberty*: "the only purpose for which power can be rightfully exercised over any member of a civilised community, against his will, is to prevent harm to others. His own good, either physical or moral, is not a sufficient warrant" (Mill 1974/1859, 68).

Paraphrasing Mill, this states that the only justification for state intervention in an individual's freedom is if that person is inflicting or is about to inflict harm on another; intervention designed to promote the individual's own good is never justified.

As is apparent, the simple definition of paternalism above has two elements that, taken together, offend this principle—the interference in freedom, and the promotion of a person's good. Very often a third element, the absence of consent, is included in definitions of paternalism to accommodate Mill's reference to the exercise of power against the individual's will.

But each of these three elements is controversial. Defining paternalism has not proved straightforward; certainly no consensus has emerged in the philosophical literature (Garren 2006). One reason for the lack of consensus is that how one defines paternalism will affect how easy it is to justify (or reject) what one has defined. A narrow definition will omit many acts that a broader definition might include as paternalistic. So someone adopting a narrow definition will be able to reject "paternalism" completely while at the same time supporting an interference in an individual's freedom that would have been included within a broader definition.[1] Questions of definition are intimately bound up with questions of justification.

---

1 For example (and as we shall discuss further below), some authors support only "soft" paternalism but then go on to describe this as "really no kind of paternalism at all" (Feinberg 1986, 16). This leaves "real" or "hard" paternalism as a narrower set of interventions that can be rejected outright.

Another reason for a lack of consensus is that people will inevitably perceive and interpret words in subtly different ways, particularly when discussing abstract terms such as freedom, autonomy, good, and consent. Further, no matter how carefully one tries to define a concept, a real-life example may not neatly and unambiguously fall within or without a definitional boundary. This has led to some highly complex definitions with many conditions, provisos, and ruminations on semantic matters. We will discuss many of these complexities before offering a simple definition that nevertheless captures what we see as the essence of paternalism—not a description of the act but rather the *reason* for acting paternalistically.

Our focus in this book is on public policy and thus on the actions of the government as the paternalist agency. Much of the philosophical literature, by contrast, is concerned with paternalism in the context of interactions and relationships between private individuals. The two scenarios raise quite different issues. We shall be concentrating on the government as paternalist; however, inevitably we draw on the rich tradition of debate about individual paternalism, and, where appropriate, we will point out where the government fits into this definitional debate.

But first we must examine in some detail the three controversial elements in existing definitions of paternalism: the interference in freedom; the promotion of good; and the question of consent.

The Interference in Freedom

Gerald Dworkin (1972, 65) has provided one of the most commonly cited definitions of paternalism: the "interference with a person's liberty of action justified by reasons referring exclusively to the welfare, good, happiness, needs, interests or values of the person being coerced."[2] Similarly, John Kleinig (1983, 18) defines paternalism as where "X acts to diminish Y's freedom, to the end that Y's good may be secured," a definition quoted and implicitly endorsed by Sarah Conly (2013, 17).[3] This definition focuses on liberty or freedom of action, understood as the absence of constraints.[4] One's physical liberty is most obviously interfered with by coercion, as Dworkin implies; if one is held up at gunpoint and offered the option of "your money or your life," for example, that is not normally considered a

---

2   Dworkin's article is perhaps the seminal piece in the modern debate on paternalism; it was originally published in Wasserstrom (1971).

3   In her important recent book, Conly actually argues for a stronger form of paternalism—what she terms coercive paternalism. We address some of her arguments in chapter 6.

4   "Liberty" is sometimes taken to refer specifically to political freedoms, although we do not imply that connotation here. See Feinberg (1986, 62–68) for a discussion of the various types of de jure and de facto liberty and freedom.

"free" choice. However, following Dworkin's article, a number of commentators noted that many kinds of interference often associated with paternalism do not restrict freedom (Gert and Culver 1976; Weale 1978). Gert and Culver provide the example of someone admitted to the hospital in need of a blood transfusion. It transpires that the person is a member of a religious sect that does not allow transfusions. While still conscious, the injured person informs the doctors of his wish not to be transfused before lapsing into a coma. If the doctors now proceed with the transfusion, they might be considered to be acting paternalistically, but they are clearly not interfering with the liberty of someone who, at the point of interference, is incapable of making decisions of any kind.

There are, of course, libertarian objections here to the doctors' failure to take account of the wishes of the patient, which could be viewed to be as offensive to liberty or freedom as an explicit act of coercion, and these we shall consider shortly. But the central point here is that it is possible to undertake a paternalistic act without any immediate coercion.

Numerous other examples have been offered of non–freedom-restricting paternalism. We may act paternalistically by declining to play tennis with a friend who is becoming upset at the frequency with which she is losing—or, rather more subtly, we may even allow the friend to win without letting her know what we are doing. In both cases we seek to improve the friend's well-being in a more or less paternalistic way. In another scenario, a doctor may not tell a terminally ill man that his daughter has just died following a road accident when he asks after her well-being (even if he specifically demands to know the worst). A converse case would also be paternalistic: telling the man that his daughter has died even if he specifically asks to remain in ignorance. Examples of these kinds often occur in the context of health care, where decisions need to be made as to whether it would be in a patient's interests to be informed of her medical condition regardless of her wishes.[5] Again, in none of these examples is there interference with an individual's liberty in any normal understanding of the term. Nevertheless, in all cases the actions of the paternalist influence the way that the recipient of the paternalism decides to conduct his or her life and probably also his or her sense of self-esteem or even happiness.

This led Gert and Culver (1976, 49) to suggest that paternalism occurs whenever an action, as well as being for the good of the paternalized individual, "involves violating a moral rule" with regard to the paternalized person. This adequately encompasses some of the cases above: the doctor and tennis player could be said to be breaking a moral rule of respect for another person's wishes and perhaps also honesty. However, some paternalistic acts do

---

5 See Buchanan (1983); further examples are discussed in Gert and Culver (1976) and G. Dworkin (1983).

not obviously break any moral rules. For example, it would be difficult to describe as immoral a householder's decision to lock up all the drugs in his apartment when a suicidal friend comes to stay—even if the friend specifically asks where they are. The drugs are the householder's property and he can do what he wishes with them (Dworkin 1983). And yet the action still seems paternalistic. Referring to "moral rules" does not ultimately succeed in pinning down the precise nature of a paternalist intervention.

If apparently paternalistic acts do not always restrict liberty, it should be equally clear that paternalism does not necessarily involve coercion. None of the individuals subject to paternalism in these examples are being threatened with any punishment if they fail to act in a certain way. However, it is possible to engage in a form of coercion *without* restricting liberty. To give patients verbal information about their condition against their will is a form of coercion—they are being "forced" to listen to bad news for their own good—but it does not restrict their freedom.[6] However, it does interfere with their *autonomy.* This is a concept that will preoccupy us a great deal in this book and for which, unfortunately, there is no simple, widely accepted definition. But at root it is an idea that emphasizes human beings' capacity for self-rule, their ability to act as deliberating agents. People may find their autonomy restricted through ill health or intoxication, while at the same time they retain the complete freedom to act. In chapter 6 we consider in detail a justification of paternalism that depends on the idea of compromised autonomy: if one has lost the capacity for self-rule, then many apparently paternalistic interventions, so it is argued, are not really paternalism at all. We will challenge this account and argue that interference in autonomy is not so easily avoided. In any event, autonomy is crucial to an understanding of paternalism; and for the purposes of the present discussion, it may be understood simply as the ability to formulate and act out one's own conception of the way one's life should go.

Gerald Dworkin (1983, 107) sought to broaden his 1972 definition of paternalism by suggesting that it is this interference with autonomy that is the crucial aspect of the concept. For paternalism to be present, "there must be a violation of a person's autonomy (which I conceive as a distinct notion from that of liberty). . . . There must be a usurpation of decision-making, either by preventing people from doing what they have decided or by interfering with the way in which they arrive at their decisions."

Thus interference in autonomy could involve coercion, omission (withholding information, refusing to cooperate), and manipulation or deceit (misinformation or trickery). So, for example, when we refuse to play tennis

---

6 Unless one believes that someone can be "free" from unwanted information. It seems more sensible, and clearer, to understand this compulsory information as burdening the patients rather than making them less free.

with an increasingly depressed opponent, we are interfering with her autonomy, not because we simply do not want to play with her—it cannot be a claim of her autonomy that we *must* play tennis with her—but because we judge, unlike her, that playing more tennis will serve to increase her unhappiness. We are taking a position on *her* autonomous judgment by rejecting her desire to play tennis with us even though we normally enjoy doing so. The point is that her judgment is being usurped by our judgment.

In two more recent contributions to the debate on the definition of paternalism, Archard and Clarke reformulate this emphasis on autonomy by simply requiring that a "choice or opportunity to choose is denied or diminished" (Archard 1990b, 36) or that one person "aims to close an option that would otherwise be open" to another (Clarke 2002, 82).[7] Clarke argues that his (and to some extent Archard's) definition should be preferred to Dworkin's because the latter definition is too narrow: some paternalism does not usurp autonomous decision making, as revealed in the case of the unconscious patient being treated by a doctor discussed above. Clarke argues that there is no autonomy to usurp, and yet the treatment is still paternalist.

It seems questionable, however, whether there is no autonomy to usurp if the patient has explicitly given his views prior to lapsing into unconsciousness. It is precisely because the patient communicated his wishes that the treatment is controversial. But we have a more significant reason for, in the end, preferring Dworkin's emphasis on the *judgment* of the individual rather than whether options have been closed off: to explain why, it will be convenient to introduce the government into the definitional debate.

It is easy to conceive of the government acting in a manner similar to the various examples given above. It can clearly coerce people with a threat of sanctions by, for example, fining motorcyclists who refuse to wear helmets, or imprisoning unlicensed doctors. It can withhold information from people by, for example, restricting the release of controversial research, or it can force them to consume information they may not want to receive.[8] And the government can tax or subsidize certain goods to make them less or more

---

7   Clarke adds that where someone chooses on behalf of someone else "in the event that [they] are unable to choose" for themselves, this is also paternalist, thus including decisions made on behalf of unconscious people.

8   In 2007 the British government proposed that all parents should be informed of their child's weight and told whether this weight constituted a dangerous level of obesity. While in the proposed policy parents are allowed to opt out of receiving the letter, the receipt of such information could be made compulsory, in the sense that a letter might be written to the parent whether or not the parent wished to have the information. Short of throwing the letter away without reading it, the parent would be coerced into receiving the information. Similarly, Shiffrin (2000, 214) suggests it is paternalistic to provide someone with a wider range of options against her will (perhaps because the individual considers she has too much choice already) even if this is technically "freedom-enhancing."

attractive. These "freedom/autonomy-coercion" combinations are shown in table 2.1.

The government can also manipulate people's decision making in ways that do not obviously fit into any one category. It can use shock tactics such as obliging manufacturers to place lurid images of diseases on cigarette packets. Or it can manipulate an individual's default position, for example, by automatically enrolling people into a national contributory pension scheme rather than leaving them to choose to opt in. We will revisit these examples in more detail.

Now it is moot whether manipulating information is closing off an option. Certainly, changing the default position seems to alter the nature of an option rather than closing it off. More clearly, where the state subsidizes goods or services it serves to *increase* the options available to individual consumers. For example, if the government makes the provision of museums or art galleries free, the individual now has a greater range of opportunities than he did before because he can now afford to go to a museum or gallery without sacrificing other pleasures.[9] And yet this, along with the other interventions just mentioned, seems intuitively paternalistic.

Some authors dissent from this intuitive position about the paternalism of specific subsidies. Archard (1990b, 37) describes a situation where a secret patron, P, provides free tickets for Q to attend various activities—including the opera—which P believes will be for Q's good, but which she suspects Q would not choose to buy ordinarily. Archard notes that it would "sound perverse to describe P's behaviour with regard to Q as paternalist" precisely because P is *adding* to the set of choices Q already has.[10] However, Archard acknowledges that P may have a paternalist *reason* for behaving as she does, even if—in his view—the effect is not paternalistic. But it no longer sounds perverse to describe the behavior as paternalistic if one accepts that P's reason is crucial: P will act in this way only if she believes there is something wrong with Q's judgment. That is where the paternalism comes in.

Now it could be argued that specific subsidies do involve coercion or the closing off of options because the subsidies have to be financed by taxation. Since taxation inevitably involves coercion, or the threat of coercion, and since it reduces the resources that taxpayers have available for private consumption, it also involves the coercive closing off of options. Should we not

9   This also applies to individual contexts. Archard (1990b) cites the example of an elderly relative using the terms of his will to persuade a young relative not to marry a certain unfavored person or else lose a substantial financial inheritance. The fact that the offer of the inheritance effectively increases the range of options open to the legatee does not alter its paternalistic nature.

10   Not all agree with this suggestion. Hershey (1985) takes the view that giving a financial donation to an individual without the person knowing *is* paternalistic even if it does *not* violate autonomy.

Table 2.1. Types of Intervention

	Coercive	Noncoercive
Freedom-restricting	Laws obliging helmets to be worn on motorcycles, or for doctors to be formally licensed	N/a—impossible to restrict freedom without being coercive
Non–freedom-restricting	Obliging people to receive information regardless of their wishes	"Sin" taxes; public subsidies of museums and the opera; withholding findings of state conducted scientific research
Non–autonomy-interfering	N/a—all interventions interfere with autonomy to some degree, if only to increase autonomy (as perhaps with public subsidies)	

view the policy concerned as a subsidy-tax combination, and hence, since the method of finance does involve coercion and the closing of options, could we not describe it as paternalistic for that reason? Here there are a number of points. First, subsidies need not be financed from taxation; they could also be financed from government borrowing or even printing money, neither of which obviously involves coercion. Putting the point another way, suppose we could unambiguously demonstrate that, say, the method of government financing of a subsidy to opera was shifted from taxation to printing money; surely this would not imply that the subsidy had in some way ceased to be paternalistic? More generally, the method of financing a subsidy policy has to be irrelevant to determining whether that policy is actually paternalistic; so, too, how the government uses the revenues from a potentially paternalistic tax, such as a tax on cigarettes, is irrelevant to the question as to whether the intention behind the imposition of the tax is actually paternalistic.[11]

11   In most countries, all forms of government revenue are pooled, and there are few or no hypothecated taxes. In such cases it is impossible to identify the specific source of revenue finances for an item of government expenditure. For further discussion of this point, though

A further problem with this argument about the source of finance is that there are two different sets of actors—taxpayers and service users—who may or may not be the same. The act of coercive taxation could be in part itself paternalistic, if the intention behind the taxation was to promote the taxpayer's own good (as with some taxes on tobacco or alcohol). The act of government subsidy is in itself paternalistic because it encourages service users to engage in one activity rather than another. In the first case, where the money goes to is irrelevant; in the second, where the money comes from is irrelevant.

In the subsidy case, it is more convincing to argue that the government activity seems paternalistic, even though it increases the individual's range of options, because the government is substituting its *judgment* for that of the individual.[12] It seeks to influence the way that the individual decides whether to go to museums. The government does not simply rely on ensuring that people's income levels are high enough to be able to afford entrance fees. Even in such circumstances, people's judgment may not lead them to choose a museum; their reasoning might be considered in some way insufficient. Only by making museums free can people be tempted to experience something they would otherwise neglect to the detriment of their well-being. Something similar is happening in all the other nongovernment examples: the tennis player is thought to misunderstand how losing at tennis is making her unhappy; the dying father is considered to have misjudged his decision to know the worst about his daughter; and so on.

The difficulty that arises from using phrases like "interfere with another" or "limitation on Q's autonomy"[13] in a definition is that there is simply too much ambiguity in what people understand by terms such as "interference" and "autonomy." Is subsidizing a theater production an interference in my autonomy? If the government fails to reveal unasked-for information, is there any effect on my autonomy? These examples may not feel like interference in the normal sense of the word, but even an expansion of my autonomy—if this is what the subsidy case amounts to—is a manipulation of the world in which I am making decisions. Surely this is an interference in, or even a limitation of, my autonomy in *some* sense? Also, not revealing the findings of research will affect the kind of decisions I am *capable* of making. Maybe these examples do constitute interference with something we call autonomy, or maybe not. Yet such ambiguity is unhelpful for definitional purposes.

---

in a different context (the assessment of the distributional impact of government spending), see Goodin and Le Grand (1987, chap. 2).

12   Here we follow Gerald Dworkin (1983, 107): "we must ascertain in each case whether the act in question constitutes an attempt to substitute one person's judgment for another's."

13   To use Gerald Dworkin's latest (2001) definitional foray.

But there is one final reason why it is preferable to focus on the poor reasoning or judgment of the individual in defining paternalism. We have seen that withholding or manipulating information, or supplying it when it has been specifically declined, can be paternalistic. But what if information is provided with no attempt to correct a judgment but merely to assist it? Take the sale of cigarettes. For many years the British government simply obliged manufacturers to state on the packet that "cigarettes can seriously damage your health." This was a piece of information that not everyone may have known. Such intervention thus helped people to make a judgment about whether to smoke. However, this kind of information provision does not call into question people's reasoning, even if in this case it is likely to deter rather than encourage the activity. Simply supplying the bald fact that cigarettes are dangerous is thus not, in this interpretation, paternalistic. Or consider an even less controversial example of a driver on a country road who is not aware of an approaching bend. He is not necessarily displaying limited reasoning if he crashes on that bend, as long as he was driving at a generally sensible speed for the conditions. He may simply have been unable to react fast enough. If the government introduces signs that warn of the impending bend, neither should this be considered paternalistic—the government would simply be improving the general supply of information about the conditions on that road.

Another way of thinking about this is to consider how it is possible to have poor information about a particular set of circumstances and yet still make a decision that maximizes well-being, given the information available. Having little information *in itself* does not impair our ability to reason.[14] Under these circumstances we must simply make a judgment about what to do given our knowledge as it stands—including, perhaps, not taking any course of action until the level or quality of information improves. One can make an analogy between human reasoning and the working of a computer. A computer can suffer from either limited or poor data (imperfect information) or corrupted, virus-ridden software (a possible case for paternalism). But an uncorrupted, well-functioning piece of software will not *in itself* be affected by the quality of the data, even if the usefulness of what it can produce will be. It will merely do the best it can with the information provided.

A famous example from John Stuart Mill ([1859] 1974, 166) reinforces the point. He described a situation in which a walker is about to cross an unsafe bridge. He argued that it would be reasonable for an official forcibly

14 Indeed, when an individual is in circumstances where there is very little information about what course of action to take—such as a trapped potholer or a kidnapped hostage—it is often observed that these individuals act with extraordinary mental clarity. Their minds work extremely well with limited distractions and maximize their chances of survival. This should be contrasted with someone overloaded with information—in the middle of a very busy and boisterous crowd, for example—where the consequence could be to panic.

to prevent the walker from crossing it if there "were no time to warn him of his danger"; otherwise "he ought, I conceive, to be only warned of the danger; not forcibly prevented from exposing himself to it." Mill was no paternalist, and he did not think providing information about the bridge, even forcibly, was paternalistic. The official is certainly intervening in the autonomy of the individual—in this case by preventing him from carrying out his decision to cross an unsafe bridge in ignorance of the bridge's condition—but is not acting paternalistically. The intervention becomes paternalistic only if the walker continues to be prevented from crossing the bridge once apprised of its condition and the risk he is about to take. By doing so, the intervening party is now making some implicit or explicit assessment about the poor-quality judgment being displayed by the walker. So by defining paternalism with reference to the judgment of the individual, rather than by describing the act itself, we avoid conflicting interpretations of what counts as an interference in autonomy.

Thus one key aspect of government paternalism is that it involves an intervention whose rationale is to address a failure of judgment or reasoning of an individual, at least as perceived by the government.[15] We should add that we are not *endorsing* government paternalism at this stage but simply trying to define the concept; the legitimacy of different kinds of paternalism is discussed later in the book.

Promoting the Good

It is central to the concept of paternalism that the intervention should be intended to further the good of the person whose judgment or reasoning ability is in question, rather than to further the good of anyone else.[16] Mill differentiated what have come to be known as "other-regarding" actions, which involve harm to others, from "self-regarding" actions, which do not, and which simply involve the individual herself acting in ways that only influence her own good. This distinction establishes the particular focus of paternalism as on actions that are self-regarding in Mill's terms—that is, actions that do not harm others. An individual's reasoning ability could be flawed and the state could act to protect others from the consequences of that person's failings, but this would not be paternalism.

15   Shiffrin (2000) is one of the few commentators who develops a definition with a similar emphasis on the motivational desire to correct or improve others' judgment. However, Shiffrin's definition contains an unusual rejection of the requirement—outlined in the next section—that the intervention should be, at least in part, for the good of that individual.

16   The good done often involves preventing harm but it may also positively promote benefit, the so-called benefit-conferring legal paternalism (Feinberg 1988, 311).

It is important to note at the outset that self-regarding actions may involve the cooperation of another person. Say I take out a loan at an exceptionally high rate of interest from a loan shark. Unless I have dependents of some kind, the decision to take out the loan is self-regarding—it harms or benefits no one else—but is undertaken through a consensual agreement with another person. If the government decides that I am likely to cause myself financial difficulties, it may outlaw such punitive interest rates. The person whose activity is restricted is the loan shark, but the prohibition on his activity is intended to prevent harm to me.

Nevertheless, the distinction between self- and other-regarding actions is not always clear-cut. Activities that have absolutely no influence on others—by giving offense or causing other types of unhappiness, for example—are few, if any.[17] Mill believed that we should not regard acts that we might find merely distasteful, such as fornication or gambling, as constituting harm to others. On the other hand, actions that are essentially self-regarding, such as getting drunk, might be viewed as potentially harmful in certain circumstances: for example, if someone predisposed to violence were to drink excessively, the government may be justified in intervening. The difficulties in establishing whether a government intervention can be justified on the basis that it is ultimately directed at behaviors that may harm others, rather than as a paternalistic intervention directed only toward the self-regarding actions of an individual, are examined in more detail in subsequent chapters.

We noted above that one element in the definition of paternalism is that it is concerned with correcting some shortcoming of an individual's judgment. The corollary of this is that the act (or omission) must also *benefit* a particular individual or group in some way relating to these shortcomings. But it should not do so merely as a side effect. Take a law designed to prevent a firm from polluting the local environment. This is a classic other-regarding harm, and the law is passed to protect the health of those third parties not involved with the business. However, the law may also serve to benefit the individual producing the pollution, to the extent that she too no longer breathes the smoke. However, this is not a paternalistic law as long as we have reason to believe that the law is intended only to benefit others. The distinction is important from a justificatory point of view: it would be odd to defend principles for a paternalistic outcome that was only a "side effect" of other laws.

Notwithstanding this proviso, one feature of paternalism universally acknowledged in the literature is that the intervention should seek to do good to the recipient and not harm. A government that acts cruelly or simply to sustain its own continuance is not acting paternalistically. So much is

---

17 Indeed Hart (1963, 5) suggests that "in an organised society it is impossible to identify classes of actions which harm no-one but the individual who does them."

uncontroversial. But we should not ignore the fact that there are a wide variety of ways in which people can in principle pursue their own good, not all of which might be obviously related to the individual's "happiness." One example would be a stoical action, such as the self-denial of material goods for reasons of a religious or spiritual nature. Amartya Sen, in particular, has argued that there are a number of ways in which people may act or choose in the world that do not seem to accord with traditional notions of well-being maximization. For example, someone who liked reading only the *Times* newspaper might feel the quality of his life was drastically reduced by a state that allowed him to read only that paper: he might give up reading it altogether because the intrinsic value of being able to choose what one wishes to read has been lost (Sen 1988). Or people may "commit" to certain acts—such as working hard or protecting the environment—even if they do not really "want" to and know that their well-being will be reduced as a result (Sen 1977, 2005). Perhaps the most controversial type of nonstandard well-being is that pertaining to moral well-being and the accompanying moral paternalism (Dworkin 2005). If the government acts to enforce morality, as long as this morality does not require or involve explicit and intentional harm to the interests of the individual, then it will be considered paternalistic rather than, say, merely cruel.

Moral paternalism is considered in more detail below. But in all these cases the "good" in question can involve valued things other than well-being per se. It will be assumed here that any interference in decisions relating to these valued things will not be discounted from the class of paternalistic actions merely because people appear to be acting in pursuit of nonwelfarist outcomes; it is enough that the interference appears to be subverting or restricting the pursuit of what the individual considers right for him or her.

The Question of Consent

The third characteristic commonly cited as being necessary for an act to be paternalistic is that, broadly speaking, there is a lack of consent. We say "broadly speaking" because the many authors who have tackled this issue have introduced subtleties into their definitions to which we cannot do justice here.[18] Nevertheless, it is a commonplace in the literature that some

18   How consent, or its absence, is characterized varies widely in the literature. Gert and Culver (1976, 50) require that paternalistic acts operate "independently of ... past, present, or immediately forthcoming (free, informed) consent"; Arneson (1980, 471) suggests that paternalistic interventions must be carried out "against [the paternalized's] present will ... or against his prior commitment"; Dworkin (1983, 106) stipulates that the person "who is being treated paternalistically does not wish to be treated that way"; VanDeVeer (1986) requires that an act or omission is contrary to the preferences of the recipient; Archard (1990b, 36) makes the point

reference is made to the fact that the individual has not acceded to the intervention.[19]

However, some authors disagree. Clarke, for example, argues that the consent clauses in all the aforementioned definitions of paternalism are redundant in his formulation, which, as we have seen, simply requires that the paternalist "aims to close an option that would otherwise be open . . . in order to promote [the paternalized's] good" (2002, 89). Clarke argues that as long as an option is closed off, this act constitutes paternalism whether the recipient of the act agrees to it, is indifferent to it, or even asks for it. For reasons already outlined, we prefer a definition that specifies that the intervention addresses reasoning or other cognitive failures rather than simply closes off options. Can we also dispense with the additional clause referring to consent?

Take the realm of individual private relationships first. If all interventions addressing shortcomings of reasoning or judgment are nonconsensual—as seems superficially plausible—then there would indeed be no need for the additional condition. How can we ever "agree" to have our reasoning interfered with? At any given time this would be logically incoherent. The individual would need to say to the intervener: "Ignore or confound the way I'm making this judgment and the decision I am now coming to." How should the potential paternalist establish which judgment or decision of such a person should be heeded?

However, it does make sense for someone to agree to have her *future* reasoning interfered with. In this case, she presumably realizes that her reasoning is going to become compromised in some way, and she wishes specifically to prepare for such an eventuality. Perhaps the most famous and oft-quoted example in all literature is that of Odysseus ordering his men to tie him to the mast of his ship and to ignore his pleas to release him to avoid the consequences of hearing the Sirens' song (having wisely told the crew to plug their own ears so that they are not affected). While Odysseus is tied to the mast, his men are interfering with his current reasoning by ignoring his

---

rather less directly, suggesting that "P [the paternalist] discounts Q's belief that P's behaviour does not promote Q's good"; and de Marneffe (2006, 73) suggests that the condition is that the paternalized "prefers [her] own situation when [her] choices are not limited" by the paternalist. Hershey (1985, 179) stipulates that the recipient's consent or dissent is not "a relevant consideration" for the paternalist. Interestingly he argues that the only extra condition for an act to be paternalistic is that it should be intended to benefit the recipient; however, this would allow the provision of cash redistribution to be counted as paternalistic.

19   Shiffrin (2000, 214) notes that simply requiring that an action is against someone's will—as did Mill—would allow for interventions that are unknown to an individual, such as having one's credit card destroyed before one received the letter containing it. In this case the individual did not will anything at all because he was ignorant of the opportunity to use the credit card coming his way. Nevertheless, the letter was his and the action was not done with his consent, rendering it paternalistic.

request to set him free. However, they are only ignoring his current entreaties because of his own previous order: it was *just this eventuality* that Odysseus had in mind when he made the original request. The refusal to obey his command does not seem paternalistic when viewed in this way because Odysseus's *prior* reasoning *is* being respected, and the earlier decision was directed at a situation when he knew his future reasoning would be compromised.[20]

In some ways the arena of government intervention is immune from these philosophical niceties. Laws apply to populations rather than individuals, and an individual cannot meaningfully consent to a law at the time of its enforcement—the law applies whether the individual consents or not. On the other hand, most laws and government policies are sufficiently controversial that there will always be some who oppose them. So we can be reasonably sure that laws will always fail to obtain the consent of some of those to whom they apply (and maybe to others too). This tends to make the definitional issue of consent redundant, at least for government paternalism.

This should not seduce us into believing that the issue of consent may not be important for the *justification* of a paternalistic law. For example, the law plays a significant role in allowing or disallowing various forms of contractual agreement between individuals. Take an individual who wishes to plan for the event of some terrible accident that leaves him severely brain damaged. This person may set out in a formal document such as a living will a wish to be helped to die. The government is not neutral in this process. It can allow such a document to stand and simply let the courts decide on whether the proposed action conforms to what was agreed, and whether the consent was genuine. Alternatively, it can disallow any such agreements that involve assisted deaths, whether apparently consensually agreed in advance or not.[21] In fact, contemporaneous consent may not be any less problematic: witness severely disabled people who wish to end their life when fully mentally competent but suffering from a physically degenerative disease. Current law in many countries does not allow such consensual acts. We may consider the law paternalistic if it is concerned with correcting the autonomous (prior) reasoning of the individual. Its status as paternalistic does not depend on

20   See Kleinig (1983, 56–58) for a general discussion of difficulties associated with prior consent. Unusually, Regan (1983) takes the view that ignoring Odysseus's cries to be released fails to acknowledge people's right to change their minds, and that as a result the "interference"—failing to set him free—needs to be justified on paternalistic grounds and not on the basis of prior commitment.

21   See Spellecy (2003) on the wider case for accepting as binding so-called Ulysses contracts (Ulysses being the Latin equivalent of the Greek Odysseus), and Richards (1992) for arguments in favor of living wills from an antipaternalist point of view; see also Davis (2002) for an argument against them in decisions relating to medical treatment.

whether people generally agree with such a law because laws will always have their opponents.[22] But whether such a law is *justified* will depend in part on our attitude toward the status of prior consent.

What about the effect of laws on that proportion of people who *do* agree with them? Are they still paternalistic for these individuals? Clarke would argue that their consent to the law is irrelevant. He gives as an example laws against prostitution that, according to his definition, are paternalistic even toward those who have no wish to engage in paying for sex. Many people consent to the measure or perhaps positively support it. But Clarke argues they are subject to an option being closed off for their own good; the law, for them, is still paternalistic. We would agree that consent is irrelevant, but according to our definition the law is *not* paternalistic because the autonomous reasoning of supportive people is not considered to be faulty.

A similar line of argument applies to those laws to which more or less everyone consents. Consider street lighting. It is not consent that excludes such public provision from the class of paternalistic interventions. The only way people can obtain public goods such as these is for the state to prevent free-riding and to oblige all those who can afford it to contribute to the cost. Thus the desires of the majority are not thwarted by a minority. A similar case is that of compulsorily providing information—say, that of the nutritional content of foods. Certainly not everyone is likely to consent, because providing accurate, clear information is not costless. Some individuals may object that the compulsory provision of information has pushed up the cost of the food. They would rather take their chances and pay the lower price. However, to accommodate these risk-takers, the state would be faced with the difficulty of providing information only to those who want it (and thus are willing to pay for it) and not to those who do not. This is not practical because those who do not pay will, again, free-ride on the benefit of the additional information.

We justify these kinds of intervention on the basis that they are devised to enable the majority to get what they want. The minority who oppose the law are not necessarily being treated paternalistically. Gerald Dworkin (1983, 110) cites the example of putting fluoride in the general water supply to improve the general state of dental health: "The restriction on the minority [who are obliged to drink fluoridated water] is not motivated by paternalistic considerations, but by the interests of a majority who wish to promote their own welfare."

---

22   It is logically possible for literally the whole population to whom a law applies to consent to that law in order that they might protect themselves from weakness of will—in other words, it is their own reasoning that is at fault, and they all recognize the problem. But this is sufficiently far-fetched to be ignored.

Even laws that are implemented for individuals' own good and that many oppose will not inevitably be paternalistic, for the same reason. For example, some pacifists may wish to do without a national defense force. But, for the majority, the only way to obtain the relevant deterrent effect is through state provision. This effectively closes off the option to do without. And yet this is not paternalistic, because the government does not believe that people's judgment or reasoning is defective; it is simply providing a service for people who do judge that they want it but can get it in no other way. The government may also believe it is for the good of those who do not approve of the service, but this is not the principal rationale behind the state intervention. Helping people to get what they want does not involve the government substituting its reasoning for that of its citizens. Thus, this "test" of whether an act is paternalistic is not passed, and a further element to the definition relating to consent is not required.

Conclusion: A Definition of Paternalism

We are now in a position to summarize the argument so far, and to provide the two conditions that define paternalistic interventions by the government.[23]

Most definitions of government paternalism involve three elements: the government restricts in some way an individual's freedom or autonomy; it engages in such restrictions to promote the individual's own good; and it does this without the individual's consent. There are problems with all these elements, but the principal difficulty is with the first: the restriction on freedom. Any definition that incorporates this element excludes interventions that most people would consider paternalistic, such as subsidizing the arts. Such acts do not restrict freedom: if anything, they seem to be freedom- or autonomy-enhancing.

In fact, for such cases, as indeed for all cases of government paternalism, the rationale for the intervention is that the government does not trust the individual's judgment.[24] It does not believe that, without the intervention, the individual will make the "right" decision—"right" in terms of promoting the individual's own good, at least as the government perceives it. Without this intervention, the individual's judgment will fail to promote her own good, or at least not promote it as successfully as it would be promoted with the intervention in place. It therefore seems preferable to define gov-

23   Or noninterventions, for we must bear in mind that paternalism can involve a failure to act. However, in most cases, particularly where the state is concerned, there will be an active intervention, and thus we use "intervention" as a convenient shorthand for both acts and nonacts.

24   Arguably, as Sarah Conly points out, this is true of all forms of paternalism, not just government paternalism. Thus "in paternalism there is a substitution of judgment; one party assumes that what you need is superior to your own judgment" (Conly 2013, 36).

ernment paternalism, not in terms of the intervention itself or of its consequences, but in terms of (a failure of) individual judgment. We should emphasize at this point that we are not addressing the questions as to why
might the government mistrust the individual's judgment, whether that
mistrust is well founded, and whether it can in fact achieve a better outcome with the intervention. Answers to those questions are provided later
in the book. Our goal here is simply to provide a definition of government
paternalism that will serve as a basis for our subsequent discussion.

The intention to promote the individual's own good must remain an
integral part of the definition, but it is now that good as defined by the
government, not necessarily as defined by the individual. Of course, the
government may accept the individual's own conception of his good as
that which ought to be promoted; indeed, later we argue that it *should* do
precisely that, and that its paternalistic interventions should be confined to
substituting its judgment for the individual's only both where there has
been a failure of the *means* by which the individual tries to achieve his
perception of the good, and where the government could do better. However, as we shall see, many proposed and actual paternalistic interventions
have as their rationale substituting the government's perception of the
good for the individual's perception; hence our definition has to include
that possibility.

The inclusion of a condition that the intervention takes place "without
the individual's consent" is redundant—unless it is assumed only to refer to
prior consent. For it would be logically incoherent for individuals to make
their own judgment concerning decisions they have to make, and simulta-
neously to consent to having that judgment replaced by the government's
judgment.

So to our definition. We conclude that a government intervention is paternalistic with respect to an individual if it is intended to

- address a failure of judgment by that individual
- further the individual's own good

However, this does not conclude the terminological discussion. For there
are important distinctions that must be made between the different types of
paternalism that fall within this definition. These we must now consider.

3   Types of Paternalism

A large number of different types of paternalism have been discussed in the literature. In this chapter we consider some of these. In particular we examine legal paternalism, soft and hard paternalism, and means and ends paternalism. As part of our discussion of means and ends paternalism, we also examine perfectionism, volitional and critical paternalism, moral paternalism, and legal moralism. Finally we consider some distinctions that are less important but nonetheless necessary to keep the terminology consistent.

Legal Paternalism

Legal paternalism is a term Feinberg (1971) originally coined to refer to the specifically lawmaking form of paternalism enacted by governments, as opposed to the paternalism that might arise from the actions of its agents or employees. As such, in chapter 2 we have already discussed some of the issues arising from legal forms of paternalism. Husak (1989, 2003) has analyzed in some depth the particular difficulties that arise when applying philosophical insights about the paternalism of personal relationships to the law. He argues that, unlike the personal, the law applies to groups of people who differ in degrees of maturity, competence, knowledge, and physical characteristics. This poses a stern challenge to those wishing to justify government paternalism, because it will be virtually impossible to specify the unique circumstances that might render an act justifiable in an individual context. For example, Husak refers to Feinberg's analysis of drug laws in which Feinberg uses a hypothetical discussion between a doctor and a patient to illustrate his case. In this discussion the doctor is able to establish whether there are any special and particular reasons for allowing certain individuals the opportunity to take a dangerous drug. However, it is difficult to extrapolate from such an analysis to the circumstances of government paternalism because it would be impractical for the government to "have a dialogue with its citizens" on an individual basis in deciding whether to act paternalistically (Husak 1989, 372). The only remedy in such a case, and one suggested by Feinberg, is to have a special statutory board to review individual claims for special dispensation from the law, something that would clearly be time-consuming and presumably open to endless legal challenge and judicial review. In practice, where the government makes laws, they will often apply indiscriminately both to individuals who would benefit from paternalism and to those who would not.[1] In chapter 7 we examine the possibility that flexible and "libertarian" forms of paternalistic policy can accommodate such concerns.

But, as we have seen, there are difficulties too in establishing the definition of a paternalistic legal act. Of particular difficulty is the requirement that such a legal act should be *intended* to address a failure of judgment by, and to be for the good of, an individual. For how can we know what was in the mind of legislators? They may not be open about the intentions of the legislation, to the wider public or perhaps even to themselves. We may never be able to pin down precisely which laws are truly paternalistic in these circumstances. Indeed, in a literal sense, no law may have ever been paternalistic if no legislator intended it to be so. Nevertheless, our approach to definition is helpful if it focuses minds on what would be the most plausible rationale for a law, that is, to correct a failure of individual judgment; in other words whether paternalism, as defined, is the "best fit" justification. In chapter 4 we discuss numerous examples of government intervention and the conditions that would make them paternalistic. And in general we favor the term "government paternalism" to "legal paternalism" because it allows for a wider range of paternalistic interventions by the government than just those that involve lawmaking.

Soft and Hard Paternalism

A major distinction often made in the literature is that between soft and hard paternalism (Feinberg 1986; Pope 2004). The distinction is important in paternalist analysis and is based on the degree to which the individual concerned is considered to be acting *autonomously* or *voluntarily*.[2] Autonomy is clearly important in thinking about paternalism, and where autonomy (or voluntariness) is compromised or absent, then a particular form of paternalism—soft paternalism—becomes a possibility. If someone is mentally ill, under the influence of drugs, or afflicted by uncontrollable com-

---

1 See also Hobson (1984) for an earlier discussion of this point.

2 These two terms are not synonymous—autonomy has a wide range of complex and subtle shades of meaning, some of which will be outlined in chapter 6. However, although "voluntarily" or "voluntariness" is normally used in discussions of soft paternalism, "autonomously" is occasionally used instead, being taken to refer to the extent of a person's capacity for self-determination (Buchanan and Brock 1989, 42; Beauchamp 2004).

pulsions, then her autonomy is restricted. It is argued that interfering in the decision making of these individuals is justified on the basis that the decision is not really their own, and thus their autonomy is not offended. Thus Feinberg (1986, 26) seeks to develop "a soft paternalistic theory of how forcible implementation of a person's will can accord with his personal autonomy."[3]

Soft paternalists consider that intervening in the decisions of people who are acting in a nonvoluntary way is not really interfering with their "true" selves at all. Rather, the intervention is a means of protecting them from harms that, owing to their lack of voluntariness, are not being chosen by them in any meaningful sense. The situation is, according to the soft paternalist, closer to that governed by the harm principle—akin to one individual being harmed by another—and really no kind of paternalism at all.

Nevertheless we have seen that not all commentators have required autonomy to be present in a definition of paternalism—some have required simply that options or choices are removed or diminished—and for these authors closing off an option for someone with severely limited autonomy would still be paternalistic. Our own definition takes a similar line: a cognitive limitation might involve a loss of autonomy, and an act intended to address that limitation would nonetheless be paternalistic. The question becomes one of when such interventions are *justified*. Indeed, antipaternalists reluctantly accept the term soft paternalism for those interventions in people's self-regarding actions where these actions are considered to be nonvoluntary. Hard paternalism, on the other hand, describes interventions in the decision making of individuals that do encroach on their autonomy, the justification for the intervention being the prevention of sufficiently serious harm. The question of whether soft paternalism does avoid offending autonomy, and thus evades the principal criticism of the antipaternalists, will be reviewed in chapter 6.

Means and Ends Paternalism

A distinction that has rarely been made in the literature, but one that is of great importance for our purposes, is that between paternalism directed at the decisions people make to achieve certain goals or ends, and paternalism directed at the ends themselves.

---

3 Conly (2013, 5–6) also refers to a distinction between hard and soft paternalism in terms of the types of paternalistic intervention, with hard paternalism referring to what she terms coercive paternalism (and what we call legal restrictions), and soft paternalism referring to other, less coercive types of intervention, such as taxes or subsidies. We do not pursue this distinction here.

Brock (1988, 561) describes the distinction between means and ends this way: first, an individual has "various aims, ends, and values that at any point in time define or give content to [the individual's] life plan and which the person appeals to in choosing between alternative courses of action," and second, there are the "choices between alternative courses of action" themselves—the means to those ends.[4]

Take someone who is choosing a school for his child and notices that its students' performance on a national examination appears to be significantly lower in the current year than in the previous year. This outcome for the school might simply be a statistical blip whereby random factors had influenced the results in the current year (several of the star students had been struck by illness on the day of the exam, perhaps). In fact, its teaching performance could have been equally good in both years, but, based purely on the exam results, the appearance was of a reduction in standards. The parent might be tempted to choose an alternative school that had previously had poor results but whose current exam results seem to show improvement (an outcome that, for similar reasons, might equally be misleading). The end that this parent desires is the best school in terms of teaching performance for his child, but his analysis of the situation may fail to provide him with the best chance of achieving that end.

Raz (1986, 423) makes an explicit reference to "means-related paternalism." He argues that some forms of government activity that restrict people's choices are acceptable if they are simply of instrumental value. Thus rules that impose safety and quality controls on manufactured goods are— for Raz—an acceptable form of paternalism precisely because people do not want unsafe goods. Clarke (2006) argues in a similar vein for paternalistic food hygiene regulations. In fact, the case for means-related paternalism is not as simple as this. Whereas people may be assumed not to want to eat food *known* to be harmful, they may wish to take the risk that the food may be harmful if it is therefore cheaper. Thus justifications for this type of paternalism involve more than simply citing the "good" of safe food because there is also the "good" of cheap food. People's true ends may be a complex mixture of the two.[5]

---

4   For other accounts that make explicit this kind of distinction, although not always in the same terms, see Scoccia (1990), Goodin (1991), Archard (1994), Wolfe (1994), Groarke (2002), and Conly (2013).

5   Clarke (2006, 119n) acknowledges that if people genuinely wanted to eat unsafe food, as a conception of the good in and of itself, then a neutral state—i.e., one that seeks to promote no particular conception of the good (Sher 1997; Wall and Klosko 2003)—would need to find ways for such people to be exempt from the regulations. However, we would suggest that a neutral but paternalist state might accept that people want to take a *risk* but misjudge the balance between potential harms and pleasures even according to their own conception of the good.

Indeed, people are almost always striving to achieve an appropriate balance between largely uncontroversial ends. If the means-related paternalist judges adversely people who seem to be failing to set aside enough money for their retirement, it may appear that the paternalist is making a judgment that the apparent ends of the individuals concerned—maximizing their present consumption—are misguided. There is a better end of having a well-provided-for old age, and this end should take precedence over the individuals' own goals. But in fact there may be no disagreement about ends. It is reasonable to suppose that individuals do not wish to have an impoverished old age. They may just hope that things will work out somehow: perhaps there will be an inheritance, or a sufficient increase in the value of their property, or they believe that their pensions will actually be sufficient for their (perhaps reduced) needs. They still wish for a comfortable and happy old age but are making a particular judgment about the balance between pleasure and happiness now and in the future. And the paternalist, as an onlooker concerned for their well-being, would not disagree about the appropriateness of these ultimate goals—both "pleasure now" and "comfort in old age" are not in dispute as goals or ends to be supported. Nor would the paternalist dispute that they have to balance the two. The paternalist might, however, disagree with them about the particular judgments they make in trying to strike that balance: the likelihood of an inheritance, for instance, or the predicted performance of pension plans they choose. And that would be the rationale for the means-related paternalist's intervention—a disagreement about means, not ends.

Thus means-related paternalism is concerned only with assisting in the *achievement* of ends that are considered to be fundamentally the individual's own—including the balance between these ends.[6] This conceptualization has echoes of Hume's notion of reason being the means to satisfy "passions": "Reason is, and ought only to be the slave of the passions, and can never pretend to any other office than to serve and obey them."[7] To intervene in this "reason" would be means-related paternalism; to question the "passions" themselves would be ends-related.

Some ends may be unchanging and unchosen. These are what we might call basic desires. We simply enjoy a Thai massage or eating chocolate brownies—we do not know why; we did not choose to enjoy them; we just do. The desires are part of "us." But other ends may change over time, and we

---

6 If an individual *genuinely* wished to live life to the absolute maximum now and risk very likely privation in old age, there would be no well-being loss for those individuals who make decisions reflecting this balancing of goals. A paternalistic policy must be mindful of the fact that some people's ends will appear odd if not downright perverse. Addressing this point will take up some of our discussion in chapter 8.

7 *A Treatise of Human Nature*, book 2, part 3, section 3.

may be able to influence them by choosing the conditions under which we live. Someone might, for example, choose to take a course in English literature in the hope that she would thereby cultivate a love of poetry or Shakespeare. Or we may act to obstruct unwelcome desires, such as avoiding shops where brownies are sold because of a concern about our weight or our long-term health.

Means and ends can easily become entangled. Take the example used earlier of the parent choosing a school. We suggested that the end was one of achieving a high quality education for his child. But perhaps there is another end lying behind this one—that the children get well-paid jobs, or secure jobs, or that they develop some aptitude to its full extent. Or perhaps the true end is yet more fundamental—that the children become simply happy or satisfied adults. Obtaining high-quality education is just a means to these ends. Sometimes this hierarchy of ends can involve a conflict. Which is the "true" end— the desire to have another cigarette or the desire to stop smoking and have a longer and healthier life? Gerald Dworkin (1988, 15–20) argues that the capacity for second-order motivations—the desire to not have the desire to smoke— is a defining quality of autonomous human beings, and that it is these "higher," more reflective and considered ends that take priority.

Questions such as these take us beyond the scope of this book. However, the distinction between means- and ends-related paternalism is nevertheless useful. For it reminds us that we can, in principle at least, either help people to achieve their own ends (while acknowledging that identifying the true end is rarely straightforward) or seek to intervene in the identification and construction of the ends themselves. For example, in developing a justification for a policy that seeks to deter people from engaging in casual sex with multiple partners, it is important to be clear about whether we wish to help people avoid excessive risk to their own health (means-related paternalism) or consider multiple sexual partners wrong in itself (ends-related paternalism). And, as we shall see, the justifications for means-related paternalism are rather different—and, in our view, much stronger—than those for the ends-related version.

Perfectionism

Ends-related paternalism has close links to perfectionism, a school of thought that has grown in significance in recent years. Perfectionism has many different varieties, and there is no unanimity about how to define or defend it,[8] but it is generally accepted that "in its broadest sense, perfection-

---

8   See, for various approaches, Raz (1986), Wall (1988), Sher (1997), Hurka (1993, 2001), Chan (2000), and Clarke (2006).

ism is the view that the state should promote valuable conceptions of the good life" (Chan 2000, 5). Thus the government is justified in taking a judgmental stance on the kinds of activities people engage in or about the character traits that should be encouraged. Perfectionists do not accept that it is only the view of the individual that counts in establishing the value of certain ends: "a perfectionist doctrine of the human good holds that what is good for its own sake for a person is fixed independently of her attitudes and opinions toward it" (Arneson 2000, 38).

Now it is reasonably easy to show how some forms of paternalism are not perfectionist. Take Sher's (1997) classification of theories of the good on a continuum from subjective to objective. For simplicity he emphasizes four points on this continuum:

- Most subjective: all value depends on people's actual preferences, choices, or affective states.
- Moderately subjective: what is valuable is not what people actually want, choose, or enjoy but what they would ideally want, choose, or enjoy if they were more instrumentally rational, better informed, or better able to imagine alternatives.
- Borderline subjective/objective: while the value of a character trait or an individual's chosen activity does depend on certain facts about the individual, the relevant facts concern neither her actual or ideal desires but certain broad capacities that all members of her species share.
- Most objective: the value of a trait or activity depends on nothing at all except its own nature; it is simply intrinsically valuable *whatever* else is the case.

The first two points constitute "subjectivist" positions, and the last two are varieties of perfectionism. It should be reasonably clear that the form of paternalism that we have termed means-related accords most closely with the second, "moderately subjectivist"—and nonperfectionist—position. Conversely, some adherents of perfectionism, such as Raz, argue specifically that the government should encourage the adoption of valuable ends. He limits the scope of such perfectionism by stipulating that these perfectionist policies should promote valuable ends only through the creation of the conditions of autonomy. Nevertheless, it is autonomy *as an end* that is important to his political philosophy, and Raz is comfortable with this being referred to as paternalistic (Raz 1986, 423).[9]

---

9 For a detailed debate on Raz's political philosophy, including a reply from the author, see the special issue of the *Southern California Law Review*: "Symposium: The Works of Joseph Raz," vol. 62, nos. 3–4 (March–May 1989).

Others develop similar arguments that, at least in part, support varieties of perfectionism on the (supposedly nonpaternalist) grounds that they do not offend autonomy because they are aimed at increasing people's range of opportunities and choices. For example, Clarke (2006) suggests that interventions that expand rather than restrict a person's options may be perfectionist but not paternalistic. So if the government makes interesting and stimulating occupations available to those stuck in dead-end jobs, it is seeking to promote a particular conception of the good as interesting and stimulating work. The kind of jobs that the government considers interesting and stimulating may not be those that the individual thinks of in this way, but Clarke argues this is not paternalistic because the individual's choices are only being expanded—he could still choose an "unstimulating" job if he wishes. However, we argued above that subsidies in general are paternalistic where they seek to increase consumption of an item or activity that, owing to some form of mistaken judgment, individuals choose not to purchase at their original price. The government could increase people's cash income as a nonpaternalist solution. This is essentially the same where it subsidizes certain jobs: it could instead raise the level of income for people to the point where they were not forced to take demeaning or menial work. Hence even these cases have a paternalistic element to them.

If perfectionism goes beyond expanding opportunities and instead supports policies that clearly *restrict* choices, then it is more obviously paternalistic. Wall (1988, 224) advocates an unequivocally restrictive policy on drugs, for example, on the basis that such prohibitions "promote and sustain social conditions that promote the flourishing of those subject to [the state's] authority." Some authors are positively supportive of the paternalist nature of perfectionist theories (Deneulin 2002).

It may be that many of the policies that emerge are nonetheless closer to means-related paternalism than they profess to be. For example, Wall's support for restrictive drug laws cites as its aim to promote the "flourishing" of the individual. Like Raz, he supports a perfectionism that promotes autonomy as the "good." But flourishing and autonomy are ends about which it is very difficult to disagree. People might well fail to achieve them by, for example, becoming addicted to drugs. They might not realize how drugs will affect them and how they will thereby be prevented from attaining their true ends. Thus the government, in outlawing drug use, is engaging in a form of means-related paternalism.

We cannot do justice to these theories here. We would simply note that, if true perfectionist theories are largely nonsubjective in Sher's taxonomy, they must make their justification based on factors other than the desires or wishes—actual or ideal—of individual citizens themselves. In the practical world of policy making this is a tall order: citizens are unlikely to look kindly on policies that make no reference at all to their own conception of their ends.[10]

Volitional and Critical Paternalism

A subtle twist to the means-ends distinction is provided by Ronald Dworkin and his understanding of "volitional" and "critical" forms of paternalism.[11] Dworkin's concern is with the various strategies, deriving from different concepts of community, that have been employed to attack what he calls "liberal tolerance," a notion he is keen to defend. Dworkin regards such a communitarian strategy as paternalistic insofar as it involves members of a community taking an active interest in, and possibly intervening coercively to support, the well-being of other members of the community for the sake of their well-being alone. But Dworkin sees this paternalism working in two distinct ways.

First, paternalism can focus on people's volitional interests—those aspects of one's well-being that simply involve people getting what they want. Volitional paternalism would intervene to assist people, possibly coercively, in getting what they already acknowledge they want. This form of paternalism is equivalent to what we termed means-related paternalism earlier. The ends are not questioned. Dworkin uses the examples of wanting good food, fewer visits to the dentist, and the capacity to sail better as volitional interests. Clearly volitional paternalism would not be relevant in all these cases, but where it could help—say by taxing sugary food so that one's teeth do not need the dentist's attention so often—it would intervene only in the means to these ends.

Second, paternalism can intervene in people's critical interests—those aspects of one's well-being that involve having or achieving something one *should* want, that is, those things without the attainment of which one's life would be a worse life. They are thus contrasted with things we want (good food, sailing better) that are not critical—although we want them, we do not think our life would be a poorer life if for some reason we did not want them. Dworkin uses the examples of having a close relationship with his children and achieving some success in his work as critical interests. Unlike volitional interests, we can make mistakes about these ends: we can misjudge

10   One difficulty for perfectionism in empirical terms is whether there is any genuine evidence for what is the good—see Sher (1997, 149–50).

11   For a full explication of his theory, see R. Dworkin (1989, 1990), and for a summary, R. Dworkin (2000). Wilkinson (2003) and Wolfe (1994) offer a critique of Dworkin's theories as they relate to paternalism.

the importance of striving for success at work, or bonding with our children.[12] This provides an opening for critical paternalism: coercion, for example, might sometimes provide people with lives that are better than the lives they now think are good.

Dworkin, while implicitly suggesting that volitional paternalism may have a role, essentially makes the point that critical paternalism is self-defeating. The components of a good life contribute to that life only if the individual endorses them. That is, people must consciously arrive at a position where they value and acknowledge the contribution a certain activity or relationship makes to the value they put on their life. But critical paternalism, in its most crude form, *imposes* a new way of life on that person without their endorsement.[13] Even if in some sense the life imposed really is a more valuable life, if the individual does not endorse it her life will not go better for her. Further, the rather more subtle forms of critical paternalism that lead people to endorse the changes they undertake also fail for Dworkin because they will tend to lessen the ability of the individual to consider the critical merits of the change in a reflective way. In particular, he rejects what he calls cultural paternalism—which removes bad options from people's imagination through educational constraints and other such devices, rather than prohibiting them outright—because this also removes the important *challenge* involved in making meaningful choices. Living well involves responding appropriately to challenges that have been rightly judged. Paternalism removes that challenge.

One problem for this approach is whether it is possible successfully to distinguish volitional from critical interests. Another question is whether all forms of paternalism—including what Dworkin terms cultural paternalism—are in fact self-defeating. He acknowledges that there are circumstances where genuine endorsement of government interventions—such as that of compulsory education—is possible. Perhaps the task for the paternalist is to build such genuine endorsement into the design of any paternalistic project that seeks to intervene in people's critical interests.

---

12   There may be some parallels here with Mill's distinction between "higher-value pleasures" and others, described in *Utilitarianism* ([1863] 1991), the higher pleasures being those that people who have experienced many different kinds of pleasure will almost always prefer as superior; see West (1977) on this point in relation to paternalism.

13   As happens to the heroes of Koestler's *Darkness at Noon* and Orwell's *1984*. In both cases the individuals come to accept the "truth" as understood by the authorities and endorse it but only as a result of unacceptable brainwashing. Alex in Burgess's *A Clockwork Orange*, on the other hand, does not endorse the "mind control" methods the authorities use on him and instead finds his *own* rationale for reforming his violent ways.

Moral Paternalism and Legal Moralism

Gerald Dworkin (2005) has differentiated a number of principles lying behind legal action intended to prevent various kinds of unwanted outcome; two of these can be described as follows.[14]

1 Legal moralism: preventing inherently immoral, though not harmful or offensive, conduct.
2 Moral paternalism: preventing moral harm (as opposed to physical, psychological, or economic harm) to the actor himself.

We have already noted that there are many types of harm that the paternalist, legal or otherwise, can seek to prevent—and goods that he can seek to promote. But here Dworkin separates the prevention of *moral* harm into a distinct category of paternalism. He further distinguishes the concept of legal moralism that seeks to prevent immoral acts where the immorality of the acts is independent of their connection with harm. The claim about legal moralism is that certain conduct—say, prostitution—is intrinsically bad. The world is a worse place for containing such conduct whether or not prostitution has harmful effects on either the persons being restrained or others.[15]

Moral paternalism, in contrast, appeals to a particular person being morally improved, with the implication that legal restrictions and prohibitions can be good for the moral character of a person. Thus a person's well-being can directly involve, and therefore be increased by, changes in her moral character and actions—changes that do not necessarily result in her being happier or healthier, and so on. A morally virtuous life might lead one to live longer if one does not indulge in excessive gluttony or hedonistic drug taking. But moral paternalism seeks to improve the moral well-being *independently of these effects*. A person can be better off just because he is morally better, just as he can be better off just because he is happier.[16]

14   They are based on Feinberg's work (1986, 1988); the other principles are legal paternalism and the harm principle, both introduced above, and the offense principle, which provides reasons for intervening to prevent offensive behavior. The distinctions here are presented in terms of their relation to harm; exactly the same distinctions can be made with respect to the promotion of good. More generally on the debate over moral paternalism, see Scoccia (2000) and Ten (1971).

15   Conversely, from a legal moralism perspective the world can also be a better place morally without any particular person being made a better person. Dworkin provides the example of the death of an evil dictator making the world a better place morally even though the moral character of everyone still alive remains unchanged.

16   Some authors discount moral paternalism from the class of paternalistic interventions altogether because the paternalist would not be acting for "the agents' own good, as defined by the agents themselves when their judgement is not in any way clouded" (Häyry 1992, 200).

Dworkin notes that such claims stretch back to Plato and the Stoic philosopher Epictetus.

According to our definition of paternalism, legal moralism is not a variant form of paternalism because it is not intended to do good to or for an individual. In fact, it is somewhat difficult to see what its status is beyond that relating to religious strictures, for if good is not made real *for anyone*, then who is to decide that it is good at all? Moral paternalism at least has in its favor that the good it promotes is a good for the person who is subject to the government intervention.

Dworkin acknowledges that, like perfectionism, moral paternalism takes a stance on the ends that people pursue. It is thus a form of what we have termed ends-related paternalism. Smokers and motorcyclists do not deny that the end of good health is valuable; but most people who watch pornography do not believe that watching pornography is morally corrupting. And yet moral paternalism takes a view on this end: it claims that the moral well-being of those who watch pornography can be improved even if they do not accept in any way that their activities are wrong, or that they would be leading a morally superior life if they refrained from them. This distinction between standard means-related paternalism and its moral cousin hinges to some extent on an empirical question: where ultimately lies the source of knowledge on the basis of which the paternalist believes she knows that there is a "mistaken judgment" about well-being that warrants the paternalistic interference? When it is only the means that are in question, one can in principle refer to the subject himself (perhaps later at a time when he is not making the relevant decision, or as part of a survey or trial, or as part of the democratic process), in order to discover whether he agrees that his ends are better achieved with the paternalist's help. With moral paternalism (and to some extent perfectionism) this is not possible because the individual is unlikely ever to agree that his ends are wrong.

Other Categories of Paternalism

There are a number of other, largely uncontroversial distinctions that can be made between various types of paternalism. We discuss these distinctions here purely for completeness, since some readers may have read only a portion of the literature and thus may be confused by terminology—especially since different authors on occasion adopt the same terminology to represent different distinctions.

First, Kleinig (1983) has made a distinction between negative and positive paternalism. Negative paternalism, for Kleinig, refers to actions that protect people from harming themselves and positive paternalism to those that promote a positive benefit. Seat belt laws are an example of the former, and subsidies for leisure facilities an example of the latter. Unfortunately this distinction has also been referred to as weak and strong paternalism, respectively (G. Dworkin 1981). To add to the confusion, some writers (for instance, Beauchamp 1983) use the weak/strong terminology to distinguish between soft and hard paternalism.

A second distinction is between mixed and unmixed paternalism (Feinberg 1986). The former refers to paternalistic policies that are combined with other motives (such as correcting market failure or promoting social justice), the latter to those motivated *only* by improvement in the well-being of the individual whose autonomy is interfered with. Again the semantics are not straightforward: Kleinig (1983, 12) refers to this distinction as between pure and impure paternalism, terms that we restrict to a rather more narrow meaning below.

The third distinction is between direct and indirect paternalism (Feinberg 1986, 1971), yet another distinction occasionally termed pure and impure (G. Dworkin 1972). Direct paternalism involves only one party, such as prohibiting suicide and drug use; indirect paternalism involves two parties so that the actions of a second person are interfered with to benefit the first, such as laws prohibiting euthanasia or drug sales. In the latter case a restriction is placed on a second party even though the first party has voluntarily entered into an arrangement with the second party that would affect only the first party's interests. The second party may be punished even though it is the first party's (supposed) misjudgment that is being addressed.

Fourth, there are paternalistic laws that require actions and there are those that forbid them: these have been termed active and passive paternalism, respectively (Kleinig 1983). For example, compelling the use of a helmet when riding a motorcycle is an active policy; outlawing the consumption of certain drugs is a passive one. This terminology, at least, has no conflicting usage.

A fifth and final distinction is between pure and impure paternalism, a distinction that, as we have already seen, is used in a variety of ways. We follow Pope (2004), using pure paternalism to refer to cases where there are consequences for the intended individual only, and impure paternalism where there are consequences both for the individual and for others.

Tables 3.1 and 3.2 in this chapter's appendix, adapted from Pope (2004), illustrate some of these distinctions. Table 3.1 categorizes paternalist interventions as to whether they are direct or indirect or mixed or unmixed; and table 3.2 as to whether they are pure or impure and again as to mixed or unmixed. So compulsory helmets for motorcyclists are pure, direct, and unmixed, whereas licensing medical professionals is impure, indirect, and mixed.

Conclusion

This chapter has distinguished between various kinds of government paternalism and pointed to the confusion in the literature concerning the different terminologies involved. Of the distinctions discussed, the most important are that between soft and hard paternalism and that between means-related and ends-related paternalism. The possible justifications for each are different, and in fact we will argue that the only forms of (potentially) justifiable government paternalism are means-related, nonperfectionist, volitional forms. And we will reject moral paternalism and legal moralism, both forms of ends-related paternalism. This will be elaborated in subsequent chapters.

Appendix

Table 3.1. Categories of Paternalism: Direct/Indirect and Mixed/Unmixed

	Intervention	
Motive	*Direct*	*Indirect*
Unmixed	Compulsory helmet laws directed at, and intended to benefit, only the motorcyclist (A)	Regulations on allowable additives directed at food manufacturers (B) to benefit consumers (A)
Mixed	Laws directed at individuals who smoke in public places (A), intended to benefit both the smoker (A) *as well as* others who breathe the smoke (C)	Laws obliging medical professionals to be licensed (B) to ensure benefits for consumers (A) *as well as* (economic) benefits to the producer (B)

Source: Adapted from Pope (2004).

Note: A is the individual whose well-being is the target of the paternalistic intervention; B is a second person whose action is restricted in some way in a two-party agreement; and C is another individual whose well-being may also benefit as a result of the paternalism but is not subject to any specific regulation.

Table 3.2. Categories of Paternalism: Pure/Impure and Mixed/Unmixed

	Consequences	
Motive	*Pure*	*Impure*
Unmixed	As in table 3.1	Regulations intended to prevent an individual harming herself—e.g., compulsory use of life vest on a boat (A)—that mean she is incidentally also able to save another life (C)
Mixed	A law banning smoking outright intending to benefit both the individual (A) and his nonsmoking family (C), but where the individual only ever smokes outside	As in table 3.1

Source: Adapted from Pope (2004).

Note: As in table 3.1.

4 Paternalism in Practice

As we defined it in chapter 2, government paternalism seeks to do good for people under circumstances whereby the government considers their judgment to be compromised. Paternalistic interventions are not concerned with protecting one individual from another, nor with helping people to achieve collectively what they cannot achieve individually, nor with ensuring that people have an adequate level of income. But such distinctions are not always obvious in practice. Those who oppose paternalism but who nonetheless are sympathetic to government intervention in key areas of society and the economy are able to cite a range of competing justifications that offer less controversial rationales for intervention, such as the harm principle, market failure, or the promotion of equity and social justice. However, as we hope to demonstrate in this chapter, such justifications are not always adequate.

First we catalog the range of government interventions that may be viewed as involving elements of paternalism. We then review various nonpaternalistic justifications for intervention and go on to examine a number of ways in which they fail satisfactorily to provide an adequate basis for particular policies. We conclude that paternalistic motivations are the most plausible explanation for many currently existing laws, regulations, and other government activities that promote well-being.

It might be noted that, in assessing the various justifications for the policies concerned, we adopt an individualist approach, concentrating on the costs and benefits to the individuals affected. This is because we consider that apparently less individualistic justifications do ultimately have to appeal to the good that is done for people in some sense. Take a justification of arts subsidies on the basis of an appeal to the preservation of tradition. For example, Shakespeare apart, it is likely that the great body of plays written over the three-hundred-year period up to, say, 1900 would seldom if ever be performed without any subsidy. Whereas the works themselves might well be preserved on the shelves of libraries,[1] the cultural understanding

---

1 Libraries themselves of course also require subsidies.

and appreciation of a significant part of cultural history would be lost to the vast majority of the population. Such a loss might be considered unacceptable to a civilized nation. But why? Surely it is not because the performance of these works is considered valuable regardless of whether anyone comes to watch or even cares that they are performed? For only if the plays are watched do people gain some pleasure or other benefit from them. Sustaining a tradition of performance would in those circumstances appear bizarre. Even if that were accepted, and plays were performed to empty halls, this might be defended on the grounds that the *knowledge* that they were being performed was valuable to people, or that the players and production staff found some kind of stimulation in putting on the plays, or—failing all that—that future generations would one day come to appreciate great works of literature if a tradition of their performance were maintained. But in each of these increasingly extreme cases, there nevertheless lurks in the justification the notion that someone, somewhere, at some time, experiences some kind of well-being gain as an individual.

Types of Government Intervention

In pursuing their aims or objectives, governments try to affect their citizens' behavior in a number of ways. The principal ones include the provision of *information*, the imposition of *legal restrictions*, the imposition of *taxation* or other forms of *negative financial incentives*, the provision of *subsidies* or other forms of *positive financial incentives*, and, in an important development, types of government intervention arising from what has been termed libertarian paternalism or nudging, including changes in the context in which people make decisions or the *architecture of choice*.

In chapter 2 we argued that the simple provision of information is not a form of paternalism. This is because it does not involve the government substituting its judgment for that of the individual; rather it is enabling the individual better to make the relevant judgments herself. However, all the other interventions could involve paternalistic elements, and in practice they often do, as we now hope to demonstrate.

The following constitutes a list of potentially paternalistic interventions that governments have used. They generally fall into the three categories of legal restrictions, negative financial incentives, and positive financial incentives. They can be found in practice in at least one country in the world and often in many more. We are not claiming that they are inevitably paternalistic—indeed, given our definition of a paternalistic act being one that seeks to address failures of judgment, it would be difficult to do so unambiguously. Nevertheless, the following have all been cited as such in the literature; the accompanying text clarifies the nature of their paternalistic elements.

Legal Restrictions on Risky Behavior

Risky behavior refers to activities where physical, psychological, or financial harm can result as an unintended consequence of the activity, sometimes many years in the future. Legal restrictions on risky behavior include

- laws requiring the wearing of helmets while riding a motorcycle
- laws requiring the wearing of seat belts while driving a car
- minimum unit pricing for alcohol
- regulations directed at ensuring safety at work or in relation to the manufacturing standards of consumer products (e.g., electrical safety; banning certain food additives)
- restrictions on dangerous leisure activities (e.g., obligations to have lifeguards at some beaches and swimming pools; prohibiting swimming at certain beaches or rivers with strong tides; restricting hill walking in dangerous locations; requirement to wear safety equipment when shooting or sailing)
- laws limiting the number of hours that can be worked per week
- laws prohibiting smoking in public places
- laws prohibiting the buying, selling, or consumption of certain drugs for recreational purposes
- usury laws limiting the maximum interest rate on loans
- various activities within medical practice, including involuntary incarceration of mentally ill people; withholding licenses for drugs considered inefficacious or potentially harmful (such as innovative therapies); and regulations restricting self-medication of licensed drugs

In some cases risk can be incurred through *in*activity: for instance, failure to take out insurance against the relevant risk. Important examples of an intervention addressed to this inactivity in the United States are some of the provisions of so-called Obamacare relating to insurance against the cost of health care, specifically,

- mandating employers or individuals to obtain private health insurance

Obligatory seat belt and helmet use are the most commonly cited examples of paternalism in action (Dworkin 1972; Kleinig 1983). The policies are paternalistic to the extent that they are intended to prevent drivers from misjudging the likelihood, and seriousness, of the harm that will result in the case of an accident. They are perhaps the paradigm case of government paternalism in practice, although even here, as we shall see below, a nonpaternalistic case is sometimes made in their defense.

Other laws that seek to minimize the risk of accidents and harm include health and safety regulations at work or for leisure activities and standards for the manufacture of consumer goods (Kelman 1981). While it might be thought that people would automatically consent to such regulations, this is not necessarily the case. Someone may wish to buy the cheaper but less rigorously designed light fixture, or to choose a higher-paid job in a more dangerous environment. Where leisure activities are concerned, the risk is often part of the pleasure. In all these cases—if the justification for government intervention is a paternalistic one—the government must take the view that people are misjudging the outcome of their decisions in balancing risk, price, income, and enjoyment.

Another commonly cited case of paternalism in action involves bans on the buying, selling, or consumption of "recreational" drugs such as marijuana (Husak 1989; Cudd 1990). Here the potential harm is not that of an accident but of long-term damage to health. For such a ban to be paternalistic, the government must believe that drug users are making an error in calculating the appropriate balance between these long-term harms and the more immediate pleasures. If the law were simply directed at preventing such drug users from being a menace to others, it would not be paternalistic.

A more controversial policy is that relating to the maximum number of hours that can be worked per week. An example would be the European Union Working Time Regulations that provide for a limit of an average of forty-eight hours per week for which a worker can be required to work. According to our definition such a policy will be paternalistic only if it addresses a cognitive error: in this case that people misjudge the relative financial benefit of taking on a job with long hours when set against the resultant additional stress. However, the government may argue that it is merely seeking to protect individuals who are in a weak position in the labor market. Later in this chapter we consider in detail whether nonpaternalistic justifications such as this offer a coherent rationale for a variety of existing laws and policies.

Laws against smoking in public places are, if paternalistic at all, an example of mixed paternalism. That is, they may have a paternalistic motive, in addition to the objective of protecting nonsmokers from the effects of secondhand smoke. But for there to be a paternalistic element, the government must believe that smokers both misjudge their own best interests *as well as* irritate and harm others.

Laws that establish maximum rates of interest on loans—so-called usury laws—have been a feature of some European countries and US states for many years. They seek to minimize harm from financial mismanagement by preventing people from taking out loans on which they cannot afford to keep up repayments. Lenders who are not prepared to lend to consumers whom they perceive to be high risk are effectively prevented from offering loans to those consumers. Again, simply requiring that people are told what the interest rate is and how much they would be liable to repay each month would not be a sufficient constraint if people are considered unable adequately to judge the impact that such borrowing would have on their future well-being.

Medical practice is fertile ground for paternalism. These matters usually arise in the context of individual personal relationships between health-care professionals and patients.[2] However, government paternalism also plays a significant role in most countries. Severely mentally ill people can be forcibly restrained to prevent them from harming both themselves and others—another mixed form of paternalism. The availability of therapeutic drugs is also commonly restricted, even when the benefits or harms affect only the patient. Newly developed therapeutic drugs may not be licensed at all, for example, even where they offer a small chance of improved life expectancy, if their use is accompanied by significantly harmful side effects. For this to be paternalistic, the government must believe that patients, even if provided with all relevant information about their disease and the impact of the drug, are still likely to misunderstand the ratio of risks to benefits, possibly because they are in desperate need or a distressed state of mind. Similarly, prohibiting the purchase of licensed therapeutic drugs without a prescription is paternalistic if the government believes people do not have sufficient understanding of their disease or what is needed to treat it—a failing that cannot be adequately rectified by providing detailed information about the medication and the dangers involved in taking it (Rainbolt 1989a).

Legal Restrictions on Intentional Behavior I: Disposing of One's Body or Life

There are also a number of legal restrictions on intentional actions, that is, where the outcome specifically desired by the individual is prohibited. The first category of restrictions on intentional behavior involves decisions over one's own body or life:[3]

- laws forbidding assisted suicide
- force-feeding hunger strikers
- laws forbidding the sale of body parts

2   See Beauchamp and Childress (2001, esp. 176–94) for an overview of the principles involved and their application to individual cases; Coulter (2002) for the general case against paternalism from a nonphilosophical viewpoint; Shinebourne and Bush (1994) and Veatch and Spicer (1994) for views from both sides of the debate about paternalism in the doctor-patient relationship; and Buchanan (1983) and Clarke (2003) specifically on the issue of withholding information.

3   For a detailed discussion of these issues, see Fabre (2006), which also covers the law relating to selling sex and reproductive surrogacy.

- ⊘ laws forbidding (the procurement of) self-mutilation
- ⊘ obligatory blood transfusions against the wishes of religious groups (such as Jehovah's Witnesses)
- ⊘ obligatory resuscitation against any patient's wish

Some actions that result in physical mutilation or even death are not just the unfortunate outcome of risky activities but may be, in the opinion of the individual concerned, precisely what he wants. Those suffering from incurable illnesses may wish to be helped to die through assisted suicide rather than suffer continued distress from the illness itself.[4] Imprisoned hunger strikers may wish to die because they consider their life meaningless unless they can pursue their ideals. Others may wish to sell an organ, such as a kidney, to raise money for themselves or their family. In each of these examples the government may judge that the ends are inappropriate—that the individuals concerned have the "wrong" goals. In such cases the laws would be examples of ends-related paternalism. Life, or one's body, might be considered to have some kind of moral sanctity that the individual would offend by intentionally dying, by mutilating, or by removing a healthy organ for a cash payment.[5] But in each case the individual must be considered to have some kind of impaired judgment. For example, it would not be paternalism to force-feed a hunger striker to prevent her from becoming a political martyr, if it were clear that was her intention.

However, means-related paternalism may also have a role in these cases if the government considers that people are in fact misjudging the achievement of ends that have become obscured in some way. In other words, although people may claim that they wish to die for their own sake, in reality they may be merely trying to relieve the stress and worry endured by their family and friends. They thus misjudge the achievement of their own ends—the balance between their own life and the burden on their caregivers—as a result of being under some form of (usually psychological) duress. However, in the case of both ends- and means-related paternalism, the individual must be considered to have some kind of failure of reasoning or of inappropriate end state. If a terminally ill person were threatened with physical abuse by a relative who wished him to die quickly and entered into a contract for assisted suicide only on this basis, then action to prevent it

---

4 Laws against assisted suicide are closely related, paternalistically speaking, to those that deny consent as an admissible defense on a murder charge; see Sneddon (2006).

5 See Arneson (2005). If the motive for outlawing assisted suicide were that it offended a religious or spiritual notion that life has a certain sanctity that must not be voluntarily cut short, then this may not be paternalistic at all because it does not serve to further the good *of the individual*. This would be closer to legal moralism.

would not be paternalistic but rather one based on the harm principle, protecting the vulnerable from exploitation.

But not all forms of interpersonal pressure are unreasonably coercive. Take the case of selling body parts. Once again, laws forbidding such sales will be paternalistic only if the individual is considered to be making some kind of reasoning failure—if, for example, she misjudges her interests in calculating that the removal of an organ and the risk this has for her health are fully compensated by a cash payment. It would not be paternalistic to prevent someone from giving up an organ if this were at the point of a gun. But an individual who has incurred a large debt may genuinely believe that selling the body part is her least worst option. She may be technically capable of settling the debt in other ways—by selling her house, for example—but would rather sell a kidney instead. She may indeed feel pressured by her family not to sell the house. But not all such pressure is unreasonable, particularly if it occurs in a context that the individual freely chooses. And we should note that a law preventing organ sales as a means of deterring undue coercion would do nothing to solve the individual's indebtedness, the original source of her troubles. Similar considerations apply to people who are denied the chance to take part in experimental drug trials because they need the money (Callahan 1986).[6]

Compulsory blood transfusions offer another example of choices on how to manage our own body. For such an action to be paternalistic, the government must believe the individual misunderstands that it is wrong in itself to die for want of a blood transfusion, or that it is misguided to believe that one's (religious) ends will in fact be achieved by doing so. However, the government would not be acting paternalistically if it believed it was acting to protect the interests of the patient's dependents.

Finally, in rare cases, people with unusual mental states—but short of derangement or psychosis—can wish to have limbs removed, known as apotemnophilia (Shafer-Landau 2005), or otherwise mutilate themselves. A law prohibiting them from undertaking such actions, or from procuring another to do it for them, will be paternalistic only if the individual is genuinely thought to have a reasoning failure. It is not a straightforward matter

---

6   The law against duelling is an interesting case of a law that apparently intervenes in how we wish to dispose of our bodies, where the question of coercion is relevant but whose rationale is complex. In this case, such a law will be means-related paternalistic if the state considers that people misjudge the best way of upholding their honor. It could also be means-related paternalistic if the state desires to correct duellers' misjudgements around risky behaviour. Or it could also be a form of legal moralism: that settling disputes through violence is morally wrong. Finally its rationale could be simply an application of the harm principle: it would simply be designed to protect people from unwarranted coercion to engage in a life-threatening activity.

establishing what constitutes a reasoning defect in such a situations and what is just eccentricity.

Legal Restrictions on Intentional Behavior II: Sexual Desires

The second category of legal restriction of intentional behavior involves decisions over one's sexual desires. Again, it is the outcome that the individual specifically wants which is prohibited or restricted:

- ⊘ laws against certain sexual activities, such as sodomy or lesbianism
- ⊘ laws restricting trade in pornography
- ⊘ laws forbidding polygamy
- ⊘ the offense of "living off immoral earnings" and restrictions on prostitution and the trade in sex

Consensual homosexuality is still proscribed in many countries around the world, and yet, even in those countries, it does not seem to be outlawed to protect the individuals concerned from physical harm.[7] For such proscriptions to be paternalistic, they must be addressing a perceived reduction in some other aspect of the person's well-being, such as their moral well-being. Moral well-being is not exclusively associated with sexual activity, but it is perhaps in this category where it is most commonly found. A *paternalistic* prohibition, it should be noted, does not aim to support the moral tenor of society as a whole nor uphold religious teachings—these motivations would be closer to what we have termed legal moralism. Rather, paternalism is concerned with the moral well-being of the individual. Thus laws preventing people from indulging in fully consensual sexual acts, where both parties evidently seek and agree to what they are doing, are paternalistic (rather than legally moralistic) only if the laws address desires perceived to affect the individuals' *own* good. This might be that their sexual activity will adversely affect their future moral well-being, or that the activity is wrong for them as an end in itself. The laws concerned are intended to "morally improve" or protect these individuals. Restrictions on pornography or prostitution, with a similar motivation, are also paternalistic—potentially to both the consumer and the supplier. Again, laws against polygamy are paternalistic only if the view is that the marriage partners have misjudged their own moral well-being.

Of course, restrictions on sexual activity and pornography may also be directed at protecting those who do not want to be exposed to sexual activity unawares—by outlawing indecent behavior, banning soliciting on the

---

7 Although some laws or regulations may have the intention of preventing the individual from contracting or spreading sexual diseases. Restrictions on their ability to form sexual relations may also be placed on people with mental disabilities (Spiecker and Steutel 2002).

public highway, or restricting sexual depiction on television. However, such laws are rarely so specific as to be clear on these counts. Indeed, the phrase "living off immoral earnings" used in English law[8]—relating to pimps and other organizers of the prostitution trade—is a rare and candid case of the law explicitly referring to morality, even if this is likely to be a type of legal moralism rather than moral paternalism.

Legal Restrictions on the Validity of Contracts

Many types of contractual agreement are legally invalid, including those that

- ◐ involve voluntary self-enslavement
- ◐ involve peonage, whereby debtors can be obliged to work to pay off debts
- ◐ waive rights to protection against sex/race/disability discrimination
- ◐ waive rights to divorce
- ◐ waive rights to sue for bankruptcy
- ◐ waive rights to an "inhabitable" dwelling in tenancy agreements
- ◐ involve agreements of any kind "in perpetuity"
- ◐ waive rights to a "cooling-off" period within which the contract can be rescinded[9]

In the case of the law invalidating certain types of contract, we are in the realm of indirect paternalism, where legal sanctions may restrict the actions of a party other than the individual who is considered liable to make a cognitive error.[10] In most of the examples given above, the law will be paternalistic if it judges that individuals are liable to misjudge their future interests when agreeing to the contract. Thus, for example, no matter how financially beneficial the terms of the contract, a paternalistic law would consider that selling oneself into slavery, or waiving rights that are there to provide some basis for mitigating unforeseen or unexpected eventualities, would be a misjudgment on the part of the individual. The possible future circumstances —a lifetime working off debts, suffering at the hands of a malign slaveholder, finding oneself in an uninhabitable dwelling or unable to extricate oneself from an unwanted marriage—would, from the paternalist's point of view, be too harmful whatever the compensation the individual received

---

8   The English Crown Prosecution Service still uses the phrase with respect to section 30 of the Sexual Offences Act 1956, whereby it is an offense for "a man knowingly to live wholly or in part on the earnings of prostitution."

9   There may be other examples in this category, such as the inalienability—that is, untradability—of voting rights.

10   See Shiffrin (2000) and Kronman (1983) for a discussion of many of these types of contracts and the case for and against their necessarily involving paternalism.

in entering into the contract. Similar thinking lies behind invalidating any contract that gives one party the right to enforce a term—such as confiscating property in the event of a payment not being made, or one that specifies terms "in perpetuity," that is, with no prospect of renegotiation. In all these cases the law is not paternalistic if it seeks merely to protect individuals from (unreasonable) coercion when a contract is agreed.

Finally, many contracts involving financial commitment give the potential consumer the chance to reconsider and withdraw his agreement—a cooling-off period. Again this would be paternalistic if the individual is thought liable to make too hasty a decision. Although we are capable of telling a salesperson that we need more time to consider such contracts, some sellers can be persuasive and threaten the removal of the offer if it is not agreed to straightaway. Requiring a cooling-off period is paternalistic if it is based on a belief that individuals tend to suffer from a cognitive weakness in such circumstances. However, the intervention is so slight—merely obliging both sides to wait a few days before the deal is finalized—that it is largely uncontroversial.

Legal Restrictions Relating to Children

Many laws restrict what children are allowed to do even with the authorization and supervision of their parents; in the case of education, the law stipulates a rare case of compulsory consumption. Examples are

- laws prohibiting the sale of babies
- laws regulating surrogacy
- compulsory education
- restrictions on working hours
- age limits for marriage/sex, smoking, drinking, and voting

Laws relating to children are in one sense the easiest to understand and accept as paternalistic, as befits the literal meaning of the term. Children need guidance for their own good, and thus the use of legal paternalism to intervene in their decision making might seem straightforward. On the other hand, parents are there to provide guidance, so why need the government become involved? Furthermore, if the interests of the child are considered to be essentially identical to those of the parent (in the sense that a parent views the interests of the child as simply an extension of her own interests), then under normal circumstances—in other words, where there is no overt abuse—the government would not be able to argue that its interventions were to protect the child from the malign actions of the parent. Thus a paternalistic law is one directed at the parents as not being able properly to judge their own (in this case synonymous with their child's) interests. The government must consider that the parents are unable to control or educate the child sufficiently or otherwise misjudge the child's needs. However, in practice this is complicated by the fact that many parents unhappily do abuse or maltreat their children. So we must qualify the normal condition for paternalism by specifying that a law is paternalistic only where the government believes there is some cognitive limitation on behalf of the parent *and* the parent is well intentioned toward the child.

Taxation of Risky Behavior

Rather than impose specific practical restrictions on risky behavior, the government may impose a tax on its consumption:

- taxes on "unhealthful" goods such as alcohol, tobacco, and the saturated fat content of food
- taxes on gambling

Taxation has the advantage, in circumstances where the activity cannot be "made safe" in other ways, of avoiding its outright prohibition while still discouraging its use, though this discouragement may disproportionately affect those on low incomes. As Mill ([1859] 1974, 171) put it in relation to specific taxation: "every increase of cost is a prohibition to those whose means do not come up to the augmented price; and to those who do, it is a penalty laid on them for gratifying a particular taste."

Taxation is paternalistic only to the extent that it seeks to benefit the individual consumer by correcting a propensity to consume excessive quantities. It is not paternalistic if its rationale is to prevent harm to others, to correct externalities, or to raise revenue to finance government expenditure. As in many of the examples given above, if the rationale is paternalistic, the consumer is considered to misjudge the balance of pleasures now against risks to health or financial security in the future. This is a form of means-related paternalism. However, drinking, smoking, and gambling have all been condemned as wrong in themselves at various times through history; if the taxation of these activities had this motivation, it would constitute a form of ends-related paternalism—and possibly a form of moral paternalism.

Subsidies to Encourage Consumption of Goods or Services

The government frequently subsidizes goods or services so as to reduce their price, sometimes to zero, to encourage their consumption. Examples are

- subsidies for museums and the arts
- subsidies or other incentives for purchasing healthful foods or sports and leisure facilities

- ⊘ public service broadcasting
- ⊘ incentives for savings for pensions, including tax allowances
- ⊘ financial incentives favoring marriage
- ⊘ in-kind rather than cash provision of welfare benefits
- ⊘ conditional cash support—for example, only where the recipient agrees to work

Subsidies are the converse of interventions involving taxation. People's level of consumption is determined in part by the market price; artificially reducing this price effectively alters how the individual judges whether or not to buy—whether to pay to visit the theater or a museum, for example. But a subsidy is paternalistic only if the government believes that people have miscalculated the good to them of consuming these services—if, for example, it thinks that people benefit from visiting theaters or museums to a greater extent than the individuals' own assessment. Similarly, subsidies for leisure activities or healthful food are paternalistic only if they are motivated by a belief that people misjudge their consumption at market prices and thus fail to maximize their well-being over a lifetime.

In the United Kingdom, the BBC, as a public service broadcaster, is not usually considered to be a subsidized service. But the "license fee" that funds it is in effect a hypothecated tax rather than a true fee because it is levied on people who own a television whether or not they use the BBC (Le Grand and New 1999). The BBC has often been described as paternalistic, not least because of its founder John Reith's dictum that it should "inform, educate, and entertain," objectives that continue to form part of the BBC's mission today.[11] However, it is truly paternalistic only if the purpose of the subsidy is, in part at least, to address a perceived misjudgment that people make when allowed to choose freely the kind of programs they wish to watch in a purely private commercial setting. Regulations rather than subsidy can also perform this function: again in the UK, another broadcaster, Channel 4, is funded through selling advertising space, but it must also broadcast programs that conform to the government's regulatory framework, notably to promote "innovation, experiment, and creativity."[12]

Private pension arrangements can also be affected through subsidy either by giving tax breaks to pension saving or by direct matching grants of various kinds (Le Grand 2006). In both cases the schemes are designed to encourage people to save more for their future than they would otherwise choose to do. There are also usually regulations of some kind of the amount that people can withdraw for their pension pot before they reach pension-

---

11   See the current Royal Charter, granted on July 19, 2006, section 5: http://www.bbc.co.uk/bbctrust/framework/charter.html.
12   From the Communications Act 2003.

able age. Such policies would be paternalistic if they seek to correct a misjudgment by individuals in assessing how much provision they should make while young for their financial security when old. The schemes would not be paternalistic if they merely redistributed cash income to promote social equality, an objective that could be achieved without the particular incentives to increase savings for pensions alone.

Similarly, government funding of health care—such as in the Medicare and Medicaid programs in the United States and the British National Health Service—will be paternalistic to the extent that it is intended to prevent people from judging that they would be better off doing without health insurance. The paternalism does not relate to how the care is delivered by professionals but only to the possibility that people miscalculate the effect of not taking out health insurance on their future well-being.

Most countries subsidize universities and other institutions of higher education. In this case the subsidy is paternalistic if it is designed to correct a perceived misjudgment by an individual that his future employment and income prospects will be satisfactory without this kind of education. The argument about whether such in-kind, universal services are indeed paternalistic is complex and will be revisited later in this chapter.

The government may also consider marriage to be "underconsumed." This may be for a number of reasons, including a desire to protect any children from harm or for reasons of legal moralism. But for a marriage incentive—say, through the tax system—to be paternalistic, it must be designed to serve the interests of the couple by addressing a failure of judgment on their part, namely, that the marriage contract will not confer any additional benefit on their relationship. Of course, many people need no encouragement to marry; it is only to those who believe it is an irrelevance to their own happiness that a financial incentive is directed. They must, according to the paternalist, be likely to misjudge how helpful the institution of marriage is in providing them with a stable and enjoyable relationship.

Nonpaternalistic Justifications for State Intervention

For John Stuart Mill, preventing harm to others was the only justifiable reason for the government forcibly infringing the liberty of individuals against their will. But the notion of harm is wider than one might first imagine. For example, many otherwise innocent and consensual economic exchanges can have spillover effects—known as externalities—that harm others, air or water pollution being merely the clearest examples. Mill also acknowledged that sometimes *failing* to act can be a form of harm, such as not providing education to a child, and that compelling education was thus allowable too in Mill's terms. Furthermore, Mill accepted that government intervention to enable collective provision might be the only way for people to obtain certain goods and services that most people want—in other words "public goods," such as a defense force.

There can also on occasion be very specific external benefits that do not help the coerced individual in any way, but the government may wish to intervene to promote these benefits as an analog of the harm principle. Feinberg calls this the "benefit-to-others principle" (1986, xvii) and largely dismisses its relevance to the criminal law by using the example of tax-funded museums (1988, 311–16). We would argue that such a subsidy is better understood as straightforward government paternalism because it serves to benefit *everyone* who is now faced with lower-cost access to a specific good. A better example of benefit-to-others would be planning laws that oblige a householder to paint her house a color she dislikes to fit in with the local aesthetic. There are also some jurisdictions that have "Bad Samaritan" laws that punish those who fail to *prevent* harm to others (Malm 1995).

Information is also a contentious issue: Mill acknowledged that intervening to provide someone with information—the famous unsafe bridge example—was not an infringement of the person's liberty because it was simply a means of ensuring he got what he really wanted. Finally, in what might be regarded as a real stretch of the harm principle, Mill saw that assistance for the very poor—to ensure they had adequate means to educate themselves, for example—was also permissible. This objective is part of what is now commonly known as equity. All these refinements of what was originally "one very simple principle" (Mill [1859] 1974, 68) have developed into an enormous field of intellectual inquiry and practical policy making. We now review the main elements in more detail.

Efficiency, Market Failures, and the Harm Principle

Economists tend to look at social issues from a perspective of efficiency, and how market organization achieves, or fails to achieve, this goal. The principal model is expected utility theory that assumes that each individual is best able to order her own preferences so as to maximize her utility or well-being. Under "perfect" market conditions—many buyers and sellers, perfect information, and well-defined property rights—suppliers competing for goods and services will result in what is known as Pareto optimality, whereby it is impossible to make one person better off without making another worse off. Individuals will be "getting what they want," and overall aggregate social well-being cannot be improved.[13] It is the understanding that these market

---

13 The Hicks-Kaldor compensation test extends the range of situations that may be called Pareto optimal by including the criterion that, if a change enables those who gain to compensate those who lose and still remain better off, this is Pareto superior. However, in most

conditions can fail, and indeed often fail to a significant degree, that lies behind the justifications for government intervention on efficiency grounds.[14] Market failures can be conveniently categorized into two areas of relevance to our discussion: imperfect excludability and nonrivalness (which incorporate the problem of externalities), and imperfect information (Gravelle and Rees 1992, 512–16).[15]

However, economists' reasons for government intervention are not unrelated to those that are behind the harm principle and that influence the criminal law. Much intervention in response to the first category of our market failures—imperfect excludability and nonrivalness—is motivated by similar concerns to those of the harm principle: that is, the government has a legitimate role in preventing one person from harming another. Such harms may be the result of individuals acting in criminal or antisocial ways, or they may be the result of the external effects of market activity. Of course, criminals generally intend, or are indifferent to, the harm they cause, whereas market harms are generally incidental to otherwise lawful activity. But, at root, intervention in both cases shares a common desire to prevent the innocent bystander from being harmed by other people's activity, whether lawful or not.

The first market failure with which we are concerned is that of externalities. Externalities occur when costs or benefits are incurred on those not directly involved in a process of exchange or consumption and are therefore outside that person's control. Thus local residents may be affected by a factory belching out smoke; neighbors may be kept awake by someone playing loud music; and travelers are incidentally affected by the beauty of a farmer's land or the aesthetic harmony of an urban environment. The problem from the point of view of economic efficiency is that those affected are external to the productive activity. As a result it is often difficult to exclude them from its harmful effects—or include those who benefit from its pleasant ones. In market contexts, the affected parties cannot influence the level of production; they are not compensated for costs or obliged to pay for benefits. As a consequence the producers do not take these external effects into account when deciding levels of production. Where there are external

---

practical circumstances this test remains theoretical (the compensation does not actually take place), and thus, if it is used to evaluate a policy change in practice, it incorporates the value judgement that if aggregate improvements in well-being are sufficiently large for some people, the reduction in well-being for others is acceptable.

14   The market may also "fail" to provide an equitable distribution of well-being or utility among its consumers. But we take this to be failure of social arrangements more generally rather than of the market per se—a market is not a mechanism designed to achieve any particular distribution of outcomes. Equity is thus considered separately.

15   There is a third major area, that of monopoly and associated problems with small numbers of buyers and/or sellers, which is less relevant to our concerns here.

costs, oversupply will result because the producer is not personally affected by costs that would otherwise limit her willingness to produce. External benefits, on the other hand, may cause the market to undersupply (or not produce the good at all) because those who benefit are known as free-riders (they can enjoy the benefits without contributing to cost) and thus do not signal a demand for increased production through the market.

The role of the government with respect to externalities is clear, if complex in practice. Either, first, establish the appropriate property rights (if practicable) so that free-riders or those affected by external costs can be excluded or compensated through the market and, if need be, the courts. Or, second, tax or subsidize producers so they are faced with a true reflection of the total social costs and benefits of their production. In both cases market production can be encouraged to fall or rise to a more socially efficient level. In nonmarket situations—such as the noisy neighbor—the government may typically need to regulate the activity directly, for example, by banning loud music outright after a certain point in the evening.

Public goods can be thought of as an extreme case of externality where a benefit is both nonexcludable *and* nonrival:[16] in addition to not being able to exclude those who benefit but do not pay, consumption of a public good's output does not affect anyone else's consumption. Perhaps the classic example is a country's national defense force: it is not possible for any individual to be excluded from the deterrent effects of the armed forces, while at the same time each person's benefit from this deterrence does not dilute—or rival—any other person's. A police force has a similar effect within a locality by generally deterring criminal activity; and policies to reduce climate change would, if successful, potentially benefit everyone in the world by protecting the human race from the malign effects of global warming. The benefit of a public good is for everyone or no one: in effect, the marginal cost of producing an extra unit of output is zero. In fact, nonrivalness produces problems for efficiency even if excludability has been achieved; under most assumptions it results in undersupply, although not all analyses concur (Cornes and Sandler 1996, 243–55). In any event, a clear case of a public good will usually require the government to step in and produce the good itself or finance another party to produce the good.

The second key area of market failure is that related to the availability or otherwise of information. Problems with information involve a failure of a fundamental assumption of microeconomics—that individuals know what goods are available, their quality and nature, and their price. However, in the real world there is often imperfect or asymmetric information. Thus the producer retains information that would be helpful to the consumer, or the

16   Some economists, such as Gravelle and Rees (1992), characterize public goods simply by their nonrivalness, regardless of whether they exhibit excludability.

consumer retains information required for the proper design of a good or service by the producer. Sometimes this may simply be a commercial supplier hiding certain risk factors of a product, such as the harmful effects of smoking, or a landlord not being candid about an apartment having a tendency to dampness. Here the government may simply compel the publication of relevant information by the manufacturer or supply that information itself through public information campaigns.

Rather more complex problems occur when there are information imbalances in insurance markets: for example, moral hazard (where the insured person hides his true lifestyle, which is likely to render the insured-against event more probable) and adverse selection (where insured people do not accurately reveal their risk factors). Moral hazard occurs in insurance markets where either consumers or suppliers act in ways more likely to incur the insured-against event. It happens because full information is not revealed by the trading parties and is particularly acute in the health-care field. Perhaps the seminal article in this context was by Kenneth Arrow (1963, 946), who argued that "virtually all the special features of [the medical care] industry ... stem from the prevalence of uncertainty." By "uncertainty" Arrow was principally referring to unpredictability and information asymmetry. Clinicians have more information than we do about our state of health and what to do about it. In private markets they have an incentive and opportunity to oversupply to increase their revenues and cause overspending on health care at an aggregate level. Some have argued that this is in itself an argument for a compulsory (universal) health-care system like the NHS (Donaldson 1998). However, it could also require simply the regulation of private markets, with people free to choose whether to be covered by insurance.

As with the harm principle, information problems also pervade justifications for intervention outside market contexts. Thus the government will provide information on dangerous tides off attractive beaches or warn of sharp corners on roads. Thus, even though there is no market exchange, it may be difficult for individuals undertaking a private activity to have sufficient knowledge to allow them to make an informed decision on whether to proceed.

In each of these cases there is a prima facie case for intervention. It is worth noting that the government also supports the general efficiency of markets through contract law, whereby freely made agreements between buyers and sellers can be enforced, or damages awarded, through the judicial system. Such legal provisions clearly support commerce and trade in all its forms by giving confidence to contractors that agreements will be honored. The general efficiency of an economic system is thus supported. Contracts are also important in nonmarket circumstances, such as marriage and adoption. Other legal provisions, such as those that ensure that the provision of a deceased person's will are effected, may also in the broadest sense promote efficiency simply by enabling people to get what they want even when no longer around themselves to undertake it.

Equity

A formal definition of equity is difficult, perhaps because most definitions actually incorporate elements of the author's preferred concept of the precise form equity should take. However, one can draw attention to the concept of a distribution—of how things are shared out between people—and the idea that this distribution should accord with a sense of fairness, that people get what is their due.[17]

Such a valued end of social arrangements goes back at least as far as Aristotle, whose original conception of distributive justice (which he carefully distinguished from retributive justice[18]) still forms the basis of many modern-day debates:

> The just, then, must be both . . . equal and relative (i.e., for certain persons) . . . if they [the persons] are not equal they will not have what is equal, [and] this is the origin of quarrels and complaints—when either equals have and are awarded unequal shares, or unequals equal shares. Further, this is plain from the fact that awards should be "according to merit"; for all men agree that what is just in distribution must be according to merit in some sense. (Aristotle 1980, 112)

In simpler terms, equals should receive what is being distributed in equal measure (sometimes known as horizontal equity), and unequals should receive it in unequal measure to the extent that their inequalities are morally relevant (a less loaded phrase than "merit" in today's language; also known as vertical equity). One important task for all those who believe distributive justice and equity have a role to play is to unravel the morally relevant, and irrelevant, differences between people—what Gutmann called the "relevant reasons" approach (1980).

Thus equity is concerned with both a "distribution," describing how some entity is shared out among people, and the "things" being distributed—there has to be a distribution of something. This distinction has been characterized

17   We should also acknowledge that distributional concerns have been argued to be irrelevant, or even counter, to notions of social justice, and measures to address them harmful to incentives. Social justice has been described as a "mirage" (Hayek 1976).

18   Aristotle used the term "rectificatory" according to the translation by Ross. And, as a semantic curiosity, Aristotle also outlined a distinction between "equity" and legal justice: here the former enters in specific cases to ameliorate the rather blunt "general" principles of law that might lead to injustices in particular cases—such as a jury acquitting of murder a doctor who killed his patient in mercy (see Aristotle 1980, 132–34). This acquittal could be termed "equitable" in an Aristotelian sense.

in terms of "combining characteristics" (which is concerned with distributional rules[19]) and "relevant personal features" (which equate to the things being distributed[20]) (Sen 1992, 73–74). For example, one can say that an equitable distribution should be equal, or it should favor those who have the least of the things, or it should reflect freely made choices, or hard work, or whatever.

Then there is a further distinction to be made between things that are themselves objects of consumption and things that enable a degree of choice over what is to be consumed. The former might include goods and services, or even some phenomenon not normally thought of as consumable nor purchasable, such as political liberties, but in any event is concerned with "final" wants and desires. The latter approximates to money, which is essentially of instrumental value: an "abstract medium of exchange value . . . [which] should be regarded as a representation of the commensurability of the meanings and values of other goods, not as a good with meaning or value in itself" (Waldron 1995, 145, 147). So if we consider income transfers— and most social security benefits fall into this category—then a decision about an equitable distribution does not include any requirement about how the money is spent. If the choice of which goods or services to consume is left to the individual, then a concern with equity amounts to a concern with how to adjust income levels to arrive at a fair distribution.

However, much government policy is actually concerned, not with income transfers, but with consumption-specific interventions. And in many cases equity is invoked to defend such interventions, such as with health (Daniels 1981), children's education (Levin 1991), and higher education (Committee on Higher Education 1963). Clearly, therefore, for these policies there is a concern that goes beyond the simple distribution of benefits, to which goods and services produce those benefits. Various terms have been used to refer to this approach in the economics and political theory literature, such as "specific egalitarianism" (Weale 1983), "categorical equity" (Feldstein 1975, 76), and the "domain" of inequality (Tobin 1970).

Do Nonpaternalist Justifications Explain Paternalist Laws and Regulations?

We outlined above a large number of possibly paternalist policies, laws, and regulations. However, we also noted that it can be difficult to disentangle the various motives for introducing such interventions. Often a regulation or law will be defended with reference to one of the justifications outlined

19 Sen includes "sum-maximisation, lexicographic priorities and maximin, equality or one of various other combining rules."

20 Here Sen includes "liberties and primary goods, rights, resources, commodity bundles and capabilities."

in the preceding section. Commonly, establishing a nonpaternalist reason for action would be more palatable politically than a paternalistic justification. In the remainder of this chapter we review a number of these nonpaternalist arguments as they relate to some of the specific examples of state intervention raised above. Specifically, we shall seek to identify where the nonpaternalist case is misused: first looking at arguments from externalities and the harm principle, then from imperfect information, and finally from equity. The nonpaternalist case for many government interventions is revealed to be weaker than is often supposed.[21]

Arguments from Externalities and the Harm Principle

Perhaps the most common strategy for supporting an existing policy in nonpaternalistic terms is to claim that a market externality or the harm principle is the reason for government intervention. There are three principal arguments of this kind: the protection of the public purse; the existence of psychic costs and caring externalities; and the misidentification of internalities as externalities, and other spurious social gains.

The first concerns the protection of the public purse. It is often argued that the reason for the state prohibition of dangerous activities such as snorkeling in treacherous but attractive waters, or of failing to wear a seat belt or a motorcycle helmet, is that they represent a financial burden on the wider community. Rescue services will be called out to people in distress, and such rescue will often be expensive—the cost will not be met by the individuals taking the risk, so why should they be allowed to undertake an activity that "harms" others financially? It is too difficult to identify those who are washed out to sea accidentally from those who willfully take risks, so the only policy is to ban the activity.

However, in many cases it would be easy to require the individual to contribute to the potential costs of her rescue. Actuarial estimates could be made about the likelihood of swimmers getting into trouble off beaches, and this charge could be made to the swimmer beforehand. Insurance companies often charge an additional premium for insuring against medical expenses incurred as a result of adventurous sports. Similar charges could be made to protect public health-care finances: for example, a tax premium could be added to motor insurance for those who wished to ride without seat belts or motorcycle helmets to cover any expected additional medical care costs.[22] Those who refuse to insure themselves could still be given med-

---

21   De Marneffe (2006) comes to a similar conclusion in arguing that the general presumption against paternalism is wrong and that many nonpaternalistic reasons for policies are less compelling than paternalistic ones.

22   For further development of this argument, see Le Grand (2013).

ical care but then charged with breaking the law and fined. No doubt some on low incomes will get away without making their "fair" contribution in such a case, but as long as the law is reasonably effective the wider community's budget would be protected.

Similar arguments from protecting the public purse are occasionally made against smokers and in other cases where it is believed there is an element of choice in undertaking the potentially health-harming activity.[23] We know smoking causes ill health, and, where there is a public health-care system, the additional medical care consumed by smokers will be met by public resources. Smoking is a matter of choice, unlike many other causes of ill health, and thus smokers are charged with causing an avoidable financial burden to be placed on the wider community.[24] This in turn leads some commentators to argue that smokers should have a weaker claim to the limited medical care resources available—particularly where this involves a nonemergency procedure such as a coronary heart bypass graft. But in fact the taxes on tobacco and cigarettes are more than sufficient to cover all the additional medical care costs incurred by smokers.[25] Indeed, this surplus tax revenue suggests that the taxes are additionally motivated by a desire to deter smoking per se. At any rate, the example of smoking demonstrates that there are mechanisms for protecting the public purse that do not require an outright ban on an activity, nor the withholding of medical treatment from people who need it.

The second externality argument concerns the existence of psychic costs and caring externalities. Take the example of protective motorcycle helmets once again. Assume we have a situation where motorcyclists are allowed to ride without a helmet on the basis that they have paid an insurance premium to cover additional costs to the wider society. We noted above that some will try to get away without paying for their insurance premium and will crash and need to be treated. We suggested that in such cases emergency services should treat the motorcyclists and then seek to recoup some of the expense through legal remedy. Implicit in this approach is that it is unthinkable that we as a society simply stand back and say, "Sorry, you haven't paid your insurance, you will have to lie there and bleed to death." The psychic

23   This is one of the factors cited in Derek Wanless, *Securing Good Health to the Whole Population* (London: HMSO, 2004).

24   In a society without public health provision, then obviously these costs would not be borne by the wider community; however, charitable and voluntary health and rescue services might still feel aggrieved that some people do not take sufficient care of their health and thus put pressure on the voluntary sector's limited resources.

25   In the UK in 2006 receipts from tobacco duty were around £8 billion (http://www.hmrc.gov.uk/statistics/receipts/info-analysis.pdf). The cost to the NHS of smoking is controversial; estimates vary between £2.7 billion and £5.2 billion, but in any case it is substantially less than the tax receipts (Allender et al. 2009; Callum, Boyle, and Sandford 2010).

costs (Dworkin 1983)—a form of external cost caused by other people's suffering—would be too great. Most people find the sight or knowledge of excessive suffering hard to bear. It is a genuine form of distress in itself.

This distress would be greater for anyone involved in the accident, and yet worse if they bore a measure of responsibility for the accidents concerned. If I cause an accident that would not normally do much harm (except to the motorbike) but that, because the other party is not wearing a helmet, kills him, then the fact that I have killed him is a heavy psychic cost for me to bear. And it could be anyone who finds himself or herself in this position of having killed another.

Thus there is a general externality argument for obliging motorcyclists to wear helmets so that these psychic costs are not incurred in the first place. After all, why should we allow motorcyclists to risk putting us in this appalling position? It is not paternalism, runs the argument, but self-protection.

Such arguments have a wide range of potential applications because any activity that involves a risk of people suffering extreme distress or harm, physically or psychologically, could equally well harm others. Even activities that cause temporary and reversible harm, such as becoming a serious drug addict, might lead society to act so as to avoid others being exposed to this suffering. The argument can also be used to support the provision of in-kind social services. Here the typical case is one where ill health cannot be prevented, as it can be with helmets and restricted swimming rights, because the ill health has not necessarily arisen from any particular cause. Rather, a service is provided for those who become sick or needy in the normal course of events but cannot afford health care. Again, many people cannot bear the thought that others should suffer from a lack of treatment in such circumstances; conversely, they gain satisfaction from knowing that the needy are cared for. This is the so-called caring externality (Culyer 1980, 183): the private market will undersupply health care under these circumstances because these external benefits are not reflected in the demand for health-care institutions. Weale (1983) considers this issue in terms of "donors"—those who are net contributors to the finance of social programs. If these donors are concerned only with the general well-being of the recipients, then cash rather than consumption-specific provision would be appropriate. However, "if donors value specific features of the circumstances of recipients, then the position is changed. For example, donors may prefer the elderly to be assured of heating or home-help services, but not worry about their consumption of tobacco or drink" (Weale 1983, 108).

Maximizing social well-being will, under these circumstances, require specifying the consumption of certain services so that those who provide the funds have *their* utility increased in addition to the benefit the recipients derive. Older people may enjoy greater utility from a cash transfer that allows them to buy plenty of drink and tobacco and minimize heating and home-help services. However, when their utility levels resulting from consumption-specific policies are added to the utility derived by the donors, the result is a greater aggregate total.

However, one of the most significant problems with the use of the psychic cost/caring externality rationale is that virtually no activity is ever entirely free from having an impact on other people's well-being if we include effects that impinge only on people's consciousness. Such an impact requires only that others are aware of an activity's existence. Knowledge of it automatically means that it is the potential source of an externality. Thus, if "others" claim that they are being harmed by this knowledge—or benefiting from it—then the government could argue, in intervening to encourage or discourage the activity, that it is simply correcting a form of market failure.

But if there are very few areas of life that in no way impinge on others' consciousness, then presumably there are very few private activities that do not lend themselves to intervention on the grounds of a psychic cost, even where this cost is not generated by someone else's suffering. So, for example, a certain type of sexual practice between consenting adults in private, which a segment of the population finds morally reprehensible (and the rest do not care about one way or the other), could be outlawed simply with reference to a judgment that the disutility experienced by disapproving "onlookers" exceeded the utility of practitioners. Such policies would be most likely to pass such a test in the case of minority practices that a majority find hard to understand.

In this example the difficulty arises as a result of the "illiberal" attitudes of some people toward others—the two groups do not agree about the legitimacy of a particular activity for others, even if the activity does not cause physical harm. This can cause tensions between liberal values (where individuals are free to pursue their own ends) and Pareto optimality (where nobody's well-being can be improved without reducing someone else's). Amartya Sen (1970) provides the example of a society of two people and one book, *Lady Chatterley's Lover*. The intuitive nature of the issue is as follows. One is a prude who does not want to read the book, the other is not a prude who does want to read it—this would be the "liberal" outcome, with both parties doing what they want. However, what if they *both prefer* that the prude rather than the nonprude reads it? This might result because the nonprude takes delight in the prude's discomfort, while the prude cannot bear the thought of anyone else actually obtaining gratification from such reprehensible material—this is the Pareto or "welfarist" solution. Given that they both prefer this latter outcome, any other permutation of reading/nonreading will make at least one of them worse off. At root, the problem arises because an assessment of well-being levels has taken into account individuals' judgments about the source of other people's well-being—the external effects of one person's pleasure or displeasure on another.

In other words, these externalities are of a very peculiar type. Normally externalities and the harm principle are concerned with the impact of certain eventualities—practical, tangible occurrences—on the utility level of third parties. But psychic costs—and we concentrate here on costs rather than benefits for simplicity—involve the nature or source of one person's utility affecting the utility of another. This could happen in two ways. Either the person is simply suffering terrible pain and distress—severe disutility— and this causes distress in the third party, or the activity providing the *source* of the utility (the unusual sexual practice, or reading of *Lady Chatterley's Lover*) is considered repugnant or offensive.[26] Either way, people are either pleased or displeased by what they perceive to be going on inside someone else's mind, or what caused that state of mind, rather than simply being concerned with how the impact of practical events around them affects their own utility. Some economists suggest that these effects are not true externalities but rather a "spiritual" variant:

> There seems to me to be a fundamental difference between the externality which arises if I receive disutility simply from my knowledge of your . . . smoking, and the externality which arises from my actually breathing your smoke. The appropriateness of the government using its powers of compulsion to intervene in spiritual externalities seems questionable at best. (Stiglitz 1989, 48)

The central point, then, is that justifications for government action based on the promotion of market efficiency by correcting external effects should confine themselves to considering external costs and benefits only when they involve actual *consumption* by a third party, and not a *judgment* about consumption—for the latter inevitably requires principles that go beyond the ordinary assessment of economic efficiency.

This leads us back to the case of compulsory helmet wearing. If spiritual or caring externalities are not true externalities, then similarly the psychic costs imposed by an injured motorcyclist cannot be sufficient justification to warrant outlawing biking bare-headed *on that basis alone*. The biker has willingly taken a risk with her health and become badly injured as a result. She has caused us to be deeply upset by what has befallen her. But this has not physically harmed us. If we wish to outlaw such risky behavior, we need to do so on the basis not of harm to us but of benefit to her—that is, through paternalism, not externalities or the harm principle.

---

26   Feinberg (1985) discusses in detail the limited number of cases in which "offense" is a legitimate reason for the sanction of the criminal law.

Another argument concerning externalities involves the misidentification of internalities as externalities, and other spurious social gains. It is often surprisingly easy to misidentify personal or "internal" benefits as an externality and thus mistakenly justify state subsidy on these grounds. Take education, a publicly delivered service that relies to a significant degree on external benefits for its justification for public subsidy. Here the state intervenes to promote increased consumption on the basis that, in an unregulated market, people calculate only their own gains from education and do not take into account the beneficial effects of their consumption on others. This principle is in some ways an analog of the harm principle—it is a relevant reason for the state to intervene in one person's decision making to ensure that a benefit is obtained for others. Children are provided with free education and an obligation to attend in order to benefit "wider society"; without it, runs the argument, we will be likely to impoverish ourselves as a nation.

Put another way, the argument is that there is a social rate of return to education that is greater than the private rate of return. The social rate of return is the sum of the private return to the individual plus the external return, the latter being the benefit to the rest of society of the individual receiving an education. If this external benefit is large, then the social rate of return will be significantly greater than the private rate of return; but since the individuals concerned will only take account of the private benefits and costs to them in making their decisions about how much to invest in their education, they may not invest enough in their own education to benefit the wider society, especially if they have to pay the full costs of that education. Hence there is a prima facie case for government subsidy to reduce those costs to the individuals concerned and hence to encourage them to make a larger investment.

Reports on higher education, particularly those in the UK by Robbins and Dearing, make repeated reference to the social or national interest. The latter's analysis of why the government should support higher education includes the following passages:

> Society as a whole has a direct interest in ensuring the UK has the level of participation in higher education which it needs for sustained economic and social viability. . . . [T]he costs of a shortfall in the numbers of those obtaining such qualifications will fall to the UK as a whole and its citizens. . . .
>
> Firms and individuals are most likely to engage in training *specific to their immediate needs*. There is therefore a danger that, if left to employers and individuals, the nature and level of higher education will not best serve the long term needs of the economy as a whole; and there will be under-investment. The state alone is able to ensure that tomorrow's workforce is equipped with the widest range of skills and attributes.

(National Committee of Inquiry into Higher Education 1997, 288, emphasis added)

More generally, high rates of return on "human capital" when compared with other factors of production can often lead commentators to argue that "with no evidence of diminishing returns to investment in higher education, somewhat larger percentage increases ... in human capital relative to the rate of increase in investment in housing, would appear to be a socially efficient investment strategy" (McMahon 1991, 291).

However, the role of externalities in education must be carefully separated from the increased productivity that education provides, and which is reflected in increased earnings of the individuals concerned.[27] These increased earnings are "internal" benefits: someone pays for education and benefits from the consequently higher income levels later in life. If the whole productivity gain is captured in this way, there is no external effect. Subsidizing education in this way would therefore actually be encouraging people to increase their investment in their own future income levels beyond what they would choose to do without government intervention. If they were refunded their tax payments and education was provided at market prices, they might spend rather less on their human capital and more on immediate pleasures: a low-income, easy life could well be more congenial to them. It is not necessarily an efficient social investment strategy to subsidize higher education if people are the best judges of their own interests.

This is not to say that true external effects do not occur in education, particularly in the realm of basic literacy and numeracy. A true external effect must influence *others*, and with education the beneficial influence is taken to be the increased ability of people to work *together*. Social skills are of limited benefit if others, with whom one has to work and live, do not possess them. Take two people on a desert island, one of whom enjoys literacy for his own sake, and another who does not. The one who does not calculates that there is insufficient benefit to be derived from teaching himself (or "paying" the other to do so) when compared with other ways he could spend his time. The literate castaway tries to reason that they would both stand to gain from literacy by being able to coordinate and communicate their activities in a more sophisticated manner. However, the illiterate castaway still estimates that the combination of the social benefit (the portion that accrues to him) and his private benefit will not quite cover his time costs in achieving literacy. In doing so, though, he does not take account of that portion of the social benefit going to his companion—adding

27   Although even this connection between education per se and increased earning power is now often questioned (Glennerster 1993).

this benefit may mean that the aggregate social benefit exceeds the aggregate cost. The literate castaway may need to pay (or "subsidize") the illiterate to learn. In a large, complex economy the state takes the role of subsidizer because of the difficulty of organizing such payments.

But higher education has little such evidence to support the government's role on this basis. One eminent commentator has concluded, "I am not convinced that the externalities are very important, as contrasted with elementary and secondary education where externalities are undoubtedly consequential. It is somewhat hard for me to visualise what these externalities would consist of" (Arrow 1993, 8).

Another argument that overuses the externality justification is that from social integration. The initial focus of interest was on welfare services such as education and health (Marshall 1950). By providing social services on a universal basis—regardless of income—the state creates a situation where service delivery involves people of all classes interacting with other members of the community, thus strengthening social bonds. Rights to receive these services are not primarily about the distribution of social benefits but about promoting social cohesion and banishing class distinctions. Thus all social classes will receive their health care in the same ward and queue up in the same waiting room. Education, on the other hand, may assist in "the emergence of 'social cohesion' by the transmission of a common cultural heritage" (Blaug 1987, 108). The latter benefit is also cited when public subsidies for the arts are debated. But the theory extends beyond welfare and the arts. Public-service broadcasting has been defended as a means of promoting a more integrated national community. When television programs enjoy high ratings, large numbers of people will be sharing in the same activity, giving a sense of social purpose and cohesion.

But do these externalities really exist? It is, at the very least, difficult to demonstrate empirically that they exist when we are discussing something as intangible as social cohesion. Who is to say what a more or less cohesive society looks like in any measurable sense, or whether a "less" cohesive society is really less functional? Some policies, such as those laws against homosexuality, are as likely to alienate people and drive them apart from others in their community and by doing so may damage society rather than sustain it. Technology may make collective activities—such as a nation watching the Olympics together on television—less frequent: multichannel broadcasting now means that we can all choose to watch a wider variety of programs with smaller audiences. It is more likely that a sense of national unity was supported by public-sector broadcasting when there was only one channel. The educational and arts "externalities" could with equal plausibility be viewed as "private" benefits, which, when aggregated, appear to reflect a "good" society. At the very least we must remain skeptical about the impact of externalities on national wealth, community, and integration. Such goals sound unobjectionable, yet they may in fact require improved individual decision making and not the correction of market failure.

Externalities are used in many ways to support government action. But very often, on closer inspection, such justifications are neither intellectually coherent nor supported by empirical evidence for the existence of the externality. Alternatively, as we have argued here, they subtly import arguments that are more supportive of the paternalist case.

Overcorrection of Imperfect Information

Imperfect information is a common reason for state action to correct both market and nonmarket situations where individuals are unable to maximize their well-being because they do not know the facts of their chosen course of action or the true nature of the goods or services available to them. But it is easy to misuse this justification by stretching it to support interventions that go beyond the mere provision of information to actually restricting behavior.

Many activities have potentially harmful side effects. The range of potentially paternalistic policies noted above included a number directed at such activities: smoking cigarettes, swimming in dangerous waters, eating certain kinds of food, or consuming recreational drugs. Information about these side effects may not be revealed by the suppliers of the products, or in the case of a dangerous natural environment there may be no active concealment and yet the danger may be difficult to perceive. In either case, the individual may do or consume more than she would have done if she were in full possession of the facts. It is equally likely that the *beneficial* outcome of activities may not be sufficiently evident to the potential consumer, in which case she would consume too little. A potential student may not be aware of the increased earnings that he is likely to earn if he goes to university, and that these earnings are likely to more than compensate him for any debt he incurs in the process. In all these examples, whether they involve dangers or benefits, the government is justified in rebalancing the information relationship by compelling certain types of declarations to be made about the potential dangers or benefits.

However, the government may go further than the simple clarification of facts and information. It may prioritize certain kinds of information over others: there are few states, for instance, that would publicize the relaxation benefits of smoking to nonsmokers, preferring instead to emphasize its dangers. Or it may engage in one of the many kinds of intervention that specifically encourage or discourage consumption. Justifications for such actions should not rely solely on imperfect information. For, as we have already noted in chapter 2, there is a distinction to be drawn between providing information and influencing how people act on that information. Take the foreword to a British government white paper on smoking, which states, "Smoking kills.... We want to help existing smokers quit the habit and help children and young people not to get addicted in the first place. These objectives can only be achieved by a concerted campaign to reduce smoking" (Secretary of State for Health et al. 1998, 2).

This does not imply a policy motivated by a concern that people are not aware of the dangers of smoking. Indeed, survey evidence now indicates that campaigns to provide information about the dangers of smoking have been so successful that people actually overestimate the probability of their suffering serious ill health (Antoñanzas et al. 2000; Viscusi 2002–3). But the governments concerned still clearly wish to prevent people from smoking.

Problems with imperfect information may also occur in nonmarket situations. Here the situation is likely to be such that it is only a single individual's interests that are at stake. Let us return to the example of our swimmer who enjoys snorkeling in attractive but dangerous waters. If she does not know that the tides are dangerous, she could be swept to her death. She has insufficient information about the dangers she faces. Under these circumstances the government is likely to provide statutory warnings about the tides or even to employ lifeguards to warn against swimming. However, if we assume that there is nothing wrong with the ability of the swimmer to reason out her best interests, then once she has full information about the state of the tides, she should be left to make up her own mind about what to do.[28] If she persists in wishing to continue with her activities in spite of the danger, and is still prevented from pursuing the activities rather than just being warned of the danger (or perhaps temporarily prevented until she was fully apprised of the situation), then this would be intervening for reasons other than simple information correction. The public official (the lifeguard) would then, on behalf of the state, be taking action based on an implicit belief that her judgment was lacking.

Government support for higher education, too, has also been justified in standard textbooks using information-based arguments.[29] And yet most countries actively subsidize such education, thus going far beyond simply providing information to students on relative lifetime earnings from undertaking various courses alongside information on the debt likely to be incurred, and then leave the student to decide what they wish to do. Some

---

28   Let us assume she has also paid her premium for the additional chance of needing to call out the rescue services.

29   See Barr (2004) for a sophisticated approach to this question, and more generally on the efficiency rationale for state intervention in welfare provision.

have argued that there are also information problems for private market lenders when they are making loans to potential students; such lenders cannot easily assess the risk of the borrower, and generally no collateral is possible for such lending (Barr 1994). Again, this may be used as an argument for subsidy. But it is not clear that there is asymmetry of information about future productive capacity: educational qualifications and being accepted by a university give a reasonable indication of ability to both student and lender. This may simply be as good as the information gets—there is no way of improving the level of information beyond what currently exists. In any event, if students are being dissuaded from taking out the necessary loans because the lenders are unwilling to provide them at sufficiently low rates of interest, this does not in itself constitute a market failure and thus is not necessarily inefficient. If there were a high risk of default, the market would be reacting quite properly by charging high interest rates.

The case for public service broadcasting also relies partly on arguments from imperfect information. The claim with broadcasting is that it is hard to know what we like in advance; furthermore, television itself may serve to shape our preferences and tastes for the future (Graham and Davies 1997). As a consequence of both these factors, the market will typically provide overly conservative viewing, based on past experience of what people watch, rather than including challenging and innovative viewing that people would enjoy more—if only they knew it. As Graham and Davies put it:

> consumers may be unavoidably myopic about their own long term interests. Consumers cannot be other than ill-informed about effects that broadcasting may have on them. . . . [I]f all television is elicited by the market, there is a very real danger that consumers will under-invest in the *development* of their *own* tastes, their *own* experience, and their *own* capacity to comprehend. (20; emphasis in original)

But this is a peculiar notion of being ill informed. We don't "know" about the future long-term effects broadcasting may have on us. It may be true that we misjudge this effect, but it is not simply a lack of information, because information involves data and descriptive facts about an item of consumption and is not the same thing as the experience of actually consuming it. Can we only be "well informed" about choices involved in purchasing a meal by actually eating it? Certainly we do not know for sure whether we will like a meal before we actually eat it (although we may have eaten many similar meals before), but information about ingredients, style, and so on are what constitute the information on which to make a judgment; the consumption itself involves the rather different assessment of what it actually did for our well-being. What about programs "educating us about future wants and desires"? Again, eating has a similar effect—but we seem quite able to educate ourselves in this respect.

Arguments from "Quality"

Support for public subsidy of the arts, film, and public-service broadcasting often makes reference to the impact a reduction in such a subsidy would have on the quality of what is produced. If the private market in these goods and services operates, and all such artistic endeavor is forced to depend on the willingness of people to pay the true cost of its production, then creativity will suffer as artists are forced to conform to people's base wants. These wants, it is argued, are typically conservative; innovation will be stifled and the quality of artistic endeavor will suffer.

This argument does not involve any specific reference to market failure of the kinds outlined thus far; it seems to rest on an ill-defined notion that the market by its very nature is inherently incapable of supplying great art. What is lacking is any specificity about the nature of the failure that is taking place. It cannot be *impossible* that great art should be associated with commercial exchange—after all, Mozart, Dickens, and Shakespeare all worked in commercial environments. Of course, the patronage of wealthy individuals through history has also supported artistic genius. But this still involved payment for a wanted product and produced any number of Renaissance geniuses. Perhaps the best argument for government subsidy on this basis would involve citing a type of "public-good" argument that true artistic talent comes along so seldom that we risk missing out altogether if we leave the nurturing of these future geniuses to the market. If a Mozart does emerge, we all benefit from his genius, and we would equally if someone else paid for it. The result may be that too few pay for the nurturing—including the prospective artists themselves, many of whom will perhaps feel that the chance of their being able to achieve success is too slim to justify the expense of their artistic training. But a public-good rationale of this kind would only justify the government supporting the *training* and nurturing of young artists, not necessarily the day-to-day subsidy of the production of artistic events.

Another argument sometimes made by those in the creative arts is that too few people can afford to pay what is necessary to achieve a certain quality standard, and so to make the production economically viable, the producers need to be subsidized. Or, alternatively, they argue that it *will* be economically viable but only to the well-off. The first line of argument merely begs the question as to why it is considered that any given artistic enterprise should, as of right, be economically viable in the first place. After all, in an ordinary market, if not enough people want to pay for something, then the typical outcome is that it is not produced. The second point is more important: the output is so "valuable" that those who make it wish it to be available to everyone no matter what their income levels. Not to make the arts available to all is unfair; the government should make them free or at least heavily subsidized for the sake of equity. However, the nonpaternalist who wishes to adopt this line of reasoning will be faced with the following response: why subsidize this particular good, rather than people's general level of income? In that way you provide people with the opportunity to experience great art but allow them the option to spend that "income subsidy" elsewhere if they wish. If the cost of the production is so expensive—world-class opera, perhaps—that income transfers would need to be very high to allow consumption, perhaps we need to reexamine just what makes this good so important that it should be available to all income levels. But this is to anticipate the next section, on equity, where we explore this type of nonpaternalistic justification for intervention in more detail.

Arguments from Equity

There are two main arguments from considerations of equity that the nonpaternalist uses to support government intervention: first, that vulnerable, disadvantaged people need protection from being able to make choices that would damage their self-interest; and second, that the provision of free or subsidized goods and services will promote equity or fairness.

Taking the argument from vulnerable people first, we can see that many of the laws and regulations outlined above are attempts to protect such individuals. Forbidding the sale of body parts, assisted suicide, euthanasia, and self-mutilation are defended as protections against desperate people being forced into doing something they do not really want to do: the poor, immigrant worker selling a kidney; the sick, elderly relative who chooses to die rather than be a burden on others; the misguided individual who asks to have his healthy leg amputated. Furthermore, those who want to restrict prostitution and pornography often do not have a moral objection to the trades concerned but want to restrict them on similar grounds: that the people supplying these services should not find themselves in such a degrading and dangerous position by reason of financial necessity. Similarly, maximum working hours and compulsory holiday entitlement are defended as a protection from overwork for people with low incomes or those who work for unscrupulous bosses. Some of the restrictions on what can be contained in a contractual agreement do the same: prohibitions on voluntary enslavement or peonage are partly defended on the grounds that people who find themselves in desperate circumstances should not be liable to exploitation. Neither is one allowed to waive one's right to protection from discrimination—the legislation seeks to help minority groups and women who are at a disadvantage, and they are not allowed to trade in that protection.

Clearly, being literally forced or coerced into any activity offends the harm principle. But the issue here is whether the prohibition on various types of activity is the right approach to the problem. Many people may well find themselves in dire circumstances, and it is certainly the role of the government to correct inequities where these result in deprivation. But in all these examples the law attempts to do this by prohibiting the very means by which the people concerned are trying to improve their situation (Callahan 1986). Is it right on grounds of equity to say that to improve the position of the people concerned we should remove what might be their *least worst option*? To prohibit them might be to make their situation worse, in their judgment.[30] If such policies instead targeted an improvement in the vulnerable person's income or circumstances, then this might address the root cause of the suffering, and in many cases people might well desist from the activity in question. But this is not inevitable: even at quite high levels of income, someone might think that selling a kidney is the best option. And for some, such as those considering assisted suicide, monetary compensation would not help their disadvantaged situation. Even where an elderly relative is considering assisted suicide to remove the burden of her care needs from relatives, and where that elderly person is being led to believe that the rest of the family would indeed be grateful—even this, reprehensible and invidious though the situation might seem, might in the judgment of the person concerned be the best outcome. This is not to say that the government should not ensure that the parties entering into all these agreements are protected from genuine threats and menaces. But once such assurances are in place, if the government wishes to go further and prevent the action, it is now doing more than simply protecting a vulnerable person—rather it may be taking away from her one of the last meaningful choices she is able to make. Hence, to justify such a potentially fundamental intrusion into an individual's decision making, paternalistic reasons must be provided as to why this choice is likely to be misguided; an appeal to equity or fairness is insufficient.

The second argument from equity is that the provision of free or subsidized goods and services will promote fairness. We have seen that the government seeks to provide many welfare services in-kind at prices close to zero, or at least heavily subsidized, at the point of consumption. Health and education services are the most obvious examples in most countries.

---

30 Indeed, according to interpretations of equity in terms of equalizing choice sets (Le Grand 1991), we might be making the situation even less equitable through closing off one way for disadvantaged people to make money and hence reducing their choice set.

This has been defended on the basis of equity. But why does equity or social justice require this, specifically, rather than simply redistributing income? In-kind provision goes beyond a simple concern with the distribution of resources, which individuals are then left to convert into utilities according to their own preferences, to a concern with particular types of well-being.

Take health care. Given health's ethically important place among the range of individual goals that constitute a worthwhile life, it is perhaps unsurprising that numerous theories of equity have been developed to justify government involvement in its provision. Most relate these claims to some notion of need for health care that, for various reasons, is claimed to be the proper basis for its provision—rather than, say, ability to pay or accident of birth. Such opinions have a long pedigree: "leaving aside preventive medicine, the proper ground of distribution of medical care is ill health: this is a necessary truth" (Williams 1964, 121). Many countries provide this medical care directly, rather than by ensuring that people have sufficient income to purchase adequate insurance.

So it is with education: schools are provided directly to address the problem of inequity. An equitable distribution of education is taken to mean that there should be universal *equality of access* that eliminates irrelevant or discriminatory criteria, such as income. This is coupled with compulsory consumption to ensure that parents do not ignore the opportunity to consume this good. Equity has also been a strong driving force in the development of higher education. The UK Robbins Report argued that "the good society desires equality of opportunity for its citizens to become not merely good producers but also good men and women" (Committee on Higher Education 1963, 8). The Dearing Report argued that "the state must . . . make sure that access to higher education is socially just" (National Committee of Inquiry into Higher Education 1997, 288).

Theories of equity that imply or require a consumption-specific policy response eventually have to justify why the particular form of consumption should be chosen. In attempting to answer this, theorists have developed highly sophisticated arguments for supporting consumption specificity. For example, Walzer (1983, 3) argues for a concept of complex equality, which involves different distributional rules for different goods in different "spheres." Thus in addition to income and wealth—which constitutes the focus of "simple" equality—there can be (in)equity in terms of "membership, power, honour, ritual eminence, divine grace, kinship and love, knowledge . . . physical security, work and leisure, rewards and punishments." As long as those who do rather better in one category do not use this advantage to obtain similar advantages in other categories, Walzer argues that domination—the true enemy of social justice—is avoided. To achieve this, boundaries must be set up between spheres, and different means of distribution will apply in each of them.

However, claiming that boundaries ought to be constructed to prevent pernicious leakages of domination between spheres involves an implicit judgment about what is in people's interests generally. Certain goods are designated as crucial to achieve this desirable state of affairs. But they are not chosen by appealing to principles of equity per se, but through an assessment (in Walzer's case by looking at the historical experience) about why they are "important" for people. Establishing importance requires a judgment that goes further than one simply relating to equity because it implies that people cannot properly assess the relative importance of consuming certain kinds of good against the potential for being dominated. For example, assume incomes alone are equalized, and there are no spheres (outside the political) where money cannot play a part. One person might wish to go fishing and travel, while another may wish to buy health and education. The former person might reasonably judge that those who choose the latter, in his opinion, will not unduly dominate him. On the other hand, he could be protected from *unfairness* in terms of how much fishing he could do, when compared with how much health care other (wealthier) people could choose, by redistributing income.

Another theorist who grappled with this problem was Norman Daniels (1981, 1985) drawing on the contribution made by Rawls (1971). Daniels specifically incorporated both "need" and health care into his theory of justice built on Rawls's foundations. He argued that health-care institutions should form part of the equality of opportunity "primary" good. This direct provision is simply the most straightforward way of dealing with unequal capabilities based on ill health. But why not offer cash equivalents instead? Daniels does not directly address this question, but the case seems to be that ill health is such a clear need that we do not have to be concerned about people having different valuations of its importance. Life, and some reasonable level of health, is an essential prerequisite—or provides the opportunity—for gaining utility. Nobody could argue differently because in this particular case it is possible to "know" that everyone needs this minimum standard of existence before a divergence of preferences makes comparison impossible.

But this does not seem quite right. Consider a severely incapacitated individual, perhaps paralyzed from the neck down. Assume this is a condition amenable to some treatment, although this will only ever offer a partial cure. If there is agreement that some kind of compensation would be fair, why should this compensation necessarily be in the form of health-care provision? The person concerned might in fact believe that, instead of the partial cure, she would prefer to use the compensatory money income to

travel the world and indulge her passion for visiting sites of historic archae-
ological interest.

We begin to see how difficult it is to establish, even in severe cases of
"need," what the appropriate response to that need should be. More generally, we can take the case of people who are healthy now but on low incomes. Just about everyone will need some expensive health care at some
point in their life, so, for Daniels, this might seem to constitute an unambig-
uous need—provide them with that health-care provision as a "right." But
can we be so sure? Would some individuals not prefer to take a chance
against their future needs and enjoy higher incomes now? The government
could ensure everyone had sufficient income to buy health insurance if they
wish—satisfying the requirements of equity—but leave those who do not to
enjoy their income in other ways.

Both Walzer and Daniels do subtly reintroduce an assumption that people should be constrained in their consumption patterns to those areas
that serve these "higher" concepts of "domination" or "normal opportunity
range." More generally, they introduce the concept that a certain need exists—that a certain important state or condition cannot be achieved without the need being satisfied. However, justifications for consumption-
specific policies do not specify why the particular decision about need
satisfaction is better taken by the government than by the individual. Instead they make great play on why, empirically and conceptually, particular
needs seem important. But why the "importance assessment" cannot be left
to the individual is evaded.

Take the case of higher education as a further example: this is heavily
subsidized in most countries. Why, and on what basis, has the choice been
made that this service, specifically, requires a universal intervention by the
government? No allowance seems to have been made for the possibility that
certain people may consider education to be an irrelevance, and that their
well-being would be better served by consuming other goods or services. In
such a case, "educational equity" would be an empty achievement for the
person concerned—in his view. The fact that some people may consider the
rejection of higher education an ill-considered, shortsighted, or even stupid
position for someone to adopt does not detract from the fact that this is one
person's (or the government's) opinion about another person's well-being.

This aspect of needs-based theories of equity is not confined to health
care and education and in particular has been applied to many aspects of
social services (Doyal and Gough 1991; Hendry 1998, iv; Brock 1998).
Needs-based theories, and those that focus on capabilities (Sen 1992), quite
reasonably emphasize the variations among people in their ability to
achieve certain valued functionings—the fact that some people find themselves in highly disadvantaged circumstances through no fault of their own.
This is not disputed here. For these people, the government must make

some judgment about the degree of this disadvantage to avoid perverse outcomes from simple money transfers. But a further distinction is less often made: between the observation and acceptance that such variations exist and the judgment about how to correct them. The correction can be provided either in money or in kind. Doing the former allows for the fact that the government may very often misjudge what is right for any particular individual, even if on average and for most people it rightly judges which needs people most highly value; furthermore, it acknowledges that even where there is agreement in general terms that a need is important (hunger, shelter, mobility), how one satisfies the need may be best undertaken by the individual utilizing monetary compensation. To do more than this, as is very common for health and education in particular, requires additional paternalistic justifications.

For one cannot simply assume that a welfare state that provides services in kind is justified by virtue of its concern with people's needs. Indeed, if needs are so important, then one might presume (given adequate incomes and leaving aside market failure) that people would be more than ready to satisfy the needs themselves. Food, after all, is of fundamental importance to us all, and yet there is no National Food Service nor any demand for one (New and Le Grand 1996, 48).

Conclusion

There are many possible nonpaternalistic justifications for government intervention in key areas of individual or social activity. These are based on (often overlapping) arguments derived from several sources, including the harm principle of John Stuart Mill, the economic theory of market failure, and various theories of equity or social justice. In many cases, however, these arguments seem insufficient to justify both the scale of government intervention and the form that it takes in practice. Often the nonpaternalistic justification for a particular intervention, such as the presence of imperfect information, would seem to justify relatively low-level interventions, such as simply the provision of information to the individuals concerned. Yet in practice the interventions concerned often go well beyond this, involving substantial levels of government finance, regulation, and provision. Moreover, the interventions often take a form that is different from that indicated by the relevant argument. So regulations on smoking are imposed where the nonpaternalistic justification concerned, such as the presence of an externality, would indicate a tax; direct provision of a service or aid-in-kind is used where a nonpaternalistic justification, such as the promotion of equity, would indicate that income supplementation would be more appropriate; and so on.

So in such cases it would seem likely that something else is going on, in both the theory and practice of government intervention. We cannot, of course, conclusively demonstrate what that something else is; we do not know what is in the minds of all the relevant policy makers, or in the minds of those providing intellectual support to the policies concerned. However, we have argued that it is not unreasonable to suppose that, at least in some of the areas involved, there are strong elements of paternalism: that, in these areas, the government is intervening in large part because it believes that the individuals concerned suffer from a failure of judgment, and that their own good will be furthered by the relevant interventions. Whether this belief is well founded, and whether it constitutes a legitimate justification for government intervention, is another set of questions—ones that will preoccupy us for the rest of the book.

5 Paternalism and Well-Being

For any theory of paternalism to have a role in public policy, there must be some basis for believing that, in making decisions about their well-being or their wider interests, people are failing in a systematic way to achieve these ends or are failing in some way to have the ends they ought to have. These failings, according to our definition of paternalism, are failures of judgment concerning various life decisions. A necessary condition for a paternalistic intervention is that there must be the potential, at least, for making better decisions. In this chapter we look at the evidence for such a potential. Unsurprisingly, perhaps, the evidence that exists largely concerns human reasoning ability and its connection to levels of well-being. In other words, it offers evidential hope to means-related paternalism. Here, at least, it is possible to test or survey people on whether they are succeeding in getting what they want. Obtaining evidence on the failings of people's ends is, on the other hand, highly problematic.

In the 1970s those sympathetic to paternalism paid less attention to the soundness of the empirical evidence. They often cited what amounted to a general acceptance that human beings are susceptible to lapses of cognitive ability and that this is one prima facie justification for paternalistic interventions. So, for example, Dworkin (1972, 82), in considering a smoker who fails even to try to give up, argues:

> what is being claimed—and what must be shown or at least argued for—is that an accurate accounting on [the smoker's] part would lead him to reject his current course of action [smoking]. Now *we all know* that such cases exist, that we are prone to disregard dangers that are only possibilities, that immediate pleasures are magnified and distorted. (emphasis added)

"We all know" sounds a little vague to twenty-first-century ears tutored in evidence-based policy making. But recently cognitive psychologists and behavioral economists have produced an increasingly rich fund of empirical evidence that reasoning failure of various kinds does indeed occur. Initially, economists took these findings and merely suggested modifications to existing descriptive theories of individuals as economic agents. But more recently they have taken a further step and proposed that the evidence collected, ipso facto, offers a potential case for paternalism:

> from the perspective of behavioral law and economics, issues of paternalism are to a significant degree empirical questions, not questions to be answered on an a priori basis. No axiom demonstrates that people make choices that serve their best interests; this is a question to be answered based on evidence. (Jolls, Sunstein, and Thaler 1998, 1545)

In this chapter we examine the classical economic model of rationality and describe how an alternative model emerged during the twentieth century; next we review the substantive evidence on how reasoning failure results in well-being loss; then we discuss the difficulty of providing evidence on the failure of people's decisions over the ends themselves.

The Classical Economic Model and Its Challengers

The starting point for such analysis of reasoning failure is the notion of "classical" economic rationality. Economists originally developed axioms of rationality so as to contribute to the development of models of consumer behavior in competitive market environments. There is some disagreement about what constitutes full rationality in this sense, but the elements that most economists accept as constituting the "classical model" are as follows (Camerer et al. 2003).

- ◎ People have well-defined preferences (or goals) and make decisions that maximize these preferences.
- ◎ These preferences accurately reflect (to the best of the person's knowledge) the true costs and benefits of the available options.
- ◎ In situations that involve uncertainty, people have well-formed beliefs about how uncertainty will resolve itself.

The most commonly discussed form of rationality in economics is known as "instrumental rationality"; this simply refers to the form of rationality that results in choices that best achieve the individual's ends or goals and is clearly of greatest relevance to means-related paternalism. A second form is "procedural rationality," which, to some extent at least, concerns itself with the rules or norms of *how* the choices are made—for example, people may adopt rules of thumb to cope with situations where they find it impossible to work out fully all the costs and benefits involved in a choice, or they may adopt choice-making behavior to fit in with social norms. Finally, "expressive rationality" is concerned with how preferences themselves are formed and involves a more reflective process whereby people might, for example, consider the kinds of preferences they would like to have. This has links with Ronald Dworkin's notion of critical interests, discussed in chapter 3. We would also note that it is a commonplace in economic discourse to argue that, under certain conditions, self-interested people operating in a competitive economy will promote the common good, an idea originating with Adam Smith's "invisible hand" in *The Wealth of Nations*. In short, an optimal economic outcome requires self-interested individuals, and as a result self-interest has also become associated with rationality (Sen 1977).

This model of rationality, as a description of reality, was gradually challenged over the second half of the twentieth century (Camerer and Loewenstein 2004). The first and most significant systematic attempt to develop a more realistic model of how people behaved came from a political scientist, Herbert Simon. He proposed notions of bounded rationality and "satisficing" that acknowledged the impossibility of people being able to assimilate all available information. Others—such as Maurice Allais—demonstrated apparently reasonable deviations from some of the axioms of the rational model. We will return to Simon's contribution below.

In a parallel development in the field of psychology, clinical psychologists were providing empirical evidence that doctors' own judgments in assessing clinical outcomes were less accurate than statistical or actuarial processes (Meehl 1954). Furthermore, normative standards for probabilistic reasoning—known as Bayesian analysis—were introduced to psychology in the 1960s, which thereby provided a standard against which psychologists could measure the actual behavior of people under experimental conditions (Gilovich and Griffin 2002). By this time economics had largely expunged psychology from its methods and intellectual debates, preferring instead what it considered the more robust and scientific approach of neoclassical economics (Camerer and Loewenstein 2004). As a result, in the 1970s psychologists were in a more favorable position to analyze the "real-life" behavior of people and subsequently began to develop descriptive theories of their own to formalize some of the departures from the classical model. Key among these were the heuristics and biases approach to human judgment and prospect theory, an alternative model of choice to expected utility theory, both developed by Daniel Kahneman and Amos Tversky.[1] Ultimately a new field of

1 The two classic articles being Tversky and Kahneman (1974) and Kahneman and Tversky (1979).

behavioral economics emerged in the 1980s,[2] focusing on the application of psychological insights to economics, and in particular to individual judgment, choice, and decision making.

Before turning to the substance of the research, a word on terminology. The classical model of individual choice often refers to how a rational individual acts. Now, "rational" and "irrational" are loaded terms in modern usage. "Irrational" has connotations of stupidity; it suggests that if one were to diverge from some highly specific rules of decision making, then this makes no sense whatsoever. But, on the contrary, many decisions that depart from these norms are perfectly sensible; furthermore, decision making that has suboptimal outcomes for the individual may be based on reasoning that is understandable in many everyday contexts. They may be based on heuristics that very often work well for people, even if they fail in specific circumstances. "Irrational" does not seem the right way to describe such decision making. Instead we use the term reasoning failure, thereby also linking it to its sister concept of market failure. Markets, like human reasoning, work well in many circumstances and for many goods and services but sometimes fail to provide what people want. The only difference is that reasoning relates to the internal and reflective processes of an individual rather than to an interaction between individuals in a "system." Having said all that, on occasion we will still refer to rationality and irrationality where other authors have used the terms or where the context demands a reference to traditional economic understanding of "homo economicus" (Weale 1992).

The Evidence on Reasoning Failure

In the remainder of this chapter we will present examples that we suggest provide evidence of reasoning failure. To distinguish between, on the one hand, substantive failures of reason and, on the other, divergences from the classical model that are trivial or occasional, we draw on experimental studies, survey evidence, and long-running philosophical inquiry to identify where there is likely to be a genuine and systematic bias in decision making. Put another way, we try to identify situations where an individual would agree to the following statements when she was confronted with a failure of reasoning which she had supposedly committed. Her decision was a nontrivial error that she would probably repeat in similar circumstances; the error was conceptual, not merely a verbal or technical misunderstanding; and she *should* have known the correct answer or procedure to find it.[3]

---

2   Perhaps the first article was Thaler (1980); see also Camerer, Loewenstein, and Rabin (2004), and, for a comprehensive history and review, Kahneman (2011).
3   Adapted from Tversky and Kahneman (1983).

In undertaking this exercise, we will be in a position to evaluate the anomalies and departures from the classic model identified by behavioral economists, and to categorize them on a coherent basis.[4] The four categories of reasoning failure that we use are

- ⊘   limited technical ability
- ⊘   limited imagination/experience
- ⊘   limited willpower
- ⊘   limited objectivity[5]

Limited Technical Ability

This category of reasoning failure describes the difficulties that people have with formal or technical analysis and perception, particularly as it applies to questions of probability and how information is presented. It covers a number of situations where people fail to maximize their well-being because they do not have the ability to perceive or process information adequately in order to achieve their preferences. This may be because the logical or causal connections between judgment and outcome are difficult to make, or because the context or frame in which information is presented deceives the decision maker in some way.

As noted above, the first significant exponent of how individuals deviate from the classical model was Herbert Simon (1972). Simon developed the idea of bounded rationality in the 1950s, arguing that because of the complexity of the world, human beings do not have the computational or decision-making capabilities to process all relevant information. But they cannot escape from the need to make a decision and so do so in one of two ways: either they adopt a highly simplified description of reality and then make their choices from this in an approximately optimal way; or they adopt what Simon terms a "satisficing" approach whereby they choose in advance an outcome that would be satisfactory rather than perfect or optimal and then look at options in the real world until they find one that provides that outcome. In both cases Simon argued that people still reason and choose rationally, but within unavoidable constraints.[6]

---

4   Useful surveys of this evidence can be found in DellaVigna (2009) and Pesendorfer (2006). See also Oliver (2013a).

5   Adapted and developed from New (1999).

6   Ullman-Margalit and Morganbesser (1977) argue that many, perhaps even most, choice situations are actually what they call "picking" ones: that is, situations where the individual is actually indifferent between the various alternatives before her and either makes no choice at all (as in the case of Buridan's ass starving to death equidistant between two identical

Kahneman and Tversky developed these ideas in the decades that followed, but they argued that the way that people simplify complex judgments is to use heuristics that are categorically different from the simplifying and satisficing heuristics that Simon proposed.[7] Importantly, Kahneman and Tversky suggested that the heuristics that people actually use can often lead to systematic biases in the way they make judgments—in particular, the processes that people use to estimate probabilities.[8] They did not argue that the heuristics were inherently suboptimal; on the contrary, the heuristics are a useful means of coming to quick judgments and may be an essential and pervasive part of everyday life. As such they are not "irrational." However, Kahneman and Tversky argued they did lead to errors of judgment as assessed by the laws of probability. The following identifies six of the most striking types of reasoning failure arising from the work of these authors and others.

First, people display a misunderstanding about the *workings of chance and the effect of small numbers*, such as sample sizes, on the accuracy of predictions about populations. For example, subjects failed to predict that in a small hospital, where there are fewer births, the likelihood on any given day of more than 60 percent of the births being boys is *greater* than in a large hospital. People seem to believe intuitively that small samples are just as likely to imitate the pattern observed in the population as large samples (Tversky and Kahneman 1974).[9] People similarly believe that in a sequence of events, such as drawing cards at random from a pack, replacing them, and then drawing again from the pack, a small string within the sequence should "look like" or represent the longer string (the large sample). For example, in one experiment subjects were asked to "imagine a sequence of 150 draws with replacement from a well-shuffled pack, including five red and five black cards, and then call aloud these binary draws" (Rapoport and Budescu 1997, 612). The results can be summarized as follows, where $Pr(A|B)$ is the probability that card A (say, a red card) would be chosen following a choice of card B (black), $Pr(A|AB)$ is the probability that a red card is chosen following red and black choices, and so on. Overall the prob-

---

bundles of food) or, rather more commonly, resorts to arbitrary rules to decide which alternative to pick. However, they do not claim that the process of picking is irrational.

7   The three original heuristics were representativeness, availability, and anchoring and adjustment. See Tversky and Kahneman (1974) for the original exposition; for an update and general review of the field in the twenty-first century, see various articles (including the 1974 paper) collected in Gilovich, Griffin, and Kahneman (2002).

8   Behavioral decision research—the arm of cognitive psychology on which much behavioral economics has drawn—typically categorizes its research into two arms: that relating to judgement and that relating to choice. Choice phenomena—the processes that people use to select among actions—include the risk-seeking and certainty effects noted above.

9   Rabin (2002) also notes that people *underappreciate* the significance of large samples.

abilities were as follows (Rabin 2002, 781, derived from Rapoport and Budescu 1997, 613, table 7):

$Pr(A|B)$	58.5%
$Pr(A|AB)$	46.0%
$Pr(A|AAB)$	38.0%
$Pr(A|AAA\ldots)$	29.8%

In fact, any sequence the subjects might have suggested is exactly as likely as any other sequence, but to produce a long sequence of red cards appears to offend some deeply felt intuition that a mixture of cards is a better match of reality. This experiment also neatly reveals the same tendency that leads to what has become known as the gambler's fallacy, namely, the belief that a long string of results of one kind—such as a string of reds on a roulette wheel—will lead to a greater likelihood of a black on the next spin. People do not see events that are independent of one another in that light; they often see chance as a self-correcting process in which a deviation in one direction—a red card or red number—requires a deviation in the other (a black) to restore a form of equilibrium.

The second type of judgment error offends probability logic, specifically the *conjunction rule*. This simply states that the probability of A and B both happening—the conjunction—cannot be greater than B happening (or A). The probability of it raining tomorrow (A) and *also* getting a phone call from an old friend (B) (i.e., both events) cannot be *more* likely than it simply raining tomorrow (whether or not you get the phone call). This seems obvious, but the way people assess probabilities can apparently lead them to break this rule. In a famous example, Tversky and Kahneman set out a description of the following female individual: "Linda is 31 years old, single, outspoken and very bright. She majored in philosophy. As a student, she was deeply concerned with issues of discrimination and social justice, and also participated in anti-nuclear demonstrations."[10]

They then offered a number of descriptions of Linda, three of which were as follows:

1 Linda is active in the feminist movement.
2 Linda is a bank teller.
3 Linda is a bank teller and active in the feminist movement.

There were five other "filler" descriptions, such as "Linda is an insurance salesperson." Subjects were then asked to rank the descriptions in order of

---

10   See Tversky and Kahneman (1983), where the authors discuss the original experiment, replications, and extensions of this work.

likelihood. The results were striking: no matter how the situation was presented to subjects, and no matter how sophisticated the subjects, a majority of people ranked or assessed descriptor 3 (the conjunction) as more likely than either of its components. It seems that people were assessing how *representative* Linda was of each of these classes, or how similar she was to them, rather than their strict likelihood, no matter how clearly this was spelled out.[11] The description of Linda is so suggestive of a feminist that people find it very hard to accept that her being only and simply a bank teller could possibly be more *likely* than being a feminist bank teller. Further, exhaustive tests were unable to establish that any number of semantic or technical blunders were the cause, rather than simply a predilection to employ the representative heuristic (Kahneman and Frederick 2002). It seems that people are simply not disposed to engage with probability judgments in an accurate way.

A third technical failure in the realm of probability is the *misperception of regression*, one that Daniel Kahneman said provided him with the greatest eureka moment in his career.[12] According to the statistical phenomenon of regression to the mean, "exceptional" cases in a distribution will tend, in subsequent measurements, to become less exceptional. Thus if a large group of students are given two aptitude tests, then the ten best-performing students on the first test will tend to do less well on the second. This "regression" is because at least some of these students performed as well as they did through an element of chance. Of course, some exceptional students will also do poorly through chance, but these chance effects will not cancel themselves out because there is a greater *opportunity* for average students to do well through chance simply because there are more average students (they are bunched around the mean). The phenomenon also applies to very poorly performing students tending to do better in a subsequent test. Indeed, Kahneman's eureka moment came when he observed flight-training instructors harshly criticize those student pilots who had done very poorly on a simulation exercise. The instructors defended their use of criticism (rather than praise) because they said that they saw improvement in the poor performers who were berated, whereas those praised after exceptional performance tended to do worse next time round. The instructors' failure to

---

11   Three strategies were used to make the relative probabilities more transparent: (1) rather than description 2, subjects were offered *Linda is a bank teller whether or not she is in the feminist movement*; (2) arguments as to why one might rank the likelihood of the descriptions in various ways were offered; and (3) subjects were invited to bet on the probabilities. None resulted in a majority of subjects ranking the conjunction below its constituents. Only when graduate students who had undertaken statistics courses took the test did a majority rank them correctly.

12   Biography submitted as part of Nobel Prize award: http://nobelprize.org/nobel_prizes/economics/laureates/2002/kahneman-autobio.html.

understand regression to the mean overestimated the influence of criticism and underestimated the effect of praise.

A fourth technical failure involves *insensitivity to prior outcomes*, or *base-rate neglect* (Tversky and Kahneman 1974; Kahneman and Frederick 2002). When people are asked to make an assessment of the likelihood that a specific case is part of one or more general classes, they need to factor in some understanding of the underlying prevalence of the members of the class in the population and not just rely on how representative the individual case appears to be of other members of a class. For example, if trying to judge whether a person you have just met is an information technology worker or a research mathematician, one needs to be aware that there are many more of the former than the latter, even if one's new companion seems to have an unhealthful interest in math. But people are very often insensitive to these base rates. For example, a group of subjects were given various descriptions of individuals and told that these individuals were selected from a group of seventy engineers and thirty lawyers; another group of subjects were offered the same descriptions but told the proportion of lawyers and engineers were reversed (Kahneman and Tversky 1973). However, both groups judged the likelihood that the descriptions were of either a lawyer or an engineer to be the same, whatever the proportions in the base group.

Then the subjects were offered the following description, designed to be neutral in terms of its representativeness of lawyers and engineers: "Dick is a 30 year old man. He is married with no children. A man of high ability and high motivation, he promises to be quite successful in his field. He is well liked by his colleagues" (242).

The subjects judged the likelihood that Dick was an engineer to be 0.5, effectively ignoring the base rates (the correct answer should be 0.7 for the 70/30 engineer/lawyer group if, as intended, the description does not describe a stereotype in either case).

Theoretical examples of base-rate neglect have also been suggested in relation to the reliability of human perception. Suppose an individual's ability to correctly identify the color of a taxicab at distance is 80 percent, and the underlying rate of cabs in a city is 85:15 blue:green. If the individual identifies a green cab, other things being equal, then the chance that the cab is actually blue is 17/29.[13] In other words, he is likely to be wrong. This has important implications for the reliability of witnesses in criminal trials— substitute "white man/black man" for taxicabs (Heap et al. 1992, 295–96)—

---

13 Imagine there are 100 cabs. There are many more blue cabs in existence, which the individual will wrongly identify as green 20 percent of the time: 0.2 * 85 = 17. He will also misidentify green cabs as blue 20 percent of the time (0.2 * 15 = 3), leaving 12 (accurately) identified green cabs. Thus 17 out of (12 + 17) 29 green cabs will on average be identified mistakenly.

leading to the potential for miscarriages of justice.[14] It also applies to medical evidence: consider a diagnostic test with 80 percent reliability that can choose between two potentially fatal diseases, one of which is more common than the other in an 85:15 ratio. If the test indicates the rare disease, it is, again, more likely to be wrong than right.

A fifth mistake commonly made in probability judgment involves the *ease with which examples can be retrieved or imagined*. This is an example of the availability heuristic whereby people rely on the extent to which a phenomenon is "available" to recall or to one's imagination in making a judgment about its probability (Tversky and Kahneman 1973). In one test, people were asked to estimate how many seven-letter words of the form "_ _ _ _ ing" would be found in a typical four-page sequence of a novel (Tversky and Kahneman 1983). A second version of the question asked how many words of the form "_ _ _ _ _ n _" would be found. As with the conjunction rule above, the former set of words are a subset of the latter set and thus *must* be less numerous. However, the median estimate of the former was 13.4 (for ". . . ing" words) against 4.7 for the latter. In another experiment, subjects were asked whether they considered more English words to begin with the letter "r" or to have "r" as their third letter; most believed the former to be true, presumably because it is easier to think of words beginning with a certain letter (Tversky and Kahneman 1974; Schwarz and Vaughn 2002). Similarly, when asked how many different committees of two people from ten, and of eight people from ten, could possibly be formed, most people believed that there were far more two-person committees possible—in fact the correct answer is forty-five in both cases. Again, this is likely to be because it is easier to imagine a sequence of different two-person committees than all the complex arrangements of eight people.

Finally, there is the *anchor and adjustment* effect, whereby people make estimates by starting from an initial value—which might have been suggested to them or which they use for some other reason—and then adjust this value to arrive at a final result. People tend to underadjust if the initial value has some relevance, but they might also adopt the initial value even if it is patently irrelevant, such as the result of a spin of a roulette wheel (Chapman and Johnson 2002). The process is not limited to probability judgments. For example, when someone is deciding how much of a particular grocery item to buy, a sign reading "Customers are permitted to buy no

---

14   The notion that such an effect might lead one to question the reliability of juries has made this a hugely controversial topic—see, for example, Cohen (1981). In the case of ethnicity and criminal trials, there may be not only a failure to take account of the simple base rate but also reference to a fictitious or prejudiced one (for example, that a criminal is more likely to be a young black man).

more than twelve items" might, according to this effect, influence people to buy more than if there were no stated limits.

Take an example of a study of willingness to pay for reducing the annual risks from death and injury from motor accidents (Jones-Lee and Loomes 2001). The study allocated people randomly to two subsamples, one who were suggested a value of £25, the other who were suggested a value of £75. The results showed that for every level of risk, the *minimum* willingness to pay was *higher* in the £75 group than the *maximum* willingness to pay in the £25 group. In this case, people might be provided with clear information on the risk of road accidents, and the costs of reducing them, and yet not be able to come to a settled position of how valuable a given reduction would be. They thus grasped at any additional information provided even where this information did not approximate any reality.

Most of the examples in this section have related to probabilities and statistical inference. This is because we are here concerned with failures of reason that can, with a reasonable degree of consensus, be judged against normative standards of logic and fact. People would, in general, accept their error if it was explained to them subsequently—and indeed in some circumstances the experimental results are supported in this way (Tversky and Kahneman 1983).[15] However, not all of the limits to technical ability involve judgments about probabilities. Some relate to the *framing* or the *context* in which decisions are made (Sunstein and Thaler 2003). Framing is a large topic and indeed is a key part of the impact that cognitive psychology has had on behavioral economics (Kahneman and Tversky 2000). It is perhaps not surprising that the framing or context of a decision is likely to influence how we take that decision. But when the two apparently different options are in fact identical, and yet individuals make different decisions because of the way in which the options are presented, we begin to see that framing *can* be a form of limited technical ability in the sense of the misunderstanding of a matter of fact. For example, the words used in posing two questions can affect the response even when the questions demonstrably make the same inquiry. In one trial, people were more likely to support a medical procedure when told that *90 percent* of the patients receiving the procedure would still be *alive* after five years than when they were told that *10 percent* of them would be *dead* after five years (Redelmeier, Rozin, and Kahneman 1993). The words used—"dead" and "alive"—elicit

---

15 It should be noted that some have argued that, from an evolutionary standpoint, human beings needed to work only with frequencies rather than probabilities, and that we are thus more adept at working with judgments couched in terms of frequencies (Pinker 1997). Although replacing probabilities with frequencies does, in some cases, improve the reasoning ability of individuals, in other cases it leaves it unchanged or even makes it worse (Gilovich and Griffin 2002).

different reactions from respondents even though, on reflection, there can be no ambiguity that the situation described in the question is the same.

Another interesting case of framing involves a classic experiment on people's attitude toward a monetary gamble. One group of subjects were given $1,000 and asked to choose either a certain $500 gain or a 50 percent chance of a $1,000 gain; the second group were given $2,000 and asked to choose between a certain loss of $500 and a 50 percent chance of losing $1,000. The majority of the first group were risk averse, choosing the sure gain, while the majority of the second group were risk seeking, choosing the gamble. However, the choice in each case was identical: a sure gain of $1,500 over the subjects' starting wealth, or a 50:50 chance of being either $1,000 or $2,000 better off. Simply using the word "losing" appeared to encourage people to adopt risk-seeking strategies (Kahneman and Tversky 1979).

Limited Imagination

The second category of reasoning failure relates to people's limited ability to imagine or predict their utility in alternative situations or at different times. It is often related to the extent and quality of our experiences. In one account of why consumer choice might be less than optimal, Burrows (1993) notes the importance of experience in contributing to the formation of preferences or preferred ends, and how very often the "thinness of experience" can constrain a fully rounded preference formation. Preferences, or the ends that an individual prioritizes, would be different if the individual had experience (rather than simply abstract knowledge or information) of all the possible outcomes of a certain activity. So drivers who habitually fail to wear a seat belt are unlikely to have had the experience of a serious car accident. Any stories they may have heard or statistical information they may have are unlikely to provide a full and emotionally vivid sensation of the injury that they might sustain in the event of a major accident.

This hypothesis—that the thinness of our experience can affect our reasoning—can be linked to research from psychology once again and has experimental evidence to support it. The psychological account derives from the notion that "losses loom larger than gains," a pervasive theme in behavioral economics and one that indirectly challenges the classical model's assumption that utility essentially derives from *states* of wealth (Kahneman 2000): that is, from the extent of wealth that an individual possesses at a given moment. People seem to feel the impact of a loss more than they enjoy the consequence of an equivalent gain. In the seat belt example, drivers refusing to wear their seat belts are weighing the experience of a (small) loss of their freedom as greater than the potentially large (but not experienced) increase in their safety in the event of a crash. In the example of the monetary gamble provided at the end of the previous section, the loss was

Table 5.1 The Endowment Effect

Group	Number of subjects	Prediction of valuation	Actual valuation
Prediction	22	$3.27 (0.48)	$4.56 (0.59)
No prediction	17	—	$4.98 (0.53)

Source: Based on Loewenstein and Adler (1995, 932, table 1). Standard errors in parentheses.

apparent rather than real in financial terms, but nevertheless a form of loss aversion was taking place.[16]

Rather than utility being derived from various states of wealth, goes the argument, it is one's departure from *a reference point* that is the significant carrier of utility; this in turn allows for individual preferences to vary depending on whether one is (or perceives oneself to be) gaining or losing.[17] One consequence is that, whereas in classical theory one's preference for a bundle of goods is independent of current assets, prospect theory suggests that whether one owns—is "endowed" with—that bundle of goods is indeed relevant. One may perceive that bundle's value differently depending on whether one owns it and is faced with losing it, or whether one does not own it and is offered the prospect of buying it. Typically, this so-called endowment effect induces a tendency to value an object more highly if it is possessed than if it is not; that is, if its possession is currently "being experienced" rather than merely imagined.

A number of experiments have been conducted to demonstrate the endowment effect (Kahneman, Knetsch, and Thaler 2000; Loewenstein, O'Donoghue, and Rabin 2003). For example, subjects randomly assigned to one group—the "prediction" group—were shown an engraved coffee mug and then told they would later be given one as a prize but would have the opportunity to exchange it for cash (Loewenstein and Adler 1995). They then filled out a form predicting what price they would be willing to accept for the mug. After a delay they were given the mug as promised and then asked to fill out the form again. A separate group were simply given the mug without making predictions and asked to fill out the form. Table 5.1 shows the typical set of results.

---

16   Loss aversion is not by itself thought to be a failure of reason; the failure in the example given at the end of the previous section related to the *perception* of loss and gain.

17   The effect does not just apply to risky choices; see Tversky and Kahneman (2000b).

Behavioral economists have termed this an example of *projection bias*: people find it hard to assess or imagine how a changed state will affect their preferences—they falsely project their current preferences into this new state. Nor is projection bias limited to the possession of inanimate objects. In another study the reaction of law students was recorded in response to two scenarios representing different legal provisions governing holidays from their employment (Sunstein 2002). In one scenario the law was taken to guarantee two weeks of vacation; students were asked to state their willingness to pay (in terms of reduced salary) for two *extra* weeks of vacation. In the second scenario the law guaranteed a mandatory, nonwaivable two-week vacation but also provided the right to two additional weeks of vacation, a right that could be "knowingly and voluntarily waived." Students were asked how much their employers would need to pay them to give up their right to the extra two weeks. In the first scenario the median willingness to pay for the extra two weeks was $6,000, and in the second the willingness to accept a loss of the two weeks was more than double, at $13,000. Here again we see evidence of an endowment effect. The different reference points of the students—"endowed" or not with the right to a vacation—caused them to arrive at remarkably different valuations of precisely the same nonmaterial good.

Thus there is a systematic *underappreciation* of how being in a different state—such as one that involves being endowed with a good or right to something—will affect an individual's preferences. This can be seen as a manifestation of the "thinness" of experience noted above. It has led researchers to distinguish "decision" from "experienced" utility, with the former constituting the classic economic assumption of utility as the weight assigned to an outcome in a decision, and the latter introducing the notion that our actual experience of utility can differ from that which we anticipated (Kahneman 1994). Where we have little experience of a state, or have forgotten what that state is truly like, we may misjudge how we value that state when it occurs. Thus although loss aversion and the endowment effect are not themselves suboptimal in well-being terms, our inability to accurately *project* or *imagine* ourselves in often quite familiar states could lead to substantial errors in circumstances where it is important to predict future preferences.

One particularly important manifestation of projection bias might be addiction. People underappreciate how difficult it will be to kick a drug habit, for example. And it may help to understand the observation that people derive less enjoyment from increased salaries, status, or even lottery wins than they thought they would, thus underappreciating the way we "adapt" to our new circumstances (Loewenstein, O'Donoghue, and Rabin 2003).

Difficulty in predicting future tastes has been combined with a commensurate difficulty in *remembering* the experience of particular states (Kahneman 1994). Two phenomena have been identified as particularly important: the *peak and end rule* and *duration neglect*. People's memory of how they enjoyed (or otherwise) an experience is best predicted by their recall of a combination of the most extreme moments of that experience, and the final moments before the experience ended (the peak and end rule). People were less impressed by how long the experience lasted (the duration effect). Experiments were conducted wherein subjects could continuously report their level of pain or discomfort, for example, by means of an "affect meter." In one trial people who had a *longer* experience of their hand being immersed in painfully cold water tended nevertheless to prefer this to a shorter period, if the final moments involved a slight warming up of the still uncomfortably cold water. In another experiment patients undergoing a colonoscopy that lasted between 4 and 6–9 minutes rated the *overall* experience of discomfort or pain *independently* of the length of time the procedure went on, but this overall assessment was strongly associated with the worst moment of pain during it, and with that during the final few moments.

A corollary of these difficulties in remembering the utility of events is the "excessive" ease with which people are able to remember events that have just occurred, leading to "hindsight bias" (Fischhoff 1975). This has been observed in juries' readiness to award damages on the basis of negligence. A negligent claim can be made only if an unwanted event happens; such an event may be very unlikely and may occur only very rarely. However, because such an event would have recently happened in a negligence case, jurors have been found to attach unreasonably high probability to it, thinking that the defendant should have foreseen it and thus are more likely to find that a defendant's course of action was the direct cause of the event.

Notwithstanding difficulties with memory and hindsight, we may presume that, even if the effect is recognizable in situations such as those where we have had experience of the particular state in question, it is likely to be most marked where we have had no such experience and we are entirely at the mercy of our imagination, or lack of it. For example, people might make a different judgment on whether to take up smoking if, in addition to having access to information about the probabilities of smoking causing disease or death, it were possible to imagine accurately the ill effects and experience of dying through lung cancer.

Limited imagination may also explain another key observation from cognitive psychology: that people display "status quo bias." In these cases people are reluctant to move from the initial, or default, position. For example, an unplanned experiment emerged in the United States in relation to motor insurance.[18] In New Jersey the default insurance position was a lower

18   Described in Sunstein and Thaler (2003).

premium for car insurance but with no right to sue; in Pennsylvania the default was a higher premium but retaining the right to sue. In both states the vast majority opted to remain in the default insurance policy. People did not have direct experience of the terms of the alternative insurance policy in the neighboring state and, even with good information about how technically these alternative insurance arrangements might affect them, had difficulty in *imagining* themselves in the alternative situation. Thus most people did nothing.

A limited imagination problem arises with intertemporal choice (Frederick, Loewenstein, and O'Donoghue 2002). The economic model of rationality allows for an assumption that people generally prefer to consume now rather than wait, other things being equal. We tend to care less about a future consequence, whether it involves a cost or a benefit, than we do about benefits and costs that can be consumed immediately.

Most people would agree that a certain amount of "discounting"—the amount by which we reduce the value or cost to us of consumption in the future—is a perfectly sensible strategy for maximizing well-being, especially in the presence of uncertainty about the future. After all, the longer we delay our pleasures, the less likely that we will be around to enjoy them. However, the assumption underlying the classical model is that this discount rate is consistent: a person's relative preference for well-being at an earlier date over a later date is the same no matter how near or far from the two dates she is asked (O'Donoghue and Rabin 1999). But this assumption is descriptively incorrect. For example, if asked about our willingness to do a piece of work some months in the future, *or* a slightly more difficult piece of work a further week later, we might choose the former over the latter. But come the night before the first task, we might change our mind—the prospect of doing the slightly easier task the next day suddenly seems less attractive than waiting a week and doing the harder. Our discount rate has risen in the intervening period so that the extent to which we diminish the impact of something a week in the future is now sufficiently great as to counteract the fact that it is a harder task. There is much evidence for some form of time-inconsistent discounting of this nature (Frederick, Loewenstein, and O'Donoghue 2002).[19]

Behavioral economists have described this phenomenon in terms of procrastination and, more formally, as "present-biased preferences" (O'Donoghue and Rabin 1999a, 103). It applies to rewards (benefits) just as much as to costs. So whereas we procrastinate over unpleasant tasks that need to be done, because their impact is lessened simply by being in the future, so pleasures tend to be consumed now because their "pleasurability" is dimin-

---

19   Although the evidence is less clear where the inconsistency lies, with the short-run or long-run self—discussed further below.

ished by waiting. In both cases there is a bias to the present—not doing the unpleasant, or doing the pleasant, now.

O'Donoghue and Rabin (1999a, 108) also work through the implications of individuals who are more or less aware of their inconsistency, referring to them as "sophisticates" if they acknowledge their weakness and "naifs" if they believe they will "do the right thing" when the time comes. Sophisticates are not suffering from limited imagination so much as from the category of reasoning failure to be discussed in the next section— limited willpower. They can be observed attempting to lock themselves into courses of action to avoid temptation, such as signing into health farms or putting their money into illiquid assets so that it is harder to spend (Laibson 1997). On the other hand, naifs are suffering from limited imagination; they imagine how they will feel in a different situation but find themselves behaving quite differently when that situation appears.

But how do we decide that the discount rate applied at the time of the choice is the wrong one (and that the long view is correct)? Are we sure that naifs are really naïve and not people who have simply mispredicted their actions but are happy with their choices as they turn out? Why are we sure that reason has been usurped by the emotions, rather than appropriately following them? For surely no one would claim that eating brownies or deferring difficult pieces of work are wrong or well-being-reducing in themselves.[20] The question turns on being able to back up the view that the long-run discount rate is the correct one—that our long-term resolutions are the best estimate of our overall well-being rather than the short-run desire for more immediate pleasure.[21] Put another way, we need to demonstrate that present-biased preferences are indeed biased.

One argument could be based on a myopic failure to recognize one's future self (Le Grand 2006). A "myopic" individual fails to give his "future self" sufficient weight when making judgments about consumption in the present. He disregards, or undervalues, the interests of his future self. Take the example of making provision for income in retirement when still young. For those exhibiting myopia, it is as though their future self is a different person.[22] They fail to acknowledge that that person has claims, and that the present individual's (in)actions now effectively impose costs on his future self, but without the latter being present to dispute those costs. There is an analogy here with external costs in the context of market failure. The reasoning failure posited here is again limited imagination. For it

20 Eating a brownie may be harmful in the long run, but this is only a probability, and it provides a great deal of immediate tastiness meanwhile.

21 See Elster (2000, 9–10) on the various strategies of precommitment people can employ to assist in intertemporal choice situations.

22 Note that Parfit (1984) claimed that even the conceptualization of one's future self as different suggested that people were being rational.

relates to a limited ability to imagine being old and needy, or a limited ability to project oneself into the state of being old and thus a reluctance to accept that those needs exist and should be planned for.

The evidence on this kind of failure is more sketchy than for other reasoning failures. Anecdotally, people behaving in this way often acknowledge they are not necessarily acting in their own best long-run interest. Our "long-run self"—the person looking months in advance, or reflecting on the experience in retrospect—might admit to foolishness. But the empirical evidence from trials or survey research is not so readily available. Indeed, a comprehensive review of time discounting and preference, which outlines a range of anomalies from the classical model, acknowledges that these anomalies may not represent individuals making "mistakes" but just be the result of descriptively inaccurate modeling (Frederick, Loewenstein, and O'Donoghue 2002).

What evidence that does exist takes the form of public surveys. Perhaps the most commonly reported examples are related to giving up smoking: here the argument from limited imagination is that the long-run self fails both to imagine how awful would be the experience of contracting lung cancer and how difficult it will be to give up once she has started smoking. Surveys conducted by the Office of National Statistics have consistently reported that around 70 percent of current smokers in Great Britain wish to give it up (Taylor et al. 2006). However, one might argue that many of these people are simply responding to a habit they now realize is unpleasant— they may by now be experiencing the harm but nonetheless cannot stop— and that the problem is, therefore, one of addiction, an important but more specific form of limited willpower. More telling would be evidence on people's reported levels of well-being, comparing those who are more strongly deterred from taking up smoking with those who live under conditions of milder deterrence. One such study measured the effect of various levels of cigarette taxes, using demographic and survey data. Would increasing the price of cigarettes, and thus making them less attractive, lead people whose demographic factors predict them to be smokers to be any happier than comparable people in areas where excise duties were lower (Gruber and Mullainathan 2002)? The results showed significant and quite substantially higher rates of happiness following tax increases in two quite independent data sets from the United States and Canada. In other words, the potential smoker has her well-being improved by being dissuaded from a myopic decision by increasing the cost to her *now*.

Another area that has had a great deal of attention in both the United States and Britain is the question of saving for retirement. In the United States, employees can elect to have part of their income paid directly into a 401(k) account (named after a US internal revenue code) and by doing so avoid taxation on that income. Many studies have looked at the possibility of automatically enrolling people into these plans rather than forcing people to choose to opt in; such studies reveal that the overwhelming majority elect to remain in the default option (Madrian and Shea 2001). Evidence in support for such proposals comes from surveys that report that between two-thirds and three-fourths of people in the United States believe that they are saving too little for their retirement.[23] Similar proposals from the Pensions Commission in the UK recommended automatic enrollment as a national scheme; this, according to the commission's own research, has overwhelming support among the public (Pensions Commission 2006), and indeed it has now been adopted as government policy in the UK. All this suggests that people do seem to support the well-being of their long-run self against their short-run decision making, at least when thinking about pensions.

Limited Willpower

The third category of reasoning failure involves limited willpower, more commonly termed by philosophers as "weakness of will" (Dworkin 1981).[24] It refers to instances where people know what they prefer in the long term and what decision is in their best interests right now but still make a choice that leads to a suboptimal outcome. A typical example would be someone who professes his good intentions to eat a healthful diet as part of a New Year's resolution and then, come January 2, succumbs to the temptations of the chocolate brownie at the end of a tiring day, resolving instead that he will commence the diet the following week. It also includes those who cannot resist spending their wages on alcohol rather than putting them into a pension plan when they have confessed that they really should be contributing to the pension.[25]

The concept of weakness of will has an intellectual heritage stretching back over two thousand years. Aristotle analyzed the concept in the *Nicomachean Ethics*; the term he used was *akrasia*: literally, incontinence or lack of self-control. It is sometimes understood as "acting against one's better judgment" (Adler 2002). Aristotle's view of happiness was "using reason well," which is to say engaging in activities deriving from reason in accordance with virtue (the latter being a "disposition, induced by our habits, to have appropriate feelings" or emotional responses).[26] *Akrasia*, for Aristotle, is a character trait wherein the individual knows what a virtuous person should

23 Surveys cited in Thaler and Benartzi (2004).
24 Dworkin termed it "weakness of *the* will," but omitting the definite article is more usual.
25 This is a different type of failure from the myopic failure noted above, but it may compound that failure with regard to pension provision; see O'Donoghue and Rabin (1999b) for a specific analysis of issues relating to the provision for retirement.
26 *Stanford Encyclopedia of Philosophy*: http://plato.stanford.edu/entries/aristotle-ethics/.

do and accepts this (rather than being simply "evil" and rejecting virtue as worthless) but suffers from the influence of the emotions or feelings that sometimes override her reason. This battle between reason and what we might term "temptation" still forms much of the debate about whether weakness of will really exists, for the idea is not so straightforward as it sounds. The problem is this: why should we discount the possibility that the desire to act in accordance with our emotions is what our reason demands *at that moment*?[27] Our emotions or feelings can often be highly effective influences on our choices.

Another aspect of weakness of will involves *visceral* decision making (Loewenstein 1996). Emotion is an important element in the decisions we make, and it occupies a complex place in explanations of behavior generally. Few would deny that emotional attachment to one's friends and lovers leads one to make many perfectly sensible choices without any obvious well-being loss. Nevertheless, we would also acknowledge that occasionally emotions can get out of hand. For example, being in love can often feel like a form of madness,[28] with good sense more or less discarded. *In extremis*, then, emotional needs can take on a visceral quality that can overwhelm the more measured decision-making capabilities. Aristotle himself distinguished this as a special form of *akrasia*. The form we have been discussing thus far Aristotle described as "weakness" (*astheneia*) because it involved something of a battle between deliberative reason leading to a choice and "passion" undermining that choice—with the passion winning. "Visceral" decision making, on the other hand, is aligned to Aristotle's notion of "impetuosity" (*propeteia*), which he suggests involves no deliberative reasoning at all. Typical visceral factors are hunger, thirst, sexual desire, cravings from drug addiction, pain (and extreme pleasure), and severe moods such as anger or depression. Many of these motivations can lead to the very outcome the individual wants, but in some cases the inability to resist a visceral urge or temptation can be highly damaging in the long term. The key example here is perhaps drug addiction, on which there is a substantial amount of theorizing and evidence.[29]

---

27   Socrates seems to argue precisely this when he suggests in Plato's *Protagoras* that no one errs willingly or knowingly—that individuals, if in a situation of knowledge and not ignorance, will not act against their own interests.

28   "And most of all would I flee from the cruel madness of love." Alfred, Lord Tennyson, *Maud*, pt. 1, sec. 4, st. 10. Rosalind in Shakespeare's *As You Like It* agrees and indeed demands paternalistic interventions: "Love is merely a madness; and, I tell you, deserves as well a dark house and a whip as madmen do" (act 3, scene 2). Love has also formally been found to produce chemical changes in the brain similar to those associated with obsessive compulsive disorder: see Marazziti et al. 1999.

29   Limited imagination in this context could contribute to mispredicting how weak one's will would be while taking drugs—a naif-like attitude.

Limited Objectivity

The final category of reasoning failure involves a failure to act sufficiently objectively and without bias toward one's own perspective. One manifestation of this has been termed *confirmatory bias* (Rabin and Schrag 1999).[30] Such biases result from the misinterpretation of information in order to confirm earlier hypotheses. This should be distinguished from the situations of technical inability that result from overly complex or rich information, and from situations where people simply ignore new information and thus display a status quo bias. In a condition of confirmatory bias, our decision making is flawed because we find it difficult to acknowledge to others that conclusions we have arrived at, and perhaps argued strongly for, are in fact wrong. To misquote Keynes, when the facts change, we find it difficult to change our minds. This might also pertain in a purely internal and reflective sense—it can be equally difficult, in the face of new information, to acknowledge to *oneself* that previous judgments were made in error, especially when we have invested a good deal of time and effort in arriving at them. This phenomenon might also help to explain why people come to hold very firm spiritual beliefs. Once one has signed up to such beliefs, it becomes necessary to reinterpret almost every empirical perception about the world so as to sustain them. Confirmatory bias might also explain other common phenomena, such as "mission creep" or "throwing good money after bad," where the individuals concerned fail to make a proper evaluation because of sunk costs (whether of money or pride) that they have "invested."

Perhaps the most striking evidence for confirmatory bias is an experiment demonstrating how providing the same ambiguous information to people who differ in their initial beliefs on some topic can move their beliefs *farther apart*.[31] Two groups of students whose answers to previous questions had revealed opposing views on capital punishment—one group pro, and one group anti—were asked to judge the merits of the same, randomly selected studies on the deterrent effect of the death penalty. The groups were then asked to rate, on a scale −8 to +8, to what extent a given study had moved their attitudes toward the death penalty generally, and toward its deterrent efficacy in particular. Those running the trial were quoted as reporting that "proponents reported that they were more in favour of capital punishment, whereas opponents reported that they were less in favour of capital punishment. . . . Similar results characterised subjects' beliefs about deterrent efficacy" (Lord, Ross, and Lepper 1979, 2104).

---

30 This form of reasoning failure is also noted in the philosophical literature by David Archard (1994).

31 Cited in Rabin and Schrag (1999).

A similar phenomenon to confirmatory bias has been termed "self-serving bias." But here the judgment of an individual who suffers from the bias acts as if furthering his own interests rather more directly, although equally unconsciously. In a US study, union representatives and employers were separately asked to choose districts comparable to their own school district in other parts of Pennsylvania (Babcock, Wang, and Loewenstein 1996). The respondents were told that the results were confidential and were to be used only to further *understanding* of teacher contract negotiations (but would have no impact on actual negotiations). The results showed the average salary in the districts listed by union presidents was $27,633, whereas the average was $26,922 for those districts listed by school board presidents. It appears that even without a strategic motivation for doing so—even when their own interests were not at stake—each side judged "comparability" in a way that favored what would have been in their interests. Acting in one's own interests is central to classical economic theory; but this study of self-serving bias indicates how difficult it is for people to make truly objective judgments even when there is no material reason for them to do otherwise.

Another form of limited objectivity is *overoptimism*. A common feature of human behavior is a belief that bad events are far less likely to happen to oneself than to others (Weinstein 1980, 1996). Sometimes this can reflect an accurate assessment of reality. Someone who is a genuinely careful driver and who doesn't drive very often will be right to say that her likelihood of a crash is less than the average. But it is clearly not true to say that a *majority* of drivers can have a lower chance than the *average (median) driver's* chance of an accident. And yet survey evidence shows that people do believe this in some areas of risky behavior. Take smoking: a large national telephone survey in the United States revealed that smokers both underestimated their increased risk of getting lung cancer when compared to the perceived risk of nonsmokers and considered their own risk of developing lung cancer as significantly less than that of the average smoker (Weinstein, Marcus, and Moser 2005).[32]

Finally, a form of hindsight bias, discussed in a previous section, can also involve elements of limited objectivity. We noted how people tended to give too much weight to an event because it actually occurred rather than being a mere possibility—it was thus easy to *imagine*. But in similar way, people may adjust their perception of what the evidence suggests after they are told what actually occurred. For example, doctors, when presented with a given

---

32   Note that people generally *overestimate* their chance of dying from lung cancer in *absolute* terms (0.06 to 0.13 statistical risk for an average smoker; 0.47 being the public assessment of the risk). Further, some authors argue that such overoptimism about one's outcomes relative to the outcomes of others does not necessarily lead to inappropriate decisions (Viscusi 2002–3); see also Antoñanzas et al. (2000) and Shapiro (1994).

set of symptoms and asked to assess the probabilities of alternative diagnoses, have been found to offer significantly different estimates depending on what they are told the actual diagnosis turned out to be (Arkes et al. 1988). They were unable to retain their objectivity about what they would have thought purely on the basis of the symptoms, in light of knowledge of the outcome.

Ends-Related Paternalism

In earlier chapters we distinguished ends-related from means-related paternalism. The latter may be justified by the reasoning failures that we have just described. Is there an equivalent ends "failure" that could justify ends-related paternalism?

Ends failure involves a putative error in establishing our "true," ultimate goals, values, and objectives. Suggesting that someone is suffering from ends failure is akin to telling a mountaineer that the thrill he experiences in the perilous ascent of the highest peaks is a delusion. The "ends-failure paternalist" would be making a judgment about something that, to the person concerned, is of the very essence of what gives her pleasure—a combination of scenic beauty, wilderness, personal challenge and danger. By contrast, reasoning failure represents an inability to achieve these ends. The "reasoning-failure paternalist" would oblige that information on the nature of the risks was presented in a vivid way; he would oblige the climber to take certain precautions and to make use of a local guide, and perhaps require a period of training during which the climber could reflect on the task ahead. This kind of paternalism would have no quarrel with the pleasures associated with scenic beauty and personal challenge—nor even with the notion that some basic wants require an element of danger. The reasoning-failure paternalist might, however, question whether the danger has been properly understood and take steps to manipulate the context in which the climber assesses and mitigates those dangers.

Now it might be argued that ends-related paternalism is actually doing something a little more subtle than simply denying the value of the ends that the individual may have chosen. Rather, it is saying that there are a variety of ends that may compete (in the case of the mountaineer, perhaps living a long life, as well as experiencing the thrills of climbing), and that the individual concerned has got the balance of those ends wrong (in this case, prioritizing climbing thrills over longevity). The means-related paternalist, on the other hand, would accept the balance of ends the individual has judged to be correct for her, unless there were a reasoning failure in assessing that balance (such as a failure properly to assess the risks associated with climbing).

It is worth relating the idea of ends-related paternalism to some of the interpretations of paternalism discussed in chapter 3, especially legal moralism and moral paternalism. Legal moralism seeks to prevent what the government views as immoral acts or behaviors where the immorality of the acts is independent of their connection with harm. Some kinds of behavior, such as prostitution or pornography, are just intrinsically bad for society, whether or not they have harmful effects on the individual concerned. Moral paternalism, in contrast, appeals to the moral harm to individuals engaging in immoral behavior, with the implication that paternalist interventions can be good for their character, and hence for them.

It should be apparent that legal moralism is not a form of ends-related paternalism because it in no way involves the ends that individuals have chosen for themselves. Those ends are irrelevant to the government's judgments of the harm to society that results from the behavior that the government is trying to restrict. Moral paternalism, on the other hand, is a form of ends-related paternalism because it is directly concerned with the "moral" ends that individuals have chosen. Under moral paternalism, the government adopts an attitude that fundamentally opposes the individual's own essential values—the basic desires and tastes that do not in turn derive from any yet more fundamental dispositions. In contrast, means-related paternalism is nonmoralistic because it seeks only to provide individuals with what they actually want, even if the means for doing so vary between the paternalist and the individual.

In many countries, the government intervenes to "correct" what it judges to be ends failure in a wide variety of areas. The most obvious areas in countries that are functioning theocracies or at least have a strong religious orientation are in those involving private sexual conduct, such as homosexuality, and in the behavior and dress of, especially, women. Even in liberal democracies there are many ends-related paternalistic interventions, including restrictions on Sunday trading, and on assisted suicide.

We take the view that such interventions cannot be justified. Why is this? The short answer is that nonmoralistic paternalism is amenable to empirical testing or logical inquiry and so is able to marshal arguments in its defense that make use of some degree of objective standards. Evidence for the reasoning failures described above derives largely from experimental inquiry or from survey questioning, or else they demonstrate compelling failures of logic. People, in principle at least, should be able to acknowledge the errors they make. At any rate, there is some standard, other than the view of the paternalist, by which the reasoning failure can be assessed.

By contrast, ends-related or moralistic "failure" is based only on the judgment of the paternalist. There is no scope for the individual subsequently to acknowledge his previous misjudgments of his fundamental interests; these interests are unchanging—or at least change only as fast as the basic character of human beings might change. Thrill seekers do not recant the thrill they enjoy from certain pursuits, although they might grow out of it or accept—as the nonmoralistic paternalist would suggest—that the dangers were perhaps more likely and more unpleasant than they imagined. There is no objective means of establishing an ends failure, and thus passing judgment on it should not form a part of any government's paternalistic policies.

It can on occasion be difficult to distinguish between ends failure and reasoning failure. How can we be sure that the thrill of mountain climbing does not for some people *depend* on their undertaking it without any preparation, on the spur of the moment and without a guide? That it is these features precisely that feed the profound desire that climbing a mountain presents? Some people might reason that unaccompanied, unprepared climbing is just the right way to achieve their ends of climbing bliss, and they might be right (for them).

To overcome this difficulty, legislators and rule makers must make every effort to gather empirical evidence that distinguishes those choices on which people change their mind from those that constitute a fundamental aspect of character. Do mountaineers ever, after a narrow escape from harm, declare that the whole enterprise of mountaineering is grossly mistaken? Or do they merely bemoan their misjudgments about the approach they adopted? As ever, the answer to this question might not be as clear-cut as we would like. Not all people suffer reasoning failure, even when it is common among the population at large. This complicates the picture, but we can at least try to ensure that any paternalist regulations that are imposed do minimal harm to such individuals. This is a point to which we shall return.

It is worth noting that some people may give the impression of recanting their fundamental desires when they are not in fact doing so. Homosexuals may claim that they no longer wish to indulge in gay sex, and that they view earlier habits as the result of inexperience or youthful indiscretion. But such attitudes may in fact be the result of social pressure to retract an *action* but fall short of a claim that the underlying desire was itself a "mistake." They may feel pressured to express guilt about what they feel, but the feeling may still be there. What is their true end in such a situation? It is undoubtedly difficult to disentangle, but we should not make the job harder by advocating in principle a version of paternalism directed toward a supposed failure that is beyond any empirical method of demonstration. The approach of the legislator must be to look at the weight of empirical evidence and couple this with appropriate paternalist mechanisms wherever possible.

Conclusion: Means-Related versus Ends-Related Paternalism

Reasoning failure involves a disjunction between the ends we want and how to get them. It is a failure of means. The evidence in this chapter suggests that we unconsciously incorporate biases or other errors into our decision making that make it likely that we misjudge the route to our own well-being. We have identified four sources of such reasoning failure: limited technical ability, limited imagination, limited willpower, and limited objectivity. It is worth noting that these failures of reasoning may be separated into two general categories: those pertaining to judgments about the appropriate course of action and those relating to the actual choices made to achieve a given objective. In terms of our categories, limited technical ability, limited imagination, and limited objectivity are examples of failures of reasoning in relation to judgment (because the individual cannot adequately compute or assess the information available); while weakness of the will is an example of a failure of reasoning in relation to choice (the individual makes a good judgment as to what is necessary to optimize her well-being but still chooses to take a different course of action).

The examples used often cite trivial decisions involving fictional scenarios or cheap goods such as coffee cups. But if the underlying judgment biases are replicated in more serious situations, such as those involving one's future health, wealth, and happiness, as they do indeed often appear to be, then their importance becomes a legitimate matter of concern for the government. It is here that means-related government paternalism has an opening.

However, experimental evidence does not exist for identifying where people might fail to have the right ends. This kind of failure would involve not acting in our best interests because, in the judgment of someone other than ourselves, either we have not properly identified our best interests or our identified best interests are simply wrong. The problem from an empirical standpoint is one of establishing evidence independently of the views of the subject. An individual may acknowledge that a given end he habitually pursues—such as the sensation of having another cigarette—is one he would prefer not to pursue. But it is difficult to see how one could challenge the latter judgment of that individual without referring to a yet more fundamental end of the person, and to do that we would require more evidence from the individual himself that this more fundamental end does exist. Evidentially, at least, we are ultimately at the mercy of what individuals tell us their (ultimate) ends are. To go beyond this and ignore what people say takes us into the realm of philosophical moral judgments and out of the empirical laboratory.

But before considering whether the government is able to fulfill any of these paternalistic roles, whether means- or ends-related, we must first consider whether anyone has the *right* to act in such a way. This is the challenge posed by the concept of autonomy, the subject of the next chapter.

6   The Nanny State:
The Challenge from Autonomy

The principal nonutilitarian objection to paternalism derives from the notion of autonomy. This is the notion of self-rule, the ability to act as a deliberating agent. Although Mill never used the term "autonomy," he is strongly associated with the notion that the individual has the right to plan and enact his life and is therefore "sovereign" over it: "In the part [of his conduct] which merely concerns himself, his independence is, of right, absolute. Over himself, over his own body and mind, the individual is sovereign" (Mill [1859] 1974, 69).

As we saw earlier, Mill considered that an individual's "own good, either physical or moral, is not a sufficient warrant" for interference (68). Indeed, one can summarize one of the fundamental tensions at the heart of paternalism as that between the paternalist's desire to do good and the individual's right to exercise his or her autonomy.

But the challenge from autonomy is not only a question of individual rights. It also underlies another fundamental criticism of paternalist policies: that they undermine an individual's intrinsic motivation to act for herself. In the view of many of its critics, the paternalist government is actually a "nanny state": a nanny who, by intervening in her protégés' autonomy ostensibly for their own good, infantilizes them and renders them incapable of exercising that autonomy. Paternalist policies can therefore defeat their own ends; for by trying to change individuals' behavior "for their own good," they deprive individuals of both the opportunity and the motivation to do it themselves. In consequence the outcome may be a worse situation than the status quo ante.

We begin this chapter by briefly elaborating on the notion of autonomy, and then considering the relationship between paternalism, autonomy, and motivation. We go on to consider in some detail the position of the so-called soft paternalists, who argue that individuals' autonomy must always be respected and not traded off for well-being gains, but who also contend that it is possible to intervene in others' lives without engaging in such trade-offs.

Their position is based on what we term autonomy failure. That is, the justification for paternalism depends crucially on a prior diminution of the individual's capacity for autonomous decision making, so that autonomy is therefore not offended by the intervention. We review the various circumstances in which this autonomy failure takes place and note the similarities with the various types of reasoning failure described in chapter 5. We then go on to consider whether the soft paternalistic strategy is successful in avoiding offending autonomy. We conclude that, as long as autonomy has as one of its essential elements individuals' *belief* that they are governing their own lives, the soft paternalistic strategy fails, for the object of the paternalistic intervention will almost always *perceive* his autonomy as being offended. The final sections consider hard paternalism; that is, those interventions that admit that autonomy will need to be compromised but that consider this to be justified by the well-being outcome for the individual.

Autonomy

Autonomy is a complex term that defies easy definition. In fact, one scholar has suggested that "it is very unlikely that there is a core meaning," given the broad range of interpretations put on it from various authors, and that "about the only features held constant from one author to another are that autonomy is a feature of persons, and that it is a desirable quality to have" (G. Dworkin 1988, 6). Nevertheless, without delving too deeply into the philosophical complexities, we must gain a definitional foothold to guide our analysis. Perhaps the most helpful starting point is to return to the Greek root of the term, namely, *auto* (self) and *nomos* (rule or law); together these terms give us the notion of self-government or self-rule. The central idea, then, is that autonomous people have the capacity to think, decide, and act for themselves. If we are autonomous, we are the authors of our own lives.

The most famous philosopher of autonomy was Immanuel Kant. For Kant, autonomy was important for morality: he believed that a human being has the "capacity to subject [him]self to (objective) moral principles" (Christman and Anderson 2005, 2), and that "autonomy is the property of the *will* of rational beings. To have a will is to be able to cause events in accord with principles" (Hill 1991, 29). This leads Kant to conceive of morality as deriving from reason and of people being in charge of their moral destiny. As a result, people must be treated as ends in themselves (by virtue of their capacity for moral self-legislation) rather than simply means to others' private interests.[1]

---

1   This is the meaning of the famous formulation, "For all rational beings stand under the law that each of them should treat himself and all others never merely as a means but al-

Subsequently the meaning of autonomy has broadened to become what is known as "personal autonomy," that is, a "morally neutral (or allegedly neutral) trait that individuals can exhibit relative to any aspects of their lives, not limited to moral obligation" (Christman and Anderson 2005, 2). It is this latter, broader conceptualization that will inform our discussions in this chapter. Autonomy in this sense is strongly associated with the idea that freedom to make decisions has intrinsic as well as consequentialist elements (Sen 1988); that is, being able to choose between options does not just give us the means to promote our own well-being but is important in itself. It is also associated with the proposition that making decisions allows us to exercise our "moral powers," and that such powers, "like the muscular, are improved only by being used" (Mill [1859] 1974, 122).

Related to such conceptions of autonomy are beliefs about the exercise of choice being essential to human dignity and the ability to be self-sufficient (Bell et al.1994). In our everyday experience, it is the value that we place on autonomy that gives us that irritable or discordant feeling when people fail to "mind their own business." Autonomy does not imply the holding of moral virtues—such as kindness or wisdom—but is considered "a necessary element in any full ideal of human character" (Feinberg 1986, 45). What is clear, at least, is that the concept does not directly refer to well-being or happiness, and as such has to be taken into account in addition to the arguments concerning well-being that emerge from the evidence of the previous chapter.

One further set of distinctions will assist our subsequent exposition. Joel Feinberg (1986) distinguished a number of ways of conceiving autonomy. First, it can be conceived of as a capacity; that is, as the ability to act in an autonomous manner as described above. This notion of autonomy sees it as a matter of degree: one can be more or less autonomous depending on, for example, whether one has had too much to drink, or whether one has suffered a brain injury. Second, one can understand autonomy as an ideal. In this sense we may never attain "true" autonomy, but we may have an idea of what it looks like, and we can strive to achieve it. Finally, we can see autonomy as a right. Feinberg argues that a person's autonomy should be considered as analogous with the right of a nation to govern over its own territory. Thus Feinberg introduces the notion of personal sovereignty over which one has the right to self-rule. Autonomy, when understood in this way, is not a matter of degree. One has the right to autonomy absolutely; it is invariable and inviolate. He contrasts this notion of right to self-government with the notion of "our own good," the typical focus of the paternalist. According to

---

ways at the same time as an end in himself. Hereby arises a systematic union of rational beings through common objective laws, i.e., a kingdom that may be called a kingdom of ends" (Kant [1785] 1981, 39).

Feinberg, when these two values conflict, personal right takes precedence, so that, even when we certainly suspect that someone will harm themselves, we should not prevent her unless we have reason to believe she is acting involuntarily. We will return to these points.

It is useful to distinguish autonomy from freedom or liberty. If we think of freedom as an absence of physical constraints, then a person may still be viewed as autonomous even if he is not free to put that choice into effect. So a person immobilized by a straitjacket can still formulate a plan of action to free himself in an "autonomous" way but is clearly not "free" in the generally understood sense of the word (Husak 1981). Not all authorities on autonomy agree: Joseph Raz (1986, 373) argues that "adequacy of options" is one component of autonomy, and that if someone is "paralyzed and therefore cannot take advantage of the options which are offered to him," he is not autonomous. This serves as an example of the lack of unanimity of authors about the meaning of autonomy. We would argue that a person should not be discounted from a description of autonomous just because of physical incapabilities; such a person is able to formulate a plan of her life and to put it into effect as long as she can obtain the practical help of others. Indeed, a wealthy paralyzed man who is able to elicit substantial assistance could reasonably be described as having a greater capacity for autonomy than a poor man who is not physically disabled.

A useful distinction can also be made between autonomous persons and autonomous decisions (Beauchamp and Childress 2001). A generally autonomous *person* can occasionally *act* with limited autonomy (when drunk or emotionally stressed); similarly a generally nonautonomous person can still make autonomous decisions, such as the mentally ill person in a care home choosing her meals. What this reminds us is that it is conceptually possible to respect the overall autonomy of a person while at the same time acknowledging that he is acting with limited autonomy in specific instances.

Autonomy and Motivation

As we noted earlier, a major challenge to paternalism (for some, perhaps the principal challenge to paternalism) arising from considerations of autonomy concerns the impact of paternalistic interventions on motivation. The damage to autonomy done by paternalistic intervention not only affects individuals' rights but also could affect any intrinsic motivation they might have to change their behavior. Excessive nannying by the state or government could infantilize the recipient, thus reducing or even negating entirely the effectiveness of the policy.

Useful insights into the relationship between autonomy and individual motivation can be obtained from the theory of self-determination as developed by psychologists Edward Deci and Richard Ryan (2000). The theory distinguishes between autonomous actions and those that are controlled or influenced by factors external to the self. Autonomous actions occur when people do something because they find it intrinsically interesting, enjoyable, or important. These actions come about because of internal or intrinsic factors: they are a product of intrinsic motivation. Controlled actions occur when individuals are motivated to perform them by some form of external pressure: they are the outcome of external or extrinsic factors— what is termed extrinsic motivation. Controlled action may be just as highly motivated as autonomous activity, but Deci and Ryan argue that the quality of the experience and performance is not as good.

Deci and Ryan (2000, 36) distinguish between kinds of controlled or extrinsic motivation according to the degree of control involved. At the extreme of heavy control is "external regulation": when behavior is motivated entirely by direct rewards or penalties. At the other extreme is "introjected regulation": when social or other external factors have engendered a sense of pride or self-worth for individuals acting in accordance with an internalized "introjected" value or standard, or guilt or shame when they do not.

They also distinguish between two types of autonomous motivation, one of which they regard as a form of intrinsic motivation and the other as extrinsic. The intrinsic motivation is the kind of autonomous motivation already referred to: that arising from the intrinsic enjoyment or interest in the task being undertaken. The extrinsic motivation is where there is a strong identification with an external value or standard: the individual identifies with the value or standard, internalizes it as part of her own morality, and regards the behavior concerned as an essential part of her identity. This is to be distinguished from the introjected regulation described in the previous paragraph, which it otherwise rather resembles, in that, with identified motivation, individuals do not feel pride if they do something socially approved of, or shame if they do not; rather, the activity concerned is simply part of their identity, and they will carry on with it regardless of changes in the outside environment.

Deci and Ryan also discuss the factors that might affect the degree of control and hence the kind of motivation that people might experience. Contextual support to decision making and situations where motivators provide a convincing rationale for undertaking a certain kind of behavior can reduce the element of perceived control and enhance feelings of autonomy, leading to introjected or even identified motivation. Conversely, threat of punishment or even the promise of a crude reward can make individuals feel controlled and less autonomous. In consequence, as noted above, the quality (and indeed quantity) of their relevant actions might diminish. A policy may thus be more effective if it is perceived as supporting or reinforcing; the policy may be less effective if it is perceived as controlling.

The concepts of introjected and identified motivation are especially relevant to the sustainability of the behavior change if the policy were withdrawn. If the internalization that has occurred is of the introjected kind, then the removal of the policy will reduce or eliminate the behavior concerned only so long as any social pressures associated with the policy are perceived to remain. But if the internalization is of the identified kind, then the change in behavior will remain even if the social pressures are withdrawn. For the internalization will then have successfully promoted people's sense of autonomy and reduced their feelings of social control.

Self-determination theory also provides clues as to the external stimuli that are likely to increase people's sense of autonomy, and thus the extent to which they identify with the policy. According to the theory, the policies concerned are more likely to promote autonomy, be successfully internalized, and lead to sustainable behavior change in harmony with the desired aim of the policy if they have a meaningful rationale, are perceived as fair, and give choice and support to the individual (Vallerand and Reid 1984; De Young 1996; Deci and Ryan 2000). More specifically, if a particular external stimulus stimulates people to engage in a form of new behavior, then this is likely to increase perceived self-efficacy and competence, which would mediate the behavioral change initiated by the incentive (de Charms 1968). The motivation, initially derived from the presence of the incentive, thus becomes internalized, making the behavior change more likely to persist even if the incentive were to be removed.

Such propositions reinforce the challenge mounted to paternalism by considerations of autonomy. Not only is that challenge a question of the policies concerned infringing or violating the rights of the individuals affected; it also concerns the effectiveness of those policies. Self-determination theory would predict that the more that an individual perceives that his autonomy is being violated by a particular policy, the less he will change his behavior in the direction in which the policy is trying to steer him; and, in consequence, any improvement in well-being may be limited, negligible, or only short term. So the search for a means-related paternalistic policy that in some way does not violate autonomy, or at least has a minimal impact on autonomy, becomes still more important.

Soft Paternalism

Soft paternalism seeks to avoid the autonomy challenge to paternalism completely.[2] As we have seen, the central argument for opposing government paternalism is that an autonomous individual should have the right to pursue her own conception of the good life in ways that seem right to her—and, moreover, that any paternalistic intervention may carry the seeds of its own failure, owing to the impact of the erosion of autonomy on the individual's intrinsic motivation. But if the ability to act as autonomous individual is not present—if there is some element of "autonomy failure"—the challenge is weakened. The soft paternalist case is that, if your capacity for autonomy is diminished and you are no longer acting voluntarily,[3] so that the decisions you make and the goals you pursue are not "yours," then an intervention in those decisions does not offend that autonomy—the intervention does not affect the "real you." Nor, by implication, will your intrinsic motivation be affected. Under such circumstances, the soft paternalist believes it is justified to intervene as long as there is a significant harm to be prevented.

The phrase "significant harm" is itself significant. For most soft paternalists, soft paternalism is decision related: if the decision is one with particularly serious or potentially harmful outcomes, then an intervention is more likely to be supported. The soft paternalist strategy might also be described as a threshold approach (Wikler 1979; Rainbolt 1989a, 46). Thus when voluntariness drops below a certain threshold (and the harm becomes significant—the two not necessarily going together), this triggers a potentially justifiable intervention. As long as people are operating above this threshold, they are all considered equally competent even if the precise degree of voluntariness varies from one person to another; they should all be allowed to undertake the activity to which the threshold applies even if it is likely to

---

2 See Pope (2004) for a detailed definition of soft paternalism that distinguishes it from hard paternalism. Those who emphasize the importance of soft (or "weak") paternalism include Beauchamp and Childress (2001) and Komrad (1983) in the context of medical care; Feinberg (1986), who articulated and defended the most sophisticated and nuanced version; and Husak (1989) in the context of drugs. See also Callahan (1986) for a discussion of how certain types of nonvoluntariness fail to justify paternalism, and Garren (2007) for a literature review.

3 Feinberg, and most who discuss soft paternalism, use the terms "voluntarily" and "voluntariness" as others use the term "autonomously" (see Brock 1988, 556; Buchanan and Brock 1989, 42; Beauchamp 2004). "Voluntarily" in this sense is similar in meaning to having the *capacity* for autonomy. It is also worth noting that Feinberg (1986, 15) argues that soft paternalism is better described as "soft anti-paternalism"—an essentially liberal position that is "really no kind of paternalism at all." Others agree. Beauchamp (1983, 138) notes that "weak paternalism applies only to substantially nonvoluntary or uninformed persons" and as such has in the final analysis "nothing to do with paternalism" (142). However, Feinberg accepts that his preferred interpretation is nevertheless best debated under the general "paternalism" heading.

cause them harm. But before returning to these matters, we must review two classes of autonomy failure, one involving external causes and the other internal causes.[4]

Autonomy Failure from External Causes

The first set of justifications based on autonomy failure involves external causes: ignorance or lack of information; coercion or compulsion from a second party; and hypnosis and drugs.

Ignorance or Lack of Information

Imperfect information, ignorance, or being unaware of relevant facts is very often considered grounds for soft paternalism. Gerald Dworkin (1981, 46) cites "ignorance," as does Feinberg (1986, 152) as one element of a justification for (soft) paternalism; Archard cites "ignorance" alongside a range of other mental incapacities (1993, 341); Goodin (1993, 234) cites being "uninformed" as the first form of justification for overriding people's preferences. There are many other examples.

We have argued above that the lack of accurate information, pure and simple, does not constitute any kind of reasoning or ends failure in an individual. We have also seen that imperfect information is one of the basic causes of market failure. Economists do not consider government interventions to correct such information failures as in any way paternalistic, and it is something of a puzzle as to why the commentators just cited—all philosophers—clearly do.[5] One explanation might be that in the philosophy literature the circumstances where paternalism takes place are not what would normally be described as a "market." Take Mill's example of a bridge whose unsafe nature is unknown to a walker, or other, similar cases such as potential swimmers unaware of the strong tides on an apparently tranquil beach, or a driver encountering an unsignaled, dangerous bend in a remote country road. None of these pieces of information is imperfectly known to consumers *in a market*. They are activities in everyday life that are typically not bought and sold: there are no market transactions between agents involved; indeed there is only one agent "transacting" with the natural world, so no

4 Many of these categories of autonomy have a long pedigree: see, for example, Hodson (1977).
5 A few authors have distinguished between imperfect information and paternalistic motivations for state intervention: see, for example, Kelman (1981), in the case of health and safety regulations, and VanDeVeer (1986, 86).

standard market failure issues arise: information asymmetry, moral hazard, adverse selection, and so on.[6]

Nonetheless, we would argue that an intervention to correct such non-market imperfect information is more properly justified through insights from market failure rationales than from paternalistic ones. As with market information failures, it is important to distinguish the adequacy of the internal intellectual process of reasoning to arrive at a judgment from the accuracy and completeness of the data to which such reasoning is applied. Few would argue that the decision to walk over a bridge in the absence of any information indicating that the bridge is unsafe demonstrates a failure of reasoning. Government interventions to correct reasoning failure are more controversial and require a more sophisticated justification than interventions aimed at correcting market failure and are best kept distinct for this reason.

Coercion by Others

Another common set of justifications for soft paternalism is those cases where an individual is being unduly forced or pressured into undertaking a particular act.[7] Some forms of coercion may be legitimately prevented directly via the harm principle. A kidnapper who forcibly binds and gags someone before carrying the victim off is subject to the criminal law on the basis that he is harming another. However, in some apparently clear examples of other-regarding acts, the target of the crime has a degree of choice. The classic example would be the mugger who asks for "your money or your life"—the person being mugged can still choose to resist, but no one would argue that this constitutes a meaningful and voluntary choice. An intervention by a police officer to prevent the mugger would be welcome and would not offend autonomy. For soft paternalists this intervention by the government would be justifiable because the person being mugged is agreeing to something (handing over her money) that pertains to her own good (saving her life) but is doing so in an overwhelmingly nonvoluntary way. The task for the soft paternalist is to assess when such consented-to harms are not truly voluntary and thus justify government intervention.

---

6 Jonathan Roberts has suggested to us that another possible explanation for information giving to be regarded as paternalist comes from the very meaning of the word paternal: that is, fatherly. Fathers certainly intervene in their children's autonomy where they deem it appropriate, but that is not all they do. Being paternal also means showing care, and making sure that children have full information when the lack of information would harm them is a protective and fatherly thing to do.

7 Feinberg (1986) distinguishes "compulsion proper," involving physical force and no choice at all (being blown about by a hurricane), from "coercion," which involves acting under duress from threats or danger.

According to our definition, however, an intervention is paternalistic only if it intends to address some reasoning or other cognitive failure. In the case of the person being mugged, there is no reason to think that she is acting according to a misconception of her situation or of the best course of action to achieve her ends. Thus the intervention by the government is not paternalistic, soft or hard. Rather, it is supported by a version of the harm principle that disallowed "offers" backed by threats of violence.

Even in a situation where there is coercion and potential harm, the government, or indeed any individual, may be doing more harm than good by intervening, regardless of whether the case is paternalistic. Consider a man being blackmailed and about to write out a check for a large sum of money to prevent the blackmailer from disclosing to his family the fact that he has had an affair. If a friend intervenes in such a situation to prevent the check being paid—because she thinks it outrageous that someone should suffer financially for such a misdemeanor—the friend may be acting against the will of the blackmailed person. He may be making a well-reasoned decision *under the circumstances in which he finds himself.* Paying the money might be precisely the right course of action to take, in his judgment, to protect himself and his family from being hurt. Preventing the payment of the money might simply lead to the blackmailer revealing her knowledge and cause greater harm than the friend set out to prevent.[8]

Nevertheless, there are cases where external coercion of some kind might be thought to be a paternalistic intervention even according to our definition. For example, in one real-life case cited by Joel Feinberg (1986, 156–59), a stuntman was "persuaded" by an impatient film crew to undertake a stunt that involved jumping over speeding cars as they approached him. He had earlier agreed to do it but then changed his mind at the last moment. The director became angry and frustrated at the waste of time and money such a delay would cause and remonstrated with the stuntman about his earlier decision. Reluctantly the stuntman agreed to do the stunt, but he was in an unhappy state of mind, the stunt went wrong, and he was left seriously injured. Subsequently legal damages were awarded against the film company, implying that the actions of the film crew were unlawfully coercive. The government's acknowledgment that the film crew were liable might be jus-

---

8 Of course there are other issues here. The man may be making a paternalistic judgement with respect to his family by deciding that their well-being lies in their not knowing. Also there are externalities involved: the blackmailer and copycats may be emboldened to commit similar offenses. Chapter 4 gives examples of how the state can often claim to be acting to protect vulnerable people in such circumstances, whereas a paternalistic rationale would be more plausible. But see also Dixon (2001) for the argument that socioeconomic circumstances can "coerce" boxers to take up the sport, thereby providing a paternalistic justification for state intervention to control it.

tified on the paternalistic grounds that the stuntman's reasoning was impaired by the pressure he was under. He was not thinking straight, and thus his "consent" to do the stunt was not given in a properly voluntary way. The government's intervention is to protect a coerced person who is thus not capable of making a sound judgment for herself. Note that the notion of not reasoning properly is related to lack of voluntariness, a point to which we will return later in this chapter.

However, we do not consider this kind of intervention to be strictly paternalistic. In fact the government is intervening only to prevent the individual from harm (or, in this case, to compensate him for the harm he has experienced)—a harm that was imposed from outside. The government's intervention is thus again better viewed as an application of the harm principle rather than motivated by a paternalistic rationale.

More difficult is the case of an individual who has been allegedly brainwashed by a religious cult. A case of brainwashing against a person's will—perhaps as a political prisoner— would allow an intervention on the basis of the harm principle to help the individuals concerned regain a sense of their "own" mind. But where the choice to join a cult was itself made voluntarily and with no apparent cognitive or ends deficiencies, and where the consequent alterations in the worldview that result from it take place with the individual's eyes wide open, then to intervene would not be justified by the harm principle and would be far from straightforward even for a soft paternalist.

Hypnosis and Drugs

It is reasonably easy to accept that an intervention to prevent a hypnotized person from walking out of a tenth-floor window is justified. Short of unconsciousness, hypnosis is possibly the nearest state to one involving a complete failure of autonomy. The relevance of the lack of autonomy is reinforced if the person were hypnotized against her will. However, people often choose to be hypnotized and thus might wish to do things that seem odd, could be embarrassing, or make them vulnerable. Nevertheless, unless we have good reason for thinking a person wishes to harm herself, the soft paternalist would feel justified on lack of autonomy grounds for intervening if harm seemed likely.

Interventions in relation to drug taking are also somewhat dependent on the circumstances. Where an individual is currently affected by an intoxicant to the extent that autonomous decision making has been seriously affected, then an intervention might be justified on soft paternalistic grounds. If the government knows that a drug induces such an effect, then prohibition of any such use in advance might also be justified. However, the situation is complicated by the fact that people often explicitly desire the intoxicating—and possibly mind-altering—properties of the drug, including any such dangers that follow. The basis for intervening in *this* kind of decision must be based on the state of mind of the individual *before* he consumes the drug. And many drugs are not particularly mind altering at all. Tobacco, for example, creates a relatively mild effect on one's mental state as, in small quantities, does alcohol.

Drugs are not simply mind altering but also addictive. Strong addiction to a narcotic substance may amount to a loss of autonomy to the extent that the "need" to have the next fix goes beyond the ability of the individual to control her decision making. Again, if such an addiction is always considered to occur, then the question becomes one of the extent to which the individual voluntarily chose this state of addiction. Drug takers may believe that the pleasure to be gained from the drug's chemical properties more than compensate for any inconveniences or expense (or even long-term health consequences) resulting from addiction.

In many such cases, then, the paternalist will need to decide whether the individual is acting truly voluntarily in making the decision to take a drug, when this is likely to damage his future health and well-being. When these prior decisions are made with a clear mind (narcotically speaking), the lack of voluntariness could derive only from a form of misjudgment about the risks and benefits—the subject of the next section. But it is worth noting at this point that such a misjudgment bears a strong resemblance to the reasoning failure of limited imagination discussed in chapter 5, where the individual fails to see with sufficient clarity the state that she will be in after taking a particular decision.[9]

Autonomy Failure from Internal Causes

Many of the most important causes of autonomy failure relate to some diminution or insufficiency of the working of our mental capabilities. These internal causes involve various forms of mental illness and disability; the immaturity of children; and the mistakes, misjudgments, or miscalculations that people make in specific circumstances.

Mental Disability, Mental Illness, and Immaturity

This category of justification for soft paternalism is the most straightforward, at least in principle, because it appears to refer to a condition of the

---

9 Of course, many prohibitive laws in relation to drugs are justified by the harm principle—that consumption is likely to cause either direct harm through the individual becoming violent, and so on, or by leading him into a life of crime to subsidize his addiction.

whole person—a general state of autonomy failure.[10] If someone has "lost her mind" though mental illness or has an organic mental disability or brain damage, then she is likely to suffer to some degree from an impaired capacity to rule her own life. Some people who suffer from mental illness or disability may be entirely incapable of looking after themselves, and such cases may be considered as rather straightforward examples of justifiable government intervention. But in fact the capacity to exercise autonomy is not usually completely absent, and the real difficulty exists in deciding *how much* intervention is justified. People with mental disability, for example, often wish to form sexual relationships (Spiecker and Steutel 2002). To what extent should this wish be respected? Particularly problematic for those who support interventions solely with reference to a lack of autonomy is to know how to focus the intervention so that it affects *only* those areas of life where autonomy is lacking. This point anticipates a difficulty we will return to in the next section when we assess whether soft paternalists really are successful in not offending autonomy. Take as an example the forcible incarceration of someone with mental illness. This can be legitimate intervention to assist the individual to the extent that he does lack autonomy, but it may, as a side effect, extinguish what little autonomy he has left.

The "whole person" situation also seems to apply to the case of children, which is why they are included under this heading. Children are not able to look after themselves—they suffer from limited autonomy—and thus we intervene on their behalf. Here the term paternalism is particularly apt—although perhaps parentalism would be even more so. But of course, just as with the cases of mental incompetence, children's autonomy varies enormously, and not least in relation to their age. The complicating factor thus becomes how much additional autonomy the child accrues as she gets older, and thus how much less warranted is the soft "parentalistic" control of her parents. Children represent a good example of how the threshold at which intervention is justified may vary—from person to person (one child is allowed to use a kitchen knife while another of the same age is not), from circumstance to circumstance (a child might be considered competent to bath himself but not to cross the road on his own), and over time (a child growing up is perpetually gaining in autonomy, and thus intervention becomes increasingly difficult to justify).

10 See Wikler (1979) for discussion of why we have a threshold conception of mental incompetence: namely, that it protects the averagely intelligent from paternalism by the super-intelligent.

"Mistakes," Misjudgment, and the Misuse of Evidence

Not all the examples of internal autonomy failure involve a general loss of mental capacity. Some involve particular circumstances, activities, or consumption choices. As we have already noted, Joel Feinberg is the chief proponent of soft paternalism, and in addition to outlining the factors noted above—coercion, children, and mental disability—he includes under the rubric of "ignorance" the following examples of various kinds of "mistake": misestimations, mistaken self-evaluations, distorted recollection of evidence, and confusion in drawing inferences from what we know (1986, 152).

As an example let us return to the case of a prospective drug user—in this case, a cannabis smoker. For Feinberg, he is not acting voluntarily (with adequate autonomy) unless

> he has accurate knowledge, at a higher level, of the scope and limits of his first level knowledge. If he knows the little that science can tell him, and knows how little that is; if he knows that conclusive evidence of the connection between nicotine and lung cancer did not accumulate until the first heavy-smoking generation had been at it for thirty years, and that there are as yet no comparable data about the effects of prolonged marijuana usage, but that such evidence could very well turn up; if he knows that there are already suspected links, based on inconclusive studies, between some amount of pot-usage and a variety of physical ailments, from loss of male hormone to diminished brain function, and that the trend has been for the discovery of more and better confirmed connections of these kinds, then he has all the relevant information there is. (160–61)

Perhaps our everyday usage of the term "voluntary" leaves us uncomfortable with this being the standard of voluntary choice. An intelligent, generally aware cannabis smoker might say, in response, "I think I'll just take the risk—there doesn't seem to be obvious or immediate damage, and there's a lot of pleasure." This may not be the correct decision, but it seems entirely voluntary.

But if the smoker does misjudge his interests, then we can begin to see a sense in which he is not making the decision voluntarily because he is not choosing what he *really* wants. He is making the choice voluntarily in the sense that no one is forcing him or tricking him into his actions; and yet we can acknowledge that mistakes can be made and that, if an individual fails to achieve his own ends, then this faulty perception of facts and suboptimal reasoning processes leave him less than fully autonomous.[11]

11   The smoker is misjudging the extent of his ignorance: he lacks adequate "metaknowledge" of the extent of his "first-level knowledge." He may not properly understand, for example, how a lack of knowledge about medicine and drugs undermines his decision making to the

A similar situation arises with respect to Feinberg's use of the concept of mental "capacity" as a factor militating against autonomy. Some incapacities are more readily recognizable than others—for instance, when one is not in control of one's cognitive faculties because the "whole self" is compromised in its function in some way, as with mental illness or hypnotism. But Feinberg (1986, 317–18) also includes the following categories of "incapacity": "Cognitive disabilities ... include ... inabilities to make correct inferences ... failures of attention or memory, failures to understand communications, and even failures to *care* about a belief's grounding and implications, leading in turn to a failure to grasp its full import, or adequately to appreciate its full significance" (emphasis in original).

We can see that these incapacities, and the various forms of "mistake" noted above, are again akin to the various forms of reasoning failure that were outlined in the previous chapter. To that extent, the soft paternalist—at least in the sophisticated version presented by Feinberg—is acknowledging, just as the behavioral economists do, that people do not always act in ways that best serve their own interests, goals, or values.[12] Reasoning failure can be viewed as a limited loss of autonomy. Every time we make a calculation, judgment, or decision that fails to achieve our ends in some way, we could reasonably be described as not acting autonomously to that extent. We are not successfully acting out and implementing our values; our self-rule fails. Reasoning failure from this perspective is a particular type of autonomy failure: it is mild and does not leave us incompetent, but it is nonetheless a failure truly to govern our own lives according to our goals. To this extent, the justification for action that reasoning failure gives to the paternalist as outlined in chapter 5 is consistent with the approach of a soft paternalist.

When Should the Soft Paternalist Intervene?

The question remains for the soft paternalist: *when* is lack of voluntariness a good enough reason to intervene? As we have seen, in Feinberg's terminology many forms of mental and cognitive processing that fall below some high level of capability will amount to a "nonvoluntary" choice. Although this conceptualization seems ill at ease with most ordinary understandings of the term "voluntary," Feinberg acknowledges that voluntariness is an elastic concept and that fully voluntary is an extremely rare, if not unattainable,

---

likely detriment of his future well-being, a case of reasoning failure/lack of voluntariness. Rainbolt (1989a, 1989b) argues that a prescription drug user *does* have good metaknowledge. See Rainbolt (1989a, 1989b) and Ten (1989) on the question of whether outlawing therapeutic drug purchases without prescription is soft or hard paternalism.

12   Feinberg would have quibbled with some of the specifics: for example, he explicitly notes that, in his view, weakness of will is consonant with fully voluntary choice—it would not, therefore, constitute a basis for state intervention.

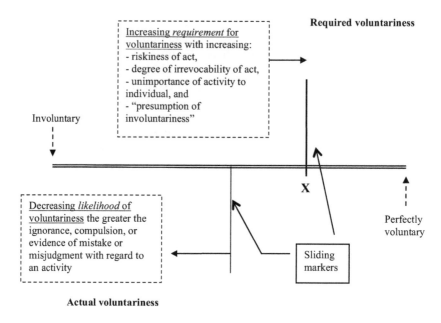

Figure 6.1. Feinberg's threshold for justified soft paternalism

ideal. At some point this side of the ideal voluntarism will dip below a threshold that justifies intervention. The question rests on where this threshold is: how voluntary is voluntary *enough*?

Feinberg's approach is as follows. Factors such as ignorance, compulsion, mistake, and incapacity act to "vitiate" or reduce voluntariness.[13] But in addition to these, a number of features of the proposed activity will serve to increase the standard of "voluntary enough." They include the degree of risk (of harm) involved in the action, the irrevocability of the harm that might result from the action (for example, if death is a distinct possibility), the extent to which the ultimate purpose of the action is important to the individual (do we think this person has always harbored a genuine desire to climb Mount Everest?), and factors that Feinberg refers to as leading to a "presumption of nonvoluntariness"—namely, the statistical unusualness of the action (such as an expressed desire to swim in waters known to be full of crocodiles) and evidence of mental illness or disturbance. The situation for the soft paternalist can be represented diagrammatically, as in figure 6.1, adapted from a representation offered by Feinberg himself (118).

---

13   We have argued that ignorance—in the sense of having imperfect information—and compulsion should not really be considered to create conditions that demand paternalistic intervention, but this does not affect the argument at this point.

Let us take a proposed activity—say smoking cannabis—with associated degrees of risk, irrevocability, and perceived importance to the individuals undertaking it.[14] In such a case, "voluntary enough" might require position X, the autonomy threshold point at which an intervention on soft paternalistic grounds becomes justified. The greater the riskiness/harmfulness of the activity—say smoking crack cocaine rather than cannabis—the further to the right the sliding marker above the line will be, and the further to the right the threshold point X will be. However, the likelihood of achieving that degree of voluntariness is reduced by the factors under the line, which are pulling this lower marker to the left. For the activity to be justified (for soft paternalism to be *unjustified*), the sliding marker below the line must be to the right of this point X: actual voluntariness must be at least as great as the required voluntariness for that activity. As the diagram is drawn, a soft paternalistic intervention in this case is justified because actual voluntariness has not reached the required level. It is worth emphasizing that Feinberg wishes to allow us to make decisions that are not fully voluntary, and that may therefore be "mistaken" in some sense, but only if they are *sufficiently* voluntary (to the right of point X, wherever this may lie) for the type of decision at hand. In the next chapter we will outline our own version of this kind of judgment. We will emphasize to a greater extent the fact that laws, and government interventions more generally, tend to act on classes of people that include individuals with different goals and cognitive abilities. We will discuss whether such overarching government interventions allow people sufficient freedom to pursue their harmful goals if they really wish to—acknowledging that not everyone who appears to take risks with their well-being is acting contrary to their interests.

But before we do, we must return to the question of autonomy: has the soft paternalist strategy really succeeded in avoiding any compromise of individuals' autonomy?

Does Soft Paternalism Avoid Offending Autonomy?

It is worth reminding ourselves that the soft paternalist strategy is not just based on an understanding that autonomy can "fail"—that people can act with insufficient voluntariness—but that this failure provides an opening for the government to intervene *without offending autonomy*. For as Feinberg makes clear, if one is operating with a concept of "de jure autonomy"—that is, autonomy as a right—and its analogy of "personal sovereignty," then

14   There is probably no "presumption of involuntariness" in this example because it is not an unusual activity, and the people undertaking it are not usually mentally disturbed, at least when not smoking.

"there is no such thing as a 'trivial interference' with personal sovereignty; nor is it simply another value to be weighed in a cost-benefit comparison. In this respect, if not others, a trivial interference with sovereignty is like a minor invasion of virginity: the logic of each concept is such that a value is respected in its entirety or not at all" (94).

This is at the heart of the soft paternalist strategy: because it refuses to countenance trading off autonomy, it must instead either demonstrate that autonomy is lacking through the concept of insufficient voluntariness or allow the individual to act in any way that she sees fit.

But there is a suspicion that, in fact, a cost-benefit analysis has been introduced by the back door. As we have seen, the more serious the potential harm, the higher the level of voluntariness we may require. It may be that autonomy is not a flexible or "tradable" value in itself, but the soft paternalist has certainly allowed that it can be present to a greater or lesser degree. The greater the harm that is likely to befall an individual, the greater the capacity for exercising autonomy he requires. The soft paternalist may not be directly trading off this autonomy, but, in judging whether the individual is considered to be acting sufficiently voluntarily, a risk-benefit frame of analysis comes into play. For example, take an individual playing Russian roulette. On one occasion he plays using blanks, and this is considered risky but allowable; but then he picks up a gun loaded with live bullets (of which he is aware), and the game is considered too risky and is disallowed. A soft paternalist might justify this by noting that, given the much higher degree of risk in the second scenario, the threshold of voluntariness shifts such that the individual's decision making is no longer "voluntary enough." But note that nothing else has changed in the two scenarios except the degree of danger: the player is exactly the same person and his level of autonomy, his state of mind, the degree of coercion, and the information available to him are all identical. All that has changed is the likelihood that he will kill himself. This, surely, is a form of risk-benefit analysis by any other name? Soft paternalists do not wish to trade off autonomy, but they arrive at very similar judgments to those who are less absolutist.[15]

---

15   Richard Arneson (2005, 268) makes a similar and detailed case against Feinberg's version of soft paternalism, arguing that "the idea of individual voluntary choice" is unable to bear "the enormous weight that the soft paternalist has to place on it," and that voluntary choice is "important but does not plausibly have the make-or-break significance that soft paternalism attaches to it." Shafer-Landau (2005) also takes issue with Feinberg's uncompromising approach to personal sovereignty and presents arguments from Feinberg's own writings that undercut his approach. Buchanan and Brock (1989, 41–47) suggest that Feinberg fails to avoid placing autonomy on the cost-benefit scales; the authors argue for a sliding scale of competence depending on risk—similar conceptually to Feinberg but squarely acknowledging that they *are* balancing autonomy with well-being. Note also DeMarco (2002), who subtly departs from these approaches by emphasizing the *evidence* for competence rather than competence itself.

But let us leave this to one side and agree that the soft paternalist intervenes simply when some degree of diminished voluntariness (this may be a form of reasoning failure) gives him an opportunity to improve the individual's well-being because the proposed action is not truly the individual's own. The question now is, does this really avoid offending autonomy *in practice?*

We would argue not. The account of the soft paternalists has been one from the perspective of political philosophy. It is, by its very nature, a highly abstract argument. There is no doubt it has a certain intellectual coherence: if your autonomy is lacking, then an intervention on that account cannot interfere with something that is not there. In extremis we can see how this would work perfectly well. Someone in a coma, to use a familiar example, is entirely lacking in autonomy. She is not conscious at all. If we take a decision to intervene in her life, we are (merely) acting in a soft paternalist way because her autonomy cannot be compromised to any greater degree than it is already. However, almost anybody who is conscious is able to reflect, no matter how incoherently, on her place in the world and what she (thinks) she wants to do next. She may do it badly, but she will be trying. She may be extremely drunk, addled by drugs, mentally ill, or mentally disabled. These are all, as we have seen, substantial cases of diminished autonomy. Paternalism may, in these cases, be justified on the grounds that the person's autonomy/reasoning is severely impaired. However, unless she actively requests or consents to such interventions, such an intervention will *feel* to her as if her autonomy is being infringed. She may even know she is acting with no sense but still resent the interference. She may consider her autonomy to be functioning—if not well, then still functioning. In practice, any government intervention will need to take this *perception* of offended autonomy into account.

The perception of autonomy loss is particularly important because of the relationship between autonomy and intrinsic motivation that we discussed earlier. An individual's intrinsic motivation to change his behavior will not be affected by a loss in autonomy that he does not perceive. But if he feels less autonomous as result of the paternalistic intervention, his intrinsic motivation to change behavior is likely to be reduced, and hence the effectiveness of the policy is also likely to be diminished.

One way in which the government can try to avoid the perception of autonomy loss is to make the intervention in a "silent" or "stealthy" way—by, for example, using framing devices in the provision of information, or by introducing opt-out mechanisms where individuals are automatically enrolled unless they choose to opt out. Such policies would clearly have to be subtly employed to work entirely silently, and there may be very few examples of a genuinely imperceptible policy—even the straightforward provision of information such as "smoking kills" can be interpreted as "nannying" by consumers. But if health advice, for example, is framed with a particular form of words—for example, in terms of lives saved rather than deaths avoided—then a silent or stealthy paternalistic effect may be achieved. We will be discussing these ideas (and their impact on autonomy) further in chapter 7, but for now it is worth noting that, in these cases, individuals are unlikely to think that they are subject to any kind of positive policy intervention, or that they are being encouraged to take one course of action rather than another.

Another example of what we might term "stealth" paternalism is the use of government subsidies. We described earlier how subsidies for certain goods are paternalistic if they seek to correct a misjudgment on the part of individuals about the appropriate level of consumption. Lowering a service's price will encourage people to use it. We argued that, even though such a policy unequivocally increases the individual's range of options, the policy is still paternalistic. But in this case it could be argued that the intervention does not diminish autonomy; in particular there is not likely to be a diminution of autonomy as perceived by the individual herself, who is pleasantly faced with lower prices for some activities and unchanged prices for the rest. Of course, the policy may not be quite silent if the consumer perceives how her choices are being conditioned; nevertheless, her experience of the government's intervention may not be felt as a restriction of her autonomy, even if she does suspect that the government would prefer her to consume more of the good in question.

This raises an interesting question about the relationship between two senses or aspects of autonomy: autonomy as normative status and autonomy as capacity. It can be argued that part of being autonomous is being recognized as autonomous, so subsidies or silent paternalism insofar as they infringe on my public standing as autonomous is a violation of it. Just what the exact causal or constitutive relationship is between these two aspects of autonomy is much contested. But one might still want to say that our public understanding of autonomy is about not just our capacities but also the relations in which we stand to one another and to the government.

But even if it is possible to find some exceptions to the problem of perceived autonomy loss from a paternalistic intervention, there is another more general difficulty for the soft paternalist. Government paternalism will find it awkward to direct its policies toward only those suffering from limited voluntariness. For example, laws requiring the wearing of motorcycle helmets will affect those individuals who really do understand the nature and consequences of the risk they are taking, as well as those who do not. Those who are not acting sufficiently voluntarily will *perceive* an infringement of their autonomy, but those who are fully voluntary in their actions will both perceive, and in fact have, their autonomy compromised. Some of these variations and distinctions are presented in table 6.1.

Table 6.1. Forms of Well-Being and Autonomy Loss

	Overt paternalistic interventions	*Silent (unnoticed by target) paternalistic interventions*
Fully voluntary before intervention (no reasoning failure or any other diminution of autonomy)	Suffers well-being loss, actual autonomy loss, and perceived autonomy loss	Suffers well-being loss and actual autonomy loss
Less than fully voluntary before intervention (e.g., reasoning failure)	Suffers perceived autonomy loss only*	Suffers no losses

* Some overt paternalistic interventions, such as the incarceration of people who are mentally ill, may restrict the individual's autonomy beyond the activity or activities that are causing concern. In this case there will be some well-being loss and actual autonomy loss too.

There are two further ways of attempting to avoid the charge of offending autonomy. The first involves what a number of authors have called hypothetical consent.[16] In short, it is argued that, if one consents to an intervention, then it is justified because the presence of consent indicates that the intervention respects autonomy. *Hypothetical* consent is the idea that people *would* consent to a certain intervention if their voluntariness were not compromised in some way. This approach to justification then typically goes on to specify what kinds of limitations to their voluntariness are preventing them from making proper decisions. The difficulty here, however, is that the consent that would indicate that there is no offense to autonomy is not real. For the person who might give consent does not exist, and thus we do not have any real additional information on what he would accede to under different circumstances. As John Kultgen (1992, 100) puts it, "Imaginary consent cannot waive actual rights since it is not an act in the real world by the subject, but an act of an imaginary agent in the world of the paternalist's imagination. As such it has no intrinsic value for the subject, no evidential value for the paternalist, and no consequentialist value for either."

16   See VanDeVeer (1986) for a particularly sophisticated account; also Hodson (1977) and G. Dworkin (1972).

The hypothetical consent approach has value only inasmuch as it reminds the paternalist that it is (or should be) the improvement in the individual's interests that are driving the intervention. It can remind us that government paternalism should ultimately do good for the individual and thus should do what she would support in some sense. But justifications from hypothetical consent do no more than that. We still need an independent means of justifying interventions on the grounds of autonomy failure—or justifying the need to compromise autonomy if this is necessary.[17]

The second way of attempting to avoid offending autonomy involves what might be called "freedom maximization." This approach takes as its cue an exception to his general principle that John Stuart Mill made in *On Liberty*. Mill ([1859] 1974, 173) argued that it was not acceptable that people should be allowed to sell themselves into slavery: "by selling himself for a slave, he abdicates his liberty; he foregoes any future use of it beyond that single act. He therefore defeats, in his own case, the very purpose which is the justification of allowing him to dispose of himself . . . the principle of freedom cannot require that he should be free not to be free."

Mill thus makes a fundamental exception to his general principle because he does not restrict this prohibition to those who are ignorant, immature, or mentally incompetent. Someone might truly wish to engage in such a contract of slavery, perhaps because in return he would be paid a lump sum that would ensure financial security for the rest of his family. There may be no reason to suspect undue coercion or monetary debts, no mental illness or depression, no intoxication or neurosis. For Mill, what seems "good" to this person must not be allowed because it offends the very principle that gave him the opportunity to so decide. Mill takes a lexicographic view of liberty whereby liberty is conceived as something that all citizens must have to some degree, regardless of their own opinion. This small portion of one paragraph in Mill's *On Liberty* has generated a significant literature of its own.[18]

These arguments have been used to support the notion that a (soft) paternalist intervention will not necessarily infringe aggregate autonomy over time. We may be justified in interfering with someone's autonomy to pre-

17   See also, on a similar theme, Kasachkoff (1994).

18   See, for example, Fuchs (2001), who argues that it is a coherent part of Mill's thought by linking it to his utilitarianism; Sneddon (2001), who suggests that selling oneself into slavery offends a notion of "deep autonomy"; Archard (1990a), who also generally supports Mill and examines whether the slavery example can be used to justify a more far-reaching paternalism; Hodson (1981), who suggests that there is no case to answer because refusal to enforce slavery contracts does not constitute a restriction of liberty in the first place, a position supported by Brown (1989); and Arneson (1980), who suggests that it is an anomaly in Mill's account. See also Kuflik (1984), who distinguishes arguments concerning the inalienability of "personal autonomy"—of relevance in Mill's slavery case—with that of "moral autonomy."

vent her from having less autonomy in the future (Dixon 2001), and we can use the same argument for justifying an intervention in terms of its potential for *increasing* future autonomy (Husak 1981; Regan 1983). Thus if it is possible to make someone in the future more autonomous than she is now, then this is a potentially powerful justification for intervening if one's principal concern is with autonomy rather than well-being. For example, the government might force-feed hunger strikers or medicate someone against his will to prolong his life.

However, it is only *future* autonomy that is protected or increased in these cases. Even if such an intervention augments the aggregate amount of autonomy over a lifetime, *current* autonomy will be sacrificed. Such an approach will inevitably involve imposing a judgment about the correct balance between a smaller quantity of (uninterfered with) autonomy now and a larger amount later. It is not self-evident that people will accept greater freedom in the future for less now, all other things being equal. People may reasonably discount the value to them of the future freedom in a way that is at odds with the paternalist. To override such a decision still offends autonomy.[19]

Overriding Autonomy: Hard Paternalism

Hard paternalism is distinguished from soft by the absence of an autonomy threshold. We have described how the soft paternalist frames the judgment he must make in terms of insufficient autonomy or voluntariness; the hard paternalist acknowledges that autonomy will be compromised but believes that there is an acceptable trade-off between autonomy and the person's well-being. Before we turn to the question of whether autonomy can indeed legitimately be traded off in this way, it is worth reviewing what the precise distinction between hard and soft paternalism amounts to in practice.

The account of soft paternalism has shown how, if we are reasonably flexible in how we interpret lack of voluntariness, a great many government interventions for paternalistic motives can plausibly be counted under that head. Mill himself supported restrictive interventions for the good of children or for what he considered backward peoples living in undeveloped states. These individuals do not have fully developed faculties and thus must be protected from their own actions. Those not in full possession of the facts may also be so protected, if only temporarily. Mill might well be called a "soft soft paternalist" on this basis because he acknowledges

19   See also Strasser (1988) in the field of medical paternalism, who argues against pretending that we are protecting autonomy when making decisions on patients' behalf, when we are really abridging autonomy for some other good.

only a limited number of cases where lack of voluntariness—to use current terminology—occurs. Feinberg, as we have seen, goes further than this and includes mistakes in estimations and confusion in drawing inferences from what we know as voluntariness-vitiating factors. This allows him to support laws prohibiting the use of recreational drugs, for example. He would no doubt reject the term, but Feinberg is thus a "hard soft paternalist." Indeed, depending on what one counts as a factor that vitiates voluntariness, it is quite possible to characterize the vast majority of interventions in the decision making of individuals for their own good as varieties of soft paternalism. Disagreements would reduce to differing understandings of what can reasonably be considered a limitation on an individual's ability to make an autonomous choice.

So what is left for the hard paternalist? As Tom Beauchamp (1983, 139) puts it, "it is not implausible to suppose that the strong [hard] paternalist, the weak [soft] paternalist, and the antipaternalist will ultimately agree that the fundamental consideration that makes legitimate apparently paternalistic interventions is the substantial nonautonomy of a particular agent."

Beauchamp's point is that it is rare indeed to come across a hard paternalist position that "makes a naked appeal to the beneficent paternalistic interest, unqualified by considerations of limited capacity or knowledge" (139). This point seems to be particularly apposite when we consider only means-related paternalism, for here the individual's ultimate ends are not being challenged. A "hard means-related" paternalist would intervene even if there were no diminution in the individual's autonomy, voluntariness, or reasoning—there might therefore be no limitation on the individual's capacity or means for making decisions. It is rare to come across such an argument in the literature because it is difficult to establish the *basis* on which such a paternalist is intervening if she identifies no diminution of decision-making capacity and her ends are to be respected. For example, George Rainbolt (1989a, 56) argues for hard paternalism in the case of prescription drug, car seat belt, and motorcycle helmet laws: "the harm prevented is great, the liberty interference is trivial and the enforcement costs are low." But if an individual's decision making is sound, and his ends are not to be challenged, then even his pursuing a course that is very likely to harm him should be accepted as his own considered choice.

If true hard means-related paternalism is something of a rarity, then "hard ends-related" paternalism emerges as the more common, if still controversial, version.[20] For here the question of whether someone's decision-

20   See, for example, Arneson (2005), who argues for a secular sanctity-of-life doctrine; Groarke (2002), who suggests that some mentally disabled individuals have the "wrong ends" and this is the source of their knowing self-harm; Deneulin (2002) for a defense of paternalist-perfectionist ends; and Scoccia (2000) generally on the possibility of justifiable moral paternalism.

making capabilities are failing or whether factors vitiating voluntariness are in evidence does not arise. Instead it is the person's ends that are lacking. The paternalist claims that an individual may be acting with full autonomy and voluntariness and yet has, or is striving toward, the wrong ends.

So whether one is a hard paternalist or a soft paternalist depends in part on one's interpretation of what counts as a factor reducing a person's voluntariness. But, either way, one's *perceived* autonomy, and very often one's actual autonomy, will be compromised in all but a limited number of paternalistic interventions. Soft paternalists, by their very nature, attempt to sustain autonomy as a lexicographic value—one that cannot be traded in for other values. But the soft paternalist strategy ultimately fails: this perceived autonomy loss is still a loss at the time it is experienced. Can any kind of paternalism (beyond the possibly exceptional case of subsidy) thus be justified?

Let us first consider the argument from lexicography. It has at least two possible rationales. First, as Feinberg put it, like virginity, one either has it all or not at all—one cannot have a portion of autonomy. In fact he was referring to autonomy as a de jure right in this context, so his point is that one cannot have part of a right: one either has a right or does not. A second view is that, following theories such as those of Joseph Raz (1986, 425), autonomy is an essential element of the good life; people's autonomy can only be infringed "to protect or promote the autonomy of those people or of others." A lexicographic argument of this kind is based on the notion that autonomy is a fundamental precondition for a good life and takes automatic precedence over other valued ends.

Set against this lexicographic view is a balancing perspective that allows for trade-offs between values. Raz (1986, 552) has described this in terms of two possible mistakes:

> On the one hand, there is the potential mistake of failing to respect an individual's right to decide for herself. . . . this mistake will consist in excessive infringement of individual autonomy. On the other hand, there is the potential mistake of failing to protect an individual from the harmful consequences of her own choices when her decision-making capacities . . . are substantially impaired or defective. . . . the task is to determine the appropriate balance between these two mistakes.

Many authors adopt the balancing view either explicitly (Brock 1988; Burrows 1995; Shafer-Landau 2005; Conly 2013)[21] or implicitly (Glover 1977;

---

21 Brock in fact rejects the notion of a simple trade-off between autonomy and well-being in favor of a trade-off between autonomy and the individual's *ability to secure her ends,* when her decision making is defective in some way. In other words, Brock would not challenge the ends pursued by the individual even if they seemed counter to her well-being.

G. Dworkin 1983; Thompson 1987; Kultgen 1992; Archard 1994; Arneson 2005).[22] They all acknowledge that autonomy can be "placed on the scales" and weighed against an individual's well-being. The arguments adopted, which we support, amount to a rejection of both reasons for promoting lexicographical values.

First, the argument against the inviolability of rights. To say that a right is absolute is to claim that no matter how small an infringement of that right, no amount of other good can compensate for it. I may have a right to walk along the street without being harassed or physically harmed. But infringements of this right can range from someone calling out to me that my shirt is a funny color, to being mugged and robbed. Autonomy too can be infringed to a greater or lesser degree. And if I am knocked to the ground by a group of people who are hurrying an ill child to a hospital, I am unlikely to have my right to a peaceful walk taken very seriously in the courts. A right is in general terms a means whereby we place a special status on some attribute that we wish to prioritize and protect (Freeden 1991), but it is not a means of excluding every other form of consideration from having any place in a world where there are competing conceptions of the good.[23] To do this would be a form of fanaticism.

Neither is autonomy necessarily more fundamental to people than other aspects of their lives, such as their well-being. If we had nothing but a life of autonomy with no well-being at all, then we would not be living. Of course, one can include a minimum amount of well-being in one's understanding of autonomy, but this is to make the concept undertake more than its core meaning. Similarly, a life where our well-being was entirely taken care of for us, where we were allowed no opportunity to formulate our own life plan, would be equally abhorrent. The point is this: to suggest that autonomy is a value purely and simply on its own is nonsense, just as to argue that well-being as a value pure and simple on its own is a nightmare. Both valued ends exist in balance with each other; to unequivocally assert one value's superiority over all others is to pervert the reality of human life, and indeed what it means to be human.

A final argument in favor of hard, means-related paternalism is put forward by Sarah Conly in her book *Against Autonomy: Justifying Coercive Paternalism* (2013). As the title suggests, she would accept that a means-related paternalistic intervention offends against autonomy but would argue that

---

22   For example, Dworkin (1983, 110): "In the final analysis, I think we are justified in requiring sailors to take along life-preservers because it minimizes the risk of harm to them at the cost of a trivial interference with their freedom"; and Thompson (1987, 154): "It is difficult to maintain that a person's own good is never a justification for the restriction of his or her liberty."

23   And indeed competing "rights." The harm principle itself can involve the balancing of rights: the right to autonomy taking a lower priority than the right not to be harmed.

this does not matter much because the very existence of the reasoning failure that justifies the paternalistic intervention undermines the value of that autonomy.[24] For that value depends in part on rationality. "From Kant to the present, people have justified deference to individual choice by reference to rational agency" (Conly 2013, 189). Although, as we have seen, choice and autonomy are not identical, and, even if they were, despite Kant's authority, autonomy must have an intrinsic value over and above our capacity to make choices, Conly surely has a point. The value of our autonomy is diminished if we make poor choices—ones that damage us as individuals, not least in terms of our own perception. If I repeatedly tried and then failed to quit smoking, I do not think I would be greatly valuing my autonomy; indeed, I might voluntarily give up some of it through deliberately going to a health farm or somewhere else where I am not allowed to smoke. Reasoning failure certainly affects our ability to promote our own wellbeing; it seems not implausible to suppose that it thereby also reduces the value of our autonomy.

However, even this argument does not change the fact that, in all probability, there will be some trade-off that will have to be made. For there remains the issue of perceived autonomy loss. If I have made a decision as result of reasoning failure and the government steps in to correct it, then I will almost certainly perceive myself as having lost a measure of autonomy. The value of that autonomy may have diminished, even in my own perception; but some value will still be there. So even Conly's government paternalist is a hard one: that is, a government that is prepared to prioritize gains in individual well-being over losses in individual autonomy, if the former are sufficiently large and the latter sufficiently small.

Conclusion

In the final analysis, soft paternalists share many of the concerns of behavioral economists: that people are not making judgments or decisions in their best interests. They couch their concerns differently, but autonomy failure—or a lack of voluntariness—is similar in many respects to reasoning failure. Furthermore, the more sophisticated soft paternalists include considerations of well-being—the (potential) harm to be prevented, or the good to be done—in their calculus of when to intervene, even if they claim that well-being can never be placed on the scales to be balanced with autonomy. And, notwithstanding the efforts of the soft paternalists, we have sug-

24 Actually Conly makes most of her argument in the context of one particular kind of paternalistic intervention—what she terms coercive paternalism—but her point applies to all forms of paternalistic intervention so long as they are means-related.

gested that *perceived* autonomy at least cannot help but be compromised in almost all cases of paternalistic intervention. Further, a loss in perceived autonomy will damage intrinsic motivation, which in turn is likely to reduce the effectiveness of the intervention concerned. Whatever way one approaches paternalism, then, we need to weigh the impact on autonomy in the scales against degrees of reasoning failure and the concomitant reduction in well-being.

In short, we need to balance the extent to which we believe people actually fail to make adequate judgments in their own interests, and how much we are willing to restrict people's (perceived) autonomy, against the amount of good that can be promoted or harm prevented as a result. This will inevitably result in the need to trade off the values of autonomy and well-being against each other, just as we do with many other good things in life. As Isaiah Berlin noted fifty years ago, values are often incommensurate, and achieving more of one will often involve having less of another (Berlin 1958, 54–57). How the government should set about making these trade-offs is the subject of subsequent chapters.

7 Libertarian Paternalism

The previous chapter identified the need for government policies aimed at correcting reasoning failure to make an appropriate trade-off between individuals' well-being and their autonomy. New and particularly influential proposals that seek to provide a practical approach to that trade-off are the so-called nudge ideas based on what has been termed "libertarian" paternalism by Richard Thaler and Cass Sunstein (Sunstein and Thaler 2003; Thaler and Sunstein 2008) and "asymmetric" paternalism by Colin Camerer, Samuel Issacharoff, George Loewenstein, Ted O'Donoghue, and Matthew Rabin (2003). These ideas and their philosophical rationale are the focus of this chapter.

The central ideas underlying both libertarian and asymmetric paternalism are simple. As we saw in earlier chapters, government paternalism is generally considered a significant interference in an individual's decision making, and thus a major affront to autonomy. This conception may derive from a belief that paternalistic interventions inevitably involve prohibition, regulation, or compulsion. But paternalistic interventions in decision making can be undertaken in rather more subtle ways. In particular, the mechanisms of reasoning failure provide a means by which the government can subtly influence behavior short of compulsion. By changing the conditions under which people make decisions over the choices that confront them—conditions that Thaler and Sunstein (2008, 3) call the "choice architecture"—individuals can be "nudged" into making the right choices. Thus the libertarian paternalists not only seek to intervene when individuals are subject to reasoning failure; they also actively manipulate reasoning failure to encourage individuals to make choices that support their own well-being.

An example of a nudge policy or libertarian paternalism in action is the switching of a pension system from one where individuals intending to participate have to opt in to the system to one where they are automatically enrolled and have to make a conscious decision to opt out if they wish not to participate. A similar example would be the changing of an organ donation program from one where people have to carry a card or a similar form of notification to confirm that they wish to donate their organs in the event of a fatal accident to one, used in several countries and US states, where people have to provide some form of notification to confirm that they do *not* wish to have their organs donated. A rather different kind of policy would be a requirement that healthful food for purchase in supermarkets or buffet restaurants should be placed in conspicuous positions (eye level on a supermarket shelf, or at the front of a buffet line). Other ideas include the proposal of a smoking permit, whereby every year smokers have to "opt in" to being a smoker through obtaining an annual permit to buy tobacco, and an exercise hour where firms automatically enroll their employees in an hour's physical exercise each week unless they explicitly opt out (Le Grand 2008).

Yet more nudge ideas are described in the publications of the British Government's Behavioural Insights Team (2010, 2011, 2012, 2013), some of which have already been successfully tried out in the United States and elsewhere. These include ideas such as schemes that encourage participants to make formal commitments to quit smoking coupled with rewards for those who pass regular smoking tests; changes to letters sent out by tax authorities to explain that most people in the local area had already paid their taxes; notifications to households of the energy consumption of similar households in the area; the enrollment of staff by employers in payroll savings plans with an opt-out provision; and the automatic increase of charitable giving payments in line with inflation, again with an opt-out provision.

In each of these ideas, a measure of individual choice is preserved, and the impact on autonomy is supposedly minimized. Hence the title "libertarian" paternalism: it is paternalism because the policies involve government intervention in individual decision making with the intention of promoting the individual's own good, but libertarian because the individual maintains a range of choices similar (indeed often identical) to those that she had without the intervention.

Definitions

Thaler and Sunstein do not have a tight definition of a libertarian paternalistic policy, but they do provide a particular definition of paternalism. In their interpretation a policy is paternalistic "if it tries to influence choices in a way that will make choosers better off, *as judged by themselves*" (2008, 5; authors' emphasis). This definition has the advantage that, unlike many of the definitions of paternalism discussed earlier in this book, it does not confine itself to interventions that restrict choice in some way—a characteristic that is obviously desirable from Thaler and Sunstein's point of view since the central feature of libertarian paternalistic interventions is that they do not restrict choice.

As Daniel Hausman and Brynn Welch (2010) have pointed out, the definition is unsatisfactory in other respects. Paternalistic interventions do not always involve choice; witness Gert and Culver's example discussed in chapter 2 of a doctor giving a blood transfusion to an unconscious patient who had earlier explicitly rejected the procedure on religious grounds. Further, there are many ways of influencing choices that will make the chooser better off and would not generally be regarded as paternalistic, such as the simple provision of information—although, as we discuss below, there might be more or less paternalistic ways of providing information. Robert Sugden (2009) has also pointed out that there are significant problems involved in finding out what would make people better off, as judged by themselves, especially in a world where people make mistakes in judgments of the very kind that the libertarian paternalists wish to exploit. In fact, he argues, the idea is essentially normative and allows the policy maker's view of what would constitute the individual's good to override that of the individual himself.

It seems reasonably clear, however, that Thaler and Sunstein's interpretation of the term is, in our terminology, a form of means-related paternalism. They appear to accept individuals' decisions about their own ends, describing these as the choices that individuals believe would make them better off, as judged by the individuals themselves. They argue that individuals in effect do not always make the choices that would best achieve those ends, and, in those situations, it is legitimate to change the environment in which they make their choices so as to nudge them in the right direction. It is these arguments that we must now address.

Nudge Ideas: The Case For

The first of the libertarian paternalist or nudge ideas that emerges from behavioral economics involves *changing the default position*. The default position refers to the current policy environment in which individuals find themselves, and which will have certain implications for them if they do nothing. The central proposal means changing that policy environment so that there is a different set of implications for individuals who continue do nothing.

We saw in chapter 5 that people have a tendency to value an object more highly when in possession of it than when they are asked to imagine that possession in the future. In short, people fail to predict accurately their future utility under changed circumstances. As a result individuals display a "status quo bias" whereby their current situation is preferred over a changed one even if other relevant factors are kept constant. But the status quo is not a given. The government has the opportunity to influence the environment in many situations pertinent to social policy goals. In the pension and organ donation programs, for example, people are automatically opted in to a plan unless they actively choose not to participate. Given people's status quo bias, they will have a tendency to remain opted in and thus will be more likely to continue with the relevant behavior than if they had actively to make the decision for themselves.

There is mounting evidence that such strategies work. For instance, if workers are automatically enrolled in a pension plan but with the freedom to opt out if they wish, most stay in. However, if they are not automatically enrolled but have to make a conscious decision to opt in, then most stay out (Madrian and Shea 2001). If an individual is required to opt in to organ donation by carrying a card that gives permission for her organs to be used for transplants in the event of her death, there will be fewer organs available for transplant than if the default is one where permission is assumed to be automatically given, and where it is the individual who does not wish to donate her organs who must deliberately elect to carry a card that expresses her wishes (Gimbel et al. 2003; Johnson and Goldstein 2004).

Changing the default may appear to be a strategy that the government can reject if it wishes: a choice, in other words, between intervention and nonintervention. But in fact matters are not so simple. Consumers must make their choices in some kind of context, and that context will often be a result of government action or inaction. Obliging people to opt in to a pension plan, rather than being automatically enrolled, will have a discernible influence on the decision the individual makes. Thaler and Sunstein argue that the government is just as responsible for creating this opt-in situation as it would be for creating an opt-out situation through automatic enrollment. There seems to be no way the government can avoid having some kind of influence on the choice that the individual will make. Some kind of paternalism with respect to the status quo will very often be inevitable.

The second way in which the government can subtly influence decision making without compulsion is by *manipulating the frame or context* in which individuals make choices. "Framing" involves the way that information is provided: as we discussed in chapter 5, a medical procedure could be described in terms of the proportion of people likely to be alive after five years, or the proportion expected to be dead. People react differently to a prospect depending on how it is described even when the content remains the same. If someone is trying to decide whether to take out a loan, for example, he will want to understand the nature of the risks he faces. Data relating to these risks may be available, but there are multiple ways in which such data can be communicated. A provider might headline an attractive repayment rate while relegating "arrangement fees" to the small print, or it might not reveal the overall cost of the loan at the end of the repayment period. People who enjoy gambling may be aware of the nature of the gamble—picking six numbers from forty-nine and hoping they match six randomly chosen numbers—but be unaware of the actual odds that such a gamble represents.

We have argued that if the government requires the provision of information, this is not paternalistic per se because it is correction of a market failure, not a reasoning failure. However, the government may also require that information is provided in certain ways. So, for example, the government may require with respect to bank loans that only interest rates that include all relevant charges, or that include the total cost of the loan at the end of the repayment period, can be advertised. Health warnings may use language known to have a greater deterrent effect or can be accompanied by pictures that more vividly portray the potential effects of the risk being taken. Those in the business of offering commercial gambles may be obliged to provide fuller descriptions of the odds involved, in ways that make it easier for gamblers to understand just how (un)likely they are to win.

Unlike the default position, the government does not *necessarily* have to make a decision about how information is provided; it can simply require that those offering goods or services are explicit about the risks and allow them to communicate those risks as they see fit. Accordingly, paternalism is not inevitable in this sense. But, given the powerful effect that framing can have, a government that wished to influence decision making could easily do so through this mechanism while preserving as much as possible the consumer's autonomy.

A third set of mechanisms open to the libertarian paternalist involves *regulating the timing of decisions.* Perhaps the most commonly used example of these is the 'cooling off' period after a purchase or loan agreement during which time a consumer can change their mind about a contractual agreement. In such cases people are not prevented from buying an item or service but simply obliged to wait for a period of time before gaining full possession. Such regulations are most common when the purchaser takes on a high level of debt, or when products are purchased from door-to-door salespeople. The rationale for such a policy is that under pressure from a salesperson, or when tempted by a well-marketed or glamorous product, people can find themselves suffering from weakness of will. A libertarian paternalist government will not wish to outlaw high levels of indebtedness, or the marketing activities of companies eager to advertise the benefits of their products. But it may reasonably require that a period of reflection on the part of the consumer is built into the consumption decision.

The smoking permit falls into this category of intervention. An individual could not spontaneously decide to continue smoking every year but would be required to go to a certain amount of trouble in obtaining a permit to do so. Again such a requirement would have the benefit of creating a conscious moment or period of reflection when individuals consider their decision to smoke.

The final set of mechanisms, *tax and subsidy*, seek to change behavior through economic incentives. They are less commonly discussed in terms of their libertarian paternalist credentials; indeed, they are explicitly rejected by Thaler and Sunstein (2008, 6) as they define nudge policies as ones that do not affect the economic incentives that individuals face. Nevertheless they share a common feature with the other mechanisms discussed here: they preserve freedom of choice to buy the relevant products while influencing the likely extent to which consumers will choose to do so. When taxes are imposed, or subsidies put in place, the cost of the good to the individual increases or decreases. Here the cost is financial, whereas in the earlier examples it is essentially a nonfinancial cost that is increased or lowered—the inconvenience of making a certain decision is increased, but without any direct financial impact.

In each of these cases, the goal of the policy is to dissuade those with reasoning failure from continuing with their harmful choices while at the same time allowing those who do not suffer from reasoning failure to pursue the activity in question. The latter individuals will inevitably suffer some harm because the government will—through the various mechanisms described above—makes it harder for them to exercise the correct decision for themselves, whether financially, psychologically, or through other transactions costs. Similarly, some with reasoning failure will slip through the net and "ignore" the liberal paternalist's incentives. The challenge will be to minimize the harm to those not suffering from reasoning failure while maximizing the benefits to those with reasoning failure.

It is here that the attractiveness of libertarian paternalist schemes becomes apparent, especially when compared with alternative forms of paternalist intervention such as compulsion or regulation. With compulsion or regulation, all individuals are forced to change their behavior. If the policy is properly designed, those who suffer from reasoning failure should experience an increase in well-being as a result of the change. But those who do not have reasoning failure will be prevented from undertaking that bundle of activities that fully promote their own well-being and will therefore suffer a loss in well-being. And there is also the loss of autonomy to consider, which is likely to be considerable for both groups.

In contrast, nudge policies can potentially improve the well-being of those who suffer from reasoning failure and at the same time limit the restrictions or harm for those who are not suffering from such failure. That these policies can come closer to achieving this than other forms of paternalism, such as prohibition or compulsion, is one of the principal attractions of the idea for Camerer et al. (2003), and the reason they termed it asymmetric paternalism. "Asymmetric paternalism is paternalistic in the sense of attempting to help people obtain their goals, but asymmetric in the sense of helping people who make irrational decisions while not harming those who make informed, deliberate decisions" (Loewenstein, Brennan, and Volpp 2007, 2416). Of course, as Conly (2013, 30–31) points out, it is implicit in much of these kinds of arguments that the people who make the choices "against" the nudge (e.g., those who do opt out of an automatic-enrollment pension plan) are in fact making the informed choices that will maximize their well-being; that is, they are not suffering from reasoning failure. But there is no guarantee that this would be the case: some of those choices may be just as mistaken as the discussions made (or not made) by those who respond to the nudge. However, since those decisions will have to involve conscious thought and deliberation—for they will require a conscious rejection of the nudge—it is likely that most will be thought through in a way that helps avoid reasoning failure.

In short, libertarian paternalism can be brought to bear in various areas of public policy—such as personal lifestyle choices—where absolute prohibition would be inappropriate and out of step with public sentiment. Rather than nannying, libertarian paternalism helps people to help themselves.

Nudge Ideas: The Case Against

Such is the case for libertarian paternalism. What is the case against? Unsurprisingly, objections come from all parts of the intellectual (and political) spectrum and are raised against all parts of the argument.[1]

First, let us consider the argument, used particularly with respect to the status quo or default position, that there is no escaping government paternalism since there always has to be a default—and keeping the default is just as much a paternalistic act as changing it. One objection to this is that, in these kinds of examples, there is always the possibility of a third, "neutral" option that might be thought of as avoiding paternalism—an option that is sometimes described as forced choice. So in the case of pensions savings, individuals could be presented on their first employment (and perhaps periodically thereafter) with pension documentation that includes a choice between two boxes—one to tick if you wish to enroll, the other to tick if you wish not to enroll. Similarly in the case of organ donation, people could be obliged to tick one of two boxes indicating whether they were willing or not willing to donate their organs in the event of a fatal accident. The only pressure, then, is that everyone must tick a box. The role of the government would then simply be to provide the document that contains all the relevant information to support the choice and to oblige individuals to tick the box of their choice.

---

1   For a libertarian critique, see Mitchell (2005).

But are such cases really avoiding paternalism? The give-away is in the use of the term "forced." For that indicates there is some government action and hence intention. In fact such interventions are really a (mild) nudge in the direction of, say, choosing to enroll in a pension plan. People are at least forced to consider the option and not ignore it altogether, which might encourage more people to enroll—though whether there was an increase in enrollment would of course be an empirical question. Rather than "manipulating the default option," this milder strategy could be said simply to "remove the default option"; but it is still paternalist.

But is keeping the default just as paternalistic as changing it—especially if the change is to move from opt in to opt out? Somehow an opt-in pension plan seems less paternalistic than an opt-out one. Perhaps this has to do with consent: that in one case, by making a conscious decision to opt in, one is explicitly consenting to the operation of the scheme on one's behalf, whereas in the other, by not opting out, one is giving only a kind of tacit consent to its operations.[2] Explicit consent is a more robust form of consent than tacit consent, and so we might require opt-out plans to need a stronger paternalistic justification than opt-in ones.

A yet more difficult case is where the government has no involvement whatsoever in the situation. Take pensions again. If there were no government, and individuals had to make their own pension arrangements, then the government would obviously have no influence on the decisions since it would not exist. Is the government being paternalist by not existing? Similarly, if the government did exist but took no interest whatsoever in individuals' pension arrangements, it would be hard to say that it was influencing choices in that arena. To claim that the government is still acting (or rather engaging in inaction) paternalistically in such situations seems rather implausible—unless acts of omission are regarded as having exactly the same status in that respect as acts of commission.

However, although it may be possible for the government through complete uninterest or nonexistence to be nonpaternalistic, it has to be acknowledged that such situations are rare in the modern world. Hence the fundamental point made by Thaler and Sunstein stands: that, at least in most policy situations, even leaving the status quo unchanged can be regarded as an act of paternalism.

There is one situation where government inaction might be regarded as just as paternalistic as government action: namely, circumstances where private interests seek to nudge individuals through exploiting reasoning failure to act in ways that may damage their well-being (and perhaps their autonomy as well). We know that in practice these circumstances occur and do so frequently. Indeed, most of the marketing techniques used by the ad-

---

2   We are grateful to David Owen for this point.

vertising and public relations industries could be viewed as involving some kind of nudge. It could be argued that in such cases the government has a duty to intervene in some way—through nudges of its own, or via some other form of intervention. Whether it does or does not intervene, it might be interpreted to be acting paternalistically. Particularly if it does intervene, the intervention will look paternalistic, insofar as the government is seeking to manipulate or protect the reasoning of the person who is harmed, and not prohibit the behaviors of the actor or organization who is doing the harming.[3]

However, such an interpretation would be wrong. In these situations neither the private interests concerned nor the government could be said to be acting paternalistically. In the case of the private interests, their intention is not to improve the welfare of the individual but merely to maximize their profits, the effect on the individual being irrelevant at least to their intention. So, if the effect were detrimental, then government intervention to prevent such would not be paternalistic either but merely intended *to prevent harm to others*; hence it would be an application of the harm principle.

A second problem of libertarian paternalism for some critics is that the policies concerned do not correct reasoning failure as such; rather they *use* reasoning failure as an attempt to correct the outcomes of that failure. So, as Ashcroft (2011, 198) says, "the idea is not to improve the quality of our decision-making but to trick ourselves." Conly (2013, 8) takes a similar position, arguing that libertarian paternalism is "manipulative." Some would argue that it may be better instead actually to try to improve the quality of our decision making. Peter John and colleagues (2009, 2011) have argued that this can be done via what they term a "think" strategy: an extension of the ideas of deliberative democracy, whereby "citizens, given the right context and framing, can think themselves collectively toward a better understanding of problems and more effective collective solutions, avoiding thereby a narrow focus on their short term self-interest" (2009, 361). The search then becomes one for the appropriate institutional mechanisms for implementing think strategies.

In fact think strategies present a challenge, not only to libertarian paternalism, but also to other forms of paternalistic intervention and indeed to paternalism in general. For if such strategies succeeded in completely correcting reasoning failure, they would remove what we have argued is the only significant justification for paternalistic policies: that they can increase the well-being of individuals subject to such failure. If no individuals have reasoning failure—or all individuals have their reasoning failure "cured" by

---

3 The attentive reader will have spotted that this is a similar argument to that employed with respect to the stuntman in chapter 6.

think strategies—then there is no case for paternalism. A successful think strategy would therefore not be paternalist, libertarian or otherwise.

However, quite apart from the well-known problems with collective decision making, think policies face extensive practical problems of implementation. Consider the long list of paternalist policies in chapter 4: is it really feasible to set up deliberative councils to discuss and debate each and every case where potentially paternalistic policy decisions are required? The problem might be even greater than this because ideally the whole population would need to be involved (and successfully so) to avoid all possible reasoning failures in the future.

But there is a more fundamental problem. Can think strategies actually cure reasoning failure? The argument in favor of think strategies, and indeed deliberative democracy overall, is that the public nature of debate has what David Miller (1992) has called a moralizing effect: that it eliminates irrational preferences based on false empirical beliefs, morally repugnant preferences that no one is willing to advance in the public arena, and self-interested preferences. But none of these is the direct source of reasoning failure that makes the case of paternalism: these are, as we described in chapter 5, limited technical ability, limited experience, limited willpower, and limited objectivity. Perhaps the problem of limited objectivity might be partly overcome by the public nature of the discussion; but there seems little reason to suppose that the individuals sitting in a collective environment would not be just as subject to the remaining set of reasoning failures (limited technical ability, limited experience, and limited willpower) as if they were on their own.

A third line of criticism of libertarian paternalist policies concerns their impact on autonomy. If one is simply concerned with improving outcomes only in terms of individual well-being, exploiting reasoning failure may not matter; but the fact that there is some trickery going on, to use Ashcroft's terminology, does seem to imply that there may be some infringement of autonomy.

Now nudge advocates would dispute this. They would argue that people who are subject to libertarian paternalistic policies remain free to make important decisions in their life as they see fit; it is merely that the contextual "choice architecture" has been changed to influence choice in one way rather than another. Such government intervention does not destroy autonomy, or even act as an irritating intrusion, but simply adjusts the context in which one can continue to exercise one's autonomy.

Critics disagree, however. Luc Bovens (2009, 209) has argued that "there is something less than fully autonomous about the patterns of decision-making that *Nudge* taps into. When we are subject to [these] mechanisms ... we are not fully in control of our actions," a point he reinforces by pointing out that, if people were told that they were being manipulated in this way, they might go to considerable lengths to self-correct. Bovens goes on to argue that the less transparent the nudge is, the greater is the threat to autonomy, citing as an extreme case the example of subliminal messages.

Dan Hausman and Brynn Welch (2010, 128) make a similar point with respect to autonomy. Defining autonomy as "the control an individual has over his or her own evaluations and choices," they argue that "if one is concerned with autonomy as well as freedom, narrowly conceived, then there does seem to be something paternalistic... in designing policies to take advantage of people's psychological foibles for their own benefit." Again they use subliminal messages as an example. They go on: "to the extent that it lessens the control agents have over their own evaluations shaping people's choices for their own benefit seems to us to be alarmingly intrusive" (131).

Thaler and Sunstein (2008, 244) are aware of the dangers posed to their arguments by the possibility that subliminal messages or other covert methods of psychological manipulation could be described as a nudge. They endeavor to circumvent these dangers by adding what they call a publicity principle, banning "government from selecting a policy that it would not be able or willing to defend publicly to its own citizens." But, as Hausman and Welch point out, it would be perfectly possible that the government could publicly—and successfully—defend the use of subliminal messages, especially in a world where many other dubious nudge mechanisms are being used by commercial interests; but there seems no reason to suppose that this would allay the concerns of those worried about the effect on autonomy of these messages, or indeed of any other nudge mechanism.

Those concerns might be partly allayed by more elaborate forms of transparency. For instance, Bovens (2009, 217) has suggested "in principle token interference transparency." This is when an alert or watchful individual could identify the intention of the change in choice architecture and "could blow the whistle if she judges that the government is over stepping its mandate." Application of this transparency condition would rule out subliminal messages and would safeguard the rights of those who do not like the use of this kind of mechanism, without requiring elaborate and possibly counterproductive processes for revealing each and every case where a nudge is being used.

Of course, as the use of the term counterproductive in the previous sentence suggests, a major problem with increasing the transparency of any kind of nudge is that it may reduce its effectiveness. If people know that a particular strategy is being employed to encourage them to change their behavior, then this may induce a reaction against that strategy and perhaps create a perverse inclination to continue with or even extend the offending behavior. There might therefore be a trade-off between transparency and effectiveness.

Oliver (2013b) makes similar points. He agrees with Bovens that if a nudge policy is made transparent it might not work, and hence that for its effectiveness to be guaranteed it might be necessary for the government to engage in a degree of covertness or deviousness that might be unacceptable in a democracy. He notes that nudge advocates could respond by arguing that, if they were aware of the nudges, those who do resent being nudged in this way could deliberately make choices in the opposite direction to which they were being nudged. He points out, however, that this would require a degree of conscious deliberation—and it is precisely the absence of conscious deliberation on which the nudge policy makers are relying for the policy to work.

But we could go further and ask: is transparency necessary at all to preserve autonomy? The answer to this question concerns the nature of autonomy itself. In chapter 6 we pointed out that *perceived* autonomy loss is important as well as actual autonomy loss; and therefore that "silent" or "stealthy" policies such as some of the libertarian paternalistic policies hold an advantage over more overt polices in that individuals might not perceive any impact on their autonomy. It might indeed be argued that in fact it is only perceived autonomy loss that matters: there is no loss to autonomy unless the individual is aware of that loss. Self-rule requires self-knowledge or self-awareness. Hence it could be claimed that nudge policies do not cause any perceived loss in autonomy and hence do not significantly affect autonomy itself. But even if that view is not accepted, it would be hard to claim that the overall loss of autonomy from a libertarian paternalistic policy is as great as that from "harder" forms of paternalism such as regulation or banning. This is a point to which we return in the next chapter.

Riccardo Rebonato (2012) puts forward another argument for transparency. He argues that the apparent innocuousness of most libertarian paternalistic interventions conceals an accountability deficit. In his view governments are not benevolent abstract entities whose only aim is to promote the well-being of their citizens; rather they are run by individuals whose motivation is suspect (vote-maximizing politicians, budget-maximizing civil servants). They are usually knaves, not knights: selfish egoists rather than public-spirited altruists (Le Grand 2006). Moreover, even when they are behaving in a knightly fashion, making decisions in the interests of their citizens rather than themselves, they may be as prone to error or bias as the citizens themselves. To keep these dangers at bay, the political system must incorporate checks and balances; and for those checks and balances to work, there is a requirement for government policies that are transparent, auditable, and easy to monitor. Libertarian paternalistic policies do not score well on any of these; indeed, in Rebonato's view they often score less well than more conventional paternalistic policies, such as an overt regulation.

Most critics accept the libertarian paternalist argument that nudge policies preserve freedom of choice, even if they disagree with the corollary that autonomy is thereby preserved. However, Rebonato challenges even this. He argues that the availability of choices (and the easy reversibility of these choices) that is a key feature of libertarian paternalist policies actually constitutes a major objection to such interventions. For nominal freedom of choice does not mean effective freedom of choice. The very fact that auto-enrollment in pension or organ donation programs results in most people staying in the program concerned indicates that their nominal freedom of choice is not effective. The fact that most do not exercise the option to opt out indicates that the choice is vacuous. Rebonato (2012, 209) links this argument with his concern about the lack of accountability when he states: "Without a real (as opposed to nominal) ability to reverse choices, we are just faced with an insidious, imperfectly visible and poorly accountable variant of old-fashioned paternalism."

With respect to the criticism that choice is nominal, and not meaningful or effective, there is evidence that some people do opt out of auto-enrollment programs. Rebonato cites a study by Johnson and Goldstein (2003) pointing out that in Austria, the "effective consent rate" for an auto-enrolled organ donation program is 99.98 percent, which presumably implies that very few opt out. Several other countries with similar programs also show very high rates of enrollment. But in Sweden, with an opt-out program, the consent rate is 85.9 percent, implying that 14.1 percent in Sweden do choose to opt out. Also, Johnson and Goldstein indicate that the high rates in Austria and in other countries are in part due to the effort involved in opting in or out: individuals are usually required to fill out forms and to negotiate other administrative hurdles. Johnson and Goldstein conducted an experiment where participants were asked to make a similar opt-out decision by simply checking a box. This resulted in an effective consent rate of 82 percent, implying that 18 percent opt out. A similar picture can be found in studies of auto-enrollment in pension and other forms of retirement savings. Again there are very high participation rates (and large differences in participation between auto-enrollment and opt-in plans), but there are always some individuals who drop out (Beshears et al. 2008).

The fact that people do opt out of auto-enrollment programs—even if only a small number—implies that the freedom of choice in these policies is not entirely vacuous or invisible. Moreover, it provides evidence for the view that these policies do not restrict freedom of choice as much as, or even in the same way as, more conventional paternalistic policies such as the legal prohibition of dangerous drugs.

Conclusion

The principal defense of libertarian paternalist policies is their effectiveness in terms of their impact on well-being and autonomy when compared to alternative paternalistic policies. It is not that libertarian policies never infringe autonomy. It is not that the mechanisms they use are concealed; many are already transparent, and those that are not can be made so perhaps by employing Bovens's idea of token transparency. The significant point is this: most of them have less impact on autonomy—or at least on perceived autonomy—than the alternatives, while still having the potential to raise well-being by at least as much if not more. This dual benefit of libertarian paternalism is discussed in greater detail in the next chapter.

8 Paternalism and Policy

The arguments in this book have so far been conducted largely at the level of principle. This is important, since, if government policy is to be consistent and coherent, the basic principles have to be resolved before the relevant policy measures are designed. The principles do need to be tested, however, to see if they may usefully guide policy when they are confronted with reality; and that is the task of this chapter.

Whether a particular paternalistic policy intervention is justified in practice will depend on the number of people affected by it and on the extent to which each person's well-being and autonomy is affected. This in turn will depend on the types of policy involved. The first section of this chapter discusses the types of people affected (or not affected) by paternalist interventions, including the group who suffer from reasoning failure and the important, though often neglected, group who do not. The second section considers the types of policy involved, distinguishing between legal restrictions, taxation, subsidy, and nudging or framing interventions. The final section illustrates the arguments by applying them in three specific areas: smoking, pensions, and assisted suicide.

The Groups Affected: Well-Being and Autonomy

For any paternalistic policy designed to affect individual behavior (say, banning smoking or subsidizing pension plans through tax relief), there are four groups of people engaging in that behavior whose well-being and autonomy are likely to be affected. First, there are those who, prior to the policy being introduced, do engage in the behavior concerned, who suffer from reasoning failure, and who are influenced by the policy. An example would be smokers suffering from reasoning failure who stop smoking as a result of a smoking ban; another would be employees not enrolled in their employer's pension plan who are incentivized to participate because of a subsidy. Since they suffer from reasoning failure, if the state intervenes in an appropriate fashion, then these individuals should have a net benefit from the policy in terms of their well-being.

Second, there are those who engage in the behavior, who do *not* suffer from reasoning failure, but who are nonetheless affected by the policy. In the case of a ban on smoking, this would be smokers without reasoning failure who fully understand and properly take account of the long-term health risks and yet have to stop smoking because of the regulation. These will suffer harm to their well-being from the policy. The employees who do not suffer from reasoning failure but who take out the pension plan will also bear a kind of well-being cost because of the subsidy; for they would have been better off if the subsidy had been given in the form of cash.

Third, there are those who engage in the behavior, who suffer from reasoning failure, but who do not change their behavior from the policy: smokers with reasoning failure who defy the law and do not stop smoking; myopic employees who still prefer to stay outside the pension plan despite the subsidy. And, fourth, there is a group whose importance is particularly emphasized by libertarian paternalists: those who engage in the behavior, who do not suffer from reasoning failure, and who also do not change their behavior. Within this group would be smokers without reasoning failure who also defy the law and do not stop smoking, and nonmyopic employees who do not take up the pension plan because of the subsidy.[1] There would be no change in either of these groups' well-being as a result of the policy—unless the transgressors were caught and punished for not changing their behavior. The latter would happen with a regulatory form of paternalistic policy, such as banning smoking, but would not with others, such as subsidizing pensions.

The justification for a paternalistic policy in terms of well-being will depend in part on the size of these four groups and how much each member is affected. More specifically a paternalistic policy is more likely to be justified in the following cases:

⊘ The average benefits in terms of well-being to individuals in the first group is large. That is, each of those who suffer from reasoning failure and who change their behavior experience a large increase in well-being as a result.

⊘ The average cost to individuals in the second group is small. That is, each of those who do not suffer from reasoning failure but who nonetheless change their behavior do not suffer greatly as a result.

---

1 For completeness we should add that there are two further categories, both involving those who do not engage in the behavior at all: those who would suffer from reasoning failure if they did engage in the behavior, and those who would not suffer in this way. But since these are not affected by the policy, they are not of interest.

⊘   The number of those in the first group is large relative to those in the second group. That is, the proportion of those who engage in the behavior, who do suffer from reasoning failure, and who do change their behavior is large, and the corresponding proportion of those who do not suffer reasoning failure, but who change their behavior, is small.

⊘   The number of those in the third group is small relative to the number in the fourth group. That is, the proportion of those who engage in the behavior, who do suffer from reasoning failure, but who do not change their behavior is small relative to the corresponding proportion of those not suffering from reasoning failure who do not change their behavior.

A few comments on some of these bullet points are in order. With respect to the first—the average benefits should be large—it is necessary to recognize that reasoning failure can accompany trivial decisions as well as significant ones, and it will be important for the state to focus on the latter. It is often emphasized that if the type of potential harm is "serious and long lasting" (Archard 1993, 342), then paternalism is more likely to be justified. As Feinberg (1986, 119) puts it, "permissible self-endangering actions should be determined by standards whose stringency varies directly with the gravity of the risked harm and with the probability of the risked harm occurring." Unsurprisingly, then, the state will maximize well-being gains by intervening in actions where the potential harm associated with those actions is greatest.[2]

Another area where an intervention will be more likely to secure large benefits involves "irrevocable decisions" (Goodin 1993, 235).[3] Some actions that result in harm, or a high probability of harm, may be reversible—such as a decision to marry an unsuitable or abusive partner. People who make such a mistake may be able to extricate themselves from the harmful situation.[4] However, decisions that are irrevocable, particularly those that involve the possibility of death such as attempted suicide, are not open to

2   In passing, it may be noted that there are demographic and other characteristics that are likely to affect the relevant values of well-being. For example, if most people in the first group were young and in good health, then a policy that discourages smoking would have greater benefit than if they were old and already suffering from irreversible damage to their health.

3   It has also been noted that if the paternalistic intervention itself is reversible, this too adds weight to the case for the intervention; or, more accurately, reduces the objections to it. See Thompson (1987).

4   Although even here there may be some element of paternalism in laws governing marriages, such as requiring certain procedures to be undertaken beforehand, and witnesses to be present at the ceremony, all of which will give those getting married some time for reflection about the decision they are making.

such corrective behavior. The state should pay particularly close attention to irrevocable decisions in designing paternalistic laws.

It is also often noted that benefits are more likely to outweigh harm when people's preferences are "unstable or weakly held" (Kelman 1981, 249), or the "more insecurely" people are attached to them (Goodin 1993, 235). Such justifications can make reference to the possibility of "second-order preferences" (Zamir 1998, 242; Frankfurt 1971): that is, preferences about other preferences, such as individuals who wish they did not have a desire to gamble or to smoke.[5] Overall the less conviction underpinning an individual's preferences for a particular good or service, the more likely that the benefit-harm calculation will favor a paternalistic intervention.[6]

The second bullet point refers to the costs that arise from the fact that some people who do not suffer from reasoning failure will nonetheless be prevented or discouraged from taking a risk or indulging in some harmful activity that they wish to undertake. Thus, for example, there will be some people who really understand and accept the probabilistic dangers of smoking—to them, the reduction in the risk of death or terrible illness from stopping smoking is insufficient to compensate for the loss in the pleasure they derive from it. Such people do not misjudge their true interests, and thus their well-being is diminished by being obliged to act in a contrary way.

The third bullet and fourth bullet points concern the proportions of those who suffer from reasoning failure and those who do not. To meet this condition, the state needs to assess in which areas of decision making reasoning failure is most likely to be prevalent, using the evidence amassed earlier. This may not always be a straightforward task because much of that evidence will probably not refer directly to the relevant areas of public policy. Furthermore, there is the added complication for the state that it will be designing paternalistic policies for classes of individuals, rather than for single people. Laws, regulations, taxes, and subsidies cannot be individualized. This makes it more difficult to pinpoint only those who are suffering from reasoning failure. This is where libertarian paternalistic interventions have a particular advantage over other types of intervention such as regulation because, as we have discussed above, they allow those who do not suffer from reasoning failure an opportunity *not* to change their behavior.

But what of autonomy? The reason the impact of a paternalist intervention matters in each case (and why we need to spend time examining that impact in some detail) is that, as we established in earlier chapters, almost

---

5   Goodin (1991) argues that public officials should refrain from paternalism only if they are sure that the individual's preferences are relevant, settled, preferred, and genuinely the individual's own.

6   However, it is not clear that such judgments are applicable to entire classes of people as required by the design of public policy.

all the individuals affected by the policy are likely to suffer a loss of perceived autonomy and, in many cases, also a loss of actual autonomy. Hence we are in the business of trading off well-being gain against autonomy loss, so the size of the gains relative to the losses matter. The autonomy loss will be felt both by those who suffer reasoning failure and by those who do not. Both will be aware that some element of their freedom to decide for themselves is being interfered with in all but the subtlest of state interventions. Even subsequent support for the policy will not eliminate a feeling that autonomy has been compromised at the point of consumption or when the activity takes place. So being forced to wear a helmet may be irritating and feel nannyish to both those who suffer from reasoning failure and those who do not. Clearly, if the restriction on liberty appears minimal, such as the inconvenience of requiring sailors to wear life jackets, or motorists to buckle their seat belts (Dworkin 1979, 1983), then this will tend to support a cost-benefit calculation in favor of paternalism. Likewise policies that retain a significant degree of choice for the individual, as with the libertarian forms of paternalism discussed in the previous chapter, may support a cost-benefit judgment in favor of a paternalistic intervention because the autonomy loss (real or perceived) is low.

Finally, it should be remembered that we are only dealing here with paternalistic justifications for policy. Many of the actual policies concerned will also have other possible justifications; so, for instance, the banning of smoking may be—and indeed usually is—defended on the grounds of the prevention of harm to third parties through passive smoking. But those justifications are not our concern here. Instead we wish to see whether paternalism, as we have defined it, can be a sufficient justification for certain kinds of policy measure, and whether it can be argued that these policy measures should therefore be implemented without needing further, non-paternalistic justifications.

Types of Policy

As we saw in chapter 4, there are four principal types of policy intervention that are potentially paternalistic: interventions involving legal restrictions, those involving taxation or negative financial incentives, those involving subsidy or positive financial incentives, and those arising from libertarian paternalism, including nudging or framing interventions.

Examples of paternalistic legal restrictions discussed in chapter 4 include the banning of smoking in public places and laws concerning the wearing of seat belts and motorcycle helmets. Another example is the ban on large soda drinks in New York introduced under Mayor Bloomberg and then ruled unconstitutional by a state appeals court. Under such measures, all affected individuals are forced to change their behavior. If the policy is properly designed, those who suffer from reasoning failure should have a (perhaps significant) increase in well-being as a result of the change. But those who do not have reasoning failure will be prevented from undertaking that bundle of activities that fully promote their own well-being, and will therefore suffer a reduction in well-being. And there is also the loss in autonomy to consider, which is likely to be considerable for both groups. Indeed any form of legal restriction could be regarded as a direct breach of their autonomy: a direct restriction on their opportunities for engaging in independent action. The overall net social gain or loss from this autonomy breach will depend on, first, the relative proportions in the population of those who suffer from reasoning failure and those who do not; second, on the average size of the well-being gains and losses in each case; and third, the value attached to the autonomy loss.

The autonomy loss may be reduced if the individuals who are being compelled to change their behavior are nonetheless offered some choices *within* the particular change being compelled. So, for instance, individuals could be compelled to save for their pension but be offered a variety of pension plans from which to choose. But, while this might mitigate the autonomy loss, it would not eliminate it. Moreover, most of the other forms of intervention discussed below can also offer similar choices, so this could not be a determining factor for a government engaged in deciding between different forms of paternalistic intervention.

As we discussed in earlier chapters, Sarah Conly (2013) justifies what she calls coercive paternalism, and we call legal restrictions, in a number of ways. One is that autonomy is not as important as generally believed, especially when there is reasoning failure; as we noted in chapter 6, there is some plausibility in this view. Another argument for legal restrictions that Conly puts forward is that this type of intervention is likely to be more effective in promoting individual well-being than any other form of intervention, since all other "softer" forms (legally) permit some people not to make the relevant changes in behavior. But, as we have seen, there are several different groups involved for each type of intervention, and we cannot assess a priori what the well-being gains and losses will be. These are ultimately empirical questions, the answers to which will vary for each group and for each intervention.

Among the principal examples of the paternalistic use of taxation or negative financial incentives are the so-called sin taxes on tobacco and alcohol levied in most countries and the tax on the saturated fat content of food that has been proposed in several countries but actually implemented and then rescinded in Denmark. Analyzing the impact of such incentives on well-being and autonomy is complicated. Some individuals will reduce their level of the taxed activity, as compared with that when it was untaxed, and some will not. Of those who do change their behavior, again those who do not suffer from reasoning failure will experience a loss in well-being, but this time for two reasons. One is because of what we might term a well-being "substitution effect": they will be substituting activities that generate less well-being for them for the ones taxed, and they will have a lower well-being as a result. The other could be termed a well-being "income effect": as a result of the increase in the price, they will have less income to spend on other sources of well-being and hence experience a loss in well-being.[7] Those who do have reasoning failure and who change their behavior as a result of the tax should experience a *gain* in long-term well-being from the substitution effect, but they will also suffer a loss in well-being from the income effect. We cannot predict a priori which will dominate. Those who do not change their behavior will suffer a loss in well-being, but this will only be due to an income effect.

In all cases, if autonomy is viewed as simply requiring the existence of choice, there will be relatively little loss in autonomy (as compared with a legal restriction) since the choice of whether to undertake the activity (or how much to undertake) remains open. If the degree of autonomy is dependent on the amount and nature of the choices available—the choice set—autonomy in this case will be reduced, since the choice set is reduced by the tax. But this reduction is unlikely to be as much as the autonomy loss under legal restrictions.

Also on the positive side of the equation would be any well-being gains that resulted from the increase in tax revenue to the government. If the extra tax paid by each individual were returned to the individual in cash, then that would cancel out the income effects noted above; there would then be simply the substitution effect on well-being for those not suffering from reasoning failure, to offset against the substitution effect benefits to those who do.

Examples of paternalistic subsidies or other forms of positive financial incentives include subsidies to public broadcasting and to opera and to the increasing experimental use of financial incentives to encourage the cessation of smoking or the eating of healthful foods. With such incentives, this time the income effects on well-being are positive for those who engage in the activity, whether or not they suffer from reasoning failure. However, here again we have to offset against this the well-being costs of the tax raised to pay for the subsidy. If the amount of subsidy that each person receives were to be to be paid back in the form of increased taxes on the people affected, then those who suffer from reasoning failure would be better off, but

7   We call these well-being income and substitution effects to distinguish them from the normal use of the terms income and substitution effects in economics: these refer to the impact of a price change on the individual's demand for a commodity, not on her well-being.

those who do not (and consequently do not change their behavior) would be worse off.

Ashcroft (2011) has considered a further way in which financial incentives (of both kinds) might affect autonomy. He points out that a threat to autonomy may occur if the individual concerned feels that the incentive in some way undermines her role as the author of her choices or her status as a person. Although this does seem possible in certain extreme cases—for instance, the offer of financial incentives for sterilization for people with large families—it seems remote for most of the cases of paternalistic interventions we have considered. Moreover, even in extreme cases, the threat to autonomy does appear to be less than that of direct compulsion or regulation.

Finally, the effect of libertarian paternalistic or nudging policies will vary according to which policy is chosen. Suppose the intervention takes the form of introducing automatic enrollment, that is, switching the "default" from not being enrolled in an activity (such as saving for a pension), so that individuals have to opt in if they wish to participate, to one where enrollment is automatic and individuals have to opt out if they do not wish to participate. Then those who are suffering from reasoning failure, were not enrolled before the change, but remain enrolled will experience an increase in well-being. Those who are not suffering from reasoning failure but would have chosen to opt in had the default not been changed will remain enrolled; they are unaffected by the change (except that they may derive a minor benefit from avoiding the transaction cost of opting in). Both those subject to and those not subject to reasoning failure and who would have consciously chosen not to opt in under the previous system can now freely choose to opt out; so their well-being levels also remain unaffected (except possibly for the minor inconvenience of having to go through the formalities of opting out).

Now let us apply some of these arguments to real-life examples where paternalistic interventions may be considered: smoking, pensions, and assisted suicide.

Smoking

Smoking is a major cause of life-threatening illnesses. It is associated with the four biggest killers in the developed world: heart disease, cancer, cerebrovascular diseases, and chronic obstructive pulmonary disease. It has been estimated that every year more than 79,000 deaths occur in England from smoking-related causes: 18 percent of all deaths of adults over age thirty-five. In the United States the Centers for Disease Control (CDC) has estimated that an average of about 440,000 annual deaths occurred between 2000 and 2004 as a result of smoking-attributable illness. This resulted in

5.6 million years of potential life lost (CDC 2008).[8] Moreover, smoking tends to be concentrated among the less well-off. In Great Britain in 2011, among adults (aged sixteen and over) living in households whose head worked in a higher professional occupation, there was a smoking prevalence rate of 9 percent; but among adults where the head was in a routine occupation, the prevalence rate was 31 percent (Office for National Statistics 2012, table 1.5).

Overall it is clear that smoking is highly dangerous. But it is also clear that, despite the well-known danger, many people continue to smoke—especially the less well-off. But the arguments of this book suggest that these facts are not sufficient on their own to justify a paternalistic policy to stop people smoking. It is possible to make a "rationalist" case for smoking: that is, a case for the proposition that a smoker who does not suffer from reasoning failure but is fully aware of the dangers of smoking should be allowed to carry on doing so. In 2004 the British secretary of state for health, John Reid, illustrated one way of making this argument when, in the context of a national debate about banning smoking in public places, he said, "Please be careful we don't patronise people. As my mother would have put it, people in those lower socio-economic categories have very few pleasures in life and one of them they regard as smoking."[9] And, given that not every smoker dies of smoking, it is possible to imagine people deciding in a perfectly rational fashion that they will take the risk—especially if they do indeed have few other pleasures in life.

To make a case for paternalistic intervention, therefore, it is necessary to demonstrate that for many individuals there is a substantial amount of reasoning failure associated with smoking. And it is relatively easy to do so. Of our four categories of such failure (limited technical ability, limited imagination/experience, limited willpower, limited objectivity), at least three would seem to apply in this case. Limited willpower is the most obvious. As we have seen, 70 percent of smokers say they want to give up, but apparently they cannot find the will to do so (Taylor et al. 2006). Limited imagination would also seem to apply: people undertaking a potentially addictive behavior such as smoking find it very difficult to imagine how they will feel once addicted, or indeed to imagine what it is actually like to die from a smoking-related disease such as lung cancer. And limited objectivity is also a problem: as we noted earlier, a large national telephone survey in the United States revealed that smokers both underestimate their increased risk of getting lung cancer when compared to the perceived risk of nonsmokers

---

8 A more conservative figure is provided by Rostron (2013), who estimates that there were 380,000 smoking-attributable deaths in the United States in 2004.

9 http://news.bbc.co.uk/2/hi/uk_news/politics/3789591.stm.

and consider their own risk of developing lung cancer as significantly less than that of the average smoker (Weinstein, Marcus, and Moser 2005).

However, the existence of reasoning failure with respect to smoking is still not sufficient to justify the introduction of a paternalistic policy to reduce the dangers from this behavior. It is necessary also to assess the well-being gains and losses and the impact on autonomy of the policy concerned; and these will vary from policy to policy.[10]

Let us consider three possible policies: banning smoking completely, raising tobacco taxes, and the introduction of a smoking permit.

Consider, first, a complete ban on smoking. What are the benefits or costs to the individuals affected? There will be well-being gains to smokers who have reasoning failure but who stop smoking as a result of the ban; and there will be well-being losses to those who do not have reasoning failure but who stop smoking. However, the experience of the prohibition of alcohol in the United States and of the "war" against illegal drugs such as heroin and cocaine in most developed countries suggests that banning smoking completely might be both socially difficult to implement and economically costly to enforce. Hence it is likely that a significant proportion of both those with reasoning failure and those without it will continue smoking. Within the group who do not stop smoking, with or without reasoning failure, there will be well-being losses (in addition to long-term health losses) for those who are caught and punished for violating the ban. For risk-averse individuals who continue smoking, there will also be a well-being loss (again in addition to the long-term health losses) even if they are not caught, since they will now be undertaking an activity for which an additional set of risks and pressures have been created (the risk of being caught and prosecuted), and this is likely sensibly to diminish any pleasure they get from smoking.

For completeness, it should be noted that there might also be backlash effects from the ban: some risk-loving individuals may derive well-being gains from the thrill of continuing to smoke in defiance of the ban. There may also be those who delight in rebelling against the authorities or who, as matter of principle, will continue to smoke (or even to take up smoking) in defiance of any form of government intervention. However, it is not clear how large the numbers of such individuals would be; and, in any case, any well-being gains they experience would have to be set against the long-term health losses from their continuing to smoke.

10   In addition, there will be many other factors that need to be taken into account in any overall assessment of the policy: in particular, the impact on tobacco firms, their shareholders, and their employees; the impact on tobacco farmers; the tax revenue impact on the government's fiscal position; the overall impact on the economy; the resources necessary to police any policy interventions; and so on. Arguably, however, these are of less importance than the central concerns of this book—the impact on well-being and autonomy.

One way or another, there are likely to be considerable well-being losses from a ban on smoking: losses that would have to be set against any gains resulting from the health benefits of the ban in calculating the net effect on well-being. At the same time, there is a substantial impact on the autonomy of smokers of any kind, whether they suffer from reasoning failure or not, or whether they stop smoking or not.

So is it possible to devise an intervention that would yield similar well-being gains in terms of the health benefits from reducing the prevalence of smoking, without some of the adverse effects on well-being and autonomy created by a complete ban? One might be to raise taxes on tobacco. The impact of these kinds of taxes on well-being and autonomy was discussed in the previous section, and we will not go through it again in detail here. But it may be recalled that one of the effects was what we termed an income effect: as a result of the increase in the price of the commodity concerned as a result of the tax, those who smoke will have less income to spend, with a negative impact on well-being. This is of particular concern in the case of tobacco, since, as we saw above, it is the less well-off who smoke the most; hence the tax increase may be regressive, hitting the poor proportionately more than the rich.

A libertarian paternalist idea that does not suffer from this problem was put forward by one of us some years ago and is now being debated in Australia: that of requiring smokers to obtain a yearly smoking permit or license (Le Grand 2008; Chapman 2012; Collin 2012). Suppose every individual who wanted to buy tobacco had to purchase a permit to do so. And suppose further that they had to do this every year. Sellers of tobacco from supermarkets to tobacconists would have to see the permit before any sale. To get a permit would not be difficult: it would simply involve filling out a form and supplying a photograph. Permits would be issued only to those over eighteen, and evidence of age would have to be provided.

In this situation, every year each individual would have to make a decision to opt in to being a smoker. Smokers would have to decide each year whether they were going to continue for the next year. Breaking the New Year's resolution not to smoke would require making a conscious decision and undertaking some action. This changes the default position from the present situation where the position for smokers is to carry on—they have to make a conscious decision to opt out—to one where the default position is to stop, and they have to make a conscious decision to carry on.

What are the problems? As with banning smoking, there are enforcement issues. Black markets, illegal sales, and smuggling of cigarettes are already widely prevalent; this might simply encourage their further expansion. Also there is the difficulty that, once someone has obtained the permit, he will feel free to smoke at least for the period for which the permit is valid. Indeed, he may even feel obliged to smoke more to justify the effort he has made to obtain the permit. However, black markets and smuggling are a problem for any system of controlling smoking, including—and perhaps especially—a complete ban, and will have to be dealt with by whatever policy measures are considered. And although obtaining the permit may provide a small incentive for some smokers to smoke more, it is hard to believe that this will have a significant impact.

So the idea may be administratively feasible. But how does it fare in terms of our arguments concerning paternalistic justification? What are the gains and losses in terms of well-being and autonomy, and how do they compare with those for a complete ban? As with those who stop smoking with the smoking ban, the average benefit to those suffering from reasoning failure who do not obtain a permit is likely to be large; for they will no longer be able to purchase tobacco, and their smoking is likely to be reduced, if not eliminated. If the numbers of people who change their behavior in other situations where the opt-in/opt-out default has been altered—as in the pensions and organ donation examples discussed in chapter 7—are a reasonable guide, the number of those who do not buy a permit and stop smoking could also be large, and possibly comparable to the number who would stop in the event of a smoking ban.

Now the average cost to smokers who do not suffer from reasoning failure may also be quite large—if they do not get a permit. However, the "if" is crucial. For the smokers without reasoning failure for whom the cost is large can in fact quite easily opt in to being a smoker; hence the proportion of such smokers who do not get a permit and thus have to change their behavior is likely to be small, as is the cost to each of them. So the well-being loss to smokers without reasoning failure is likely to be small—and much smaller than their loss under a smoking ban.

It is plausible to argue that the backlash effects would also be small: the government intervention is much less draconian than a complete ban, and defying it would likely create fewer thrills of any kind. Of course, in a paradoxical way, this could reduce the overall well-being gain from the intervention, as compared with the smoking ban, because fewer people would derive well-being from defying it. However, since there would also be fewer people smoking for that reason, there would be an offsetting gain in health-related well-being. In any case, both effects are likely to be small and not likely to affect the overall assessment.

There might be a perceived or symbolic loss in autonomy. The need to get a permit for an activity (purchasing tobacco) that was previously unrestricted may be viewed as a challenge to autonomy and arouse political or individual hostility for that reason. However, the degree of autonomy loss from the permit policy is likely to be much less that from a ban. The options—to smoke or not to smoke—remain the same as if there had been no intervention. The "cost" of being a smoker has gone up a little owing to the slight bureaucracy involved in getting a permit, but it would be hard to see this as a major intrusion on autonomy. And the policy would be overt; there is no hidden loss of autonomy so that people are unaware of being nudged in the direction that the government wants.

On balance, therefore, in terms of minimizing the impact on autonomy, the permit proposal scores better than the complete ban. The analysis of the impact on well-being also suggests that it is unlikely that any group would be worse off with the permit policy than with a ban, and at least one important group would be better off: smokers who do not suffer from reasoning failure. Unlike the tax increase proposal, there is no income effect so the permit does not discriminate against the less well-off in that respect. Of course, any government considering these policies would have to take other comparative factors into account, such as their relative ease of enforcement, but, at this level of analysis, the permit idea at least seems to be worthy of serious consideration.

Pensions

In general people do not save enough for their pension. As life expectancies increase, so too does the length of time for which we are retired. On average in England and Wales, a sixty-five-year-old man can expect to live for a further eighteen years, and a woman for a further twenty-one years (Office for National Statistics 2013). In consequence we need to spend a larger proportion of our life in retirement. An analysis of the UK state health service (NHS) pension scheme suggests, for instance, that "A female pensioner . . . who retired at the age of 60 in 2010 could expect to spend around 45% percent of their adult life in retirement compared to around 30 percent for pensioners in the 1950s" (Independent Public Service Pensions Commission 2011, 22). Yet the extent of savings to support these extended periods of retirement is quite inadequate. A recent estimate implied that in 2012 around eleven million British adults (aged twenty-two to the state retirement age) were still facing inadequate retirement incomes (DWP 2012). In the United States a report on the 401(k) retirement plan concluded that the average American has accumulated only one-fifth of what he or she needs for a secure retirement (White 2008); and it has been suggested that 51 percent of US households are at risk of being unable to maintain their standard of living into retirement (Munnell et al. 2009).

Now at least two of our sources of reasoning failure seem to be implicated in the pension decision. Partly because of the various tax provisions associated with pension contributions, the information requirements involved in making the relevant decisions are often highly complex; hence many people, perhaps most, are likely to suffer technical processing difficulties. But a more important source of reasoning failure is limited imagination—in the particular form of myopia. The best advice on pensions is to begin contributing to a scheme as young as possible: say, before thirty. Yet it is very difficult in one's twenties to imagine oneself in one's sixties or seventies. It is as though one is contemplating a different person: one to whom one has a connection, certainly, but a fairly tenuous one. As we have noted several times, distances in time lead to serious failures of imagination, with the magnitude of the failure increasing as the time distance increases.

The two most common ways that governments have of dealing with the pension shortfall are legal compulsion and fiscal subsidy through tax relief. More specifically, governments often compel their citizens to contribute to some form of pension scheme. In most countries the contribution is exacted either through general taxation or through social insurance contributions; some countries rely on mandated or compulsory contributions to private plans. Alternatively or as well, governments frequently offer tax relief of various kinds to make pensions attractive. This may include income tax relief for pension contributions or exempting pension payments from income tax.

How do the compulsory schemes fare in terms of well-being and autonomy? The answer is problematic. Individuals who suffer from the sources of reasoning failure that we have specified, especially that of limited imagination—call them myopics—are likely to experience a net rise in well-being, viewed from the perspective of their lifetime, with the increase in the long run when their pension is realized outweighing the cost in the short run due to their having to forgo more current consumption than they would have forgone in the absence of the restriction. However, individuals who do not have reasoning failure—call them farseers—and who, prerestriction, are saving as much or as little as they want to will experience a significant loss in net well-being as a result of being compelled to save. And there is obviously a significant loss in autonomy for all groups, both perceived and actual.

What of the subsidies associated with the tax relief? Those suffering from reasoning failure who are incentivized to take out a pension will experience a net increase in well-being. This is likely to be greater than those who take out a pension under compulsion, because, owing to the subsidy, the short-term financial cost, and hence the current consumption forgone, is less. And although, as we have argued above, they may suffer some loss in autonomy, it is unlikely that this will be as great as under compulsion. So in terms of the *average* well-being gain and autonomy loss for this group, tax relief is likely to score well as compared with compulsion. However, the size of the group will be different, with that under compulsion likely to be larger than that under subsidy alone; hence the total gain in well-being (the average gain multiplied by the number in the group) under compulsion might well be larger than under tax relief. But the numbers increase also means that there would be an increase in the total loss in autonomy for that group.

Those without reasoning failure—the farseers—are of particular interest in this case since they are the ones who "suffer" most from compulsion, in terms of both well-being and autonomy. Farseers who are already in the pension plan get an income benefit through the subsidy. Hence they will have an increase in well-being, but they may experience a small loss in perceived autonomy. Farseers who are not in the pension plan and who continue to stay out of it do not receive any tax benefit but maintain their autonomy.

However, there is a particular equity concern with respect to tax relief for pensions that parallels the tax incentive issues for smoking. Tax relief can be highly regressive in impact, with higher-income groups benefiting more both in absolute terms and as a proportion of their income than lower-income groups (Agulnik and Le Grand 1998). A policy that preserves freedom of choice but without this adverse consequence is the libertarian paternalistic policy whereby people are automatically enrolled in a pension plan unless they opt out. The average well-being benefit to myopics is likely to be quite large; but the average cost to those who are made to save but who are farseers could also be large—if they stay automatically enrolled. However, as with the subsidy case, the "if" is crucial. For the farseers for whom the cost is large can in fact opt out; hence the proportion of farseers who have to change their behavior is likely to be small, as is the cost to each of them. Moreover, since enrollment is automatic, the proportion of myopics who do not stay in the scheme is likely to be small; indeed, if the automaticity works properly, it will be zero. Again there may be little loss in autonomy.

Of course there are several other important factors that will have to be taken into account in any practical applications of the policy concerned; notably enforcement issues in the case of compulsory contributions and the losses in government tax revenues that will be a consequence of the tax relief program. As we noted above, there will also be equity issues to consider, especially with respect to the regressivity of tax relief. However, it seems reasonably safe to conclude that, certainly in terms of autonomy and possibly in terms of average well-being, compulsion fares the worst of all three types of policy measure, and that tax relief fares worst in terms of equity.

Assisted Suicide

Situations in which people voluntarily end their own lives with the assistance of others are already subject to prohibitive legislation in many countries. In this section we ask whether there is too much paternalism in this area, rather than too little as in the other activities we have discussed.

There are various means of helping someone to end her life, and there are numerous categories of individual who might wish to do so. The two principal methods are, first, assisted suicide, whereby a doctor or other assistant will provide the means for the individual to take her own life but will not perform the act themselves; and second, voluntary euthanasia whereby the doctor performs the killing himself but with the express consent of the individual. Here we will focus on a group of particular interest to the paternalistic debate: the generic case of mentally competent adults who are suffering from an incurable disease and who wish to curtail their suffering, either because they are already approaching the end of their life or simply because life is intolerable whether the illness is terminal or not. In both cases the illness renders them incapable of ending their own life without assistance. We will not pursue further the relative merits of assisted suicide compared with voluntary euthanasia and will use the former term to cover any method by which a person is assisted in ending his life.

As we have suggested before, it is not clear that prohibiting assisted suicide is paternalistic. The current law could be defended as a means of preventing "other-regarding" harm, the most commonly cited example being that of family members putting pressure on an old and burdensome relative to end her life. However, such concerns could be resolved by legal safeguards that require independent observers to be assured that undue pressure is not being brought to bear, rather than through outright prohibition. It will never be possible to achieve absolute confidence that the interests of family members have not been influential, but neither should we seek to do so. The individual can legitimately take into account how her death will ease the burden on her caregivers without ceasing to act voluntarily.

Another set of justifications for absolute prohibition is the "slippery slope" argument (Warnock and Macdonald 2008). This does not argue that assisted suicide is wrong in principle. Rather, the claim is that it would be impossible in practice to distinguish a legitimate from an illegitimate case (for example, what constitutes undue pressure from relatives, or what makes an adult mentally competent to make such a decision), leading to a "creeping" liberality in interpreting the law. In addition it is argued that the legal safeguards or the thresholds themselves would inevitably be weakened over time, leading to a legal framework unintended by the original policy makers.

However, these are practical matters; on their own they do not give cause to reject the principle that people should have the right to choose to end their own lives. The need for a practical means to distinguish suitable from unsuitable cases may well present difficult decisions in the case of particular individuals, but the point of principle still needs to be analyzed: if there is no legitimacy in principle, then the practical problems become academic. And, although in practice the outcome of a change in law is hard to predict, it does not seem to be a legitimate argument to say that a law must remain in place simply because it is difficult to see how it may develop in the hands of future legislators. The case for change should always be made in principle initially, and then at every stage at which a further change is proposed. Our purpose here is to establish whether the principle of a right to end one's own life with the help of others is justified.

An objection to assisted suicide that is often made on principle is known as the sanctity of life argument (Warnock and Macdonald 2008). This may be a form of legal moralism: the idea that if life is not sacred, then the whole community is somehow poorer. Or it falls into the category of ends-related paternalism: the government is making the judgment that the individual has inappropriate ends (in this case, not considering his or her own life in terms of its absolute value or sanctity) and replaces the individual judgment about ends with its own judgment. In earlier chapters we concluded that legal moralism was difficult to justify since it seemed to give the community a kind of mystical status that was independent of the actual consequences for individuals in the community. And we also argued that ends-related paternalism was not justified because the alleged ends-failure had no empirical basis, often relying instead on religious or quasi-religious arguments—as, arguably, is happening in this case.

But principled arguments against assisted suicide are not always quasi-religious. The final category of argument that supports an absolute prohibition is a form of means-related paternalism. It can be argued that individuals are likely to misjudge their future levels of well-being: that is, they think that they will be better off dead than in their present state of intolerable pain, depression, or other form of discomfort. In doing so they are engaging in a form of reasoning failure.

One might question whether it is sensible to talk about well-being at all in this context. How can well-being be improved if one is choosing to die? The point turns on whether one accepts that some forms of existence can be so unpleasant for the individual that death is preferable. If we take death and assign it a nominal value of zero well-being, then states worse than death would have a negative value. A move from one of these states to death would thus constitute a well-being gain even if that well-being is not directly experienced.

If we accept that an element of means-related paternalism is operating in the case of assisted suicide, then it immediately becomes clear that it is not a form of libertarian paternalism. The restriction on decisions to end one's own life is prohibitive; it does not attempt to influence the decision of the individual but simply denies any choice. Thus in terms of our groups discussed at the beginning of this chapter, all are affected by the policy because no one can choose to ignore it.

Nor is it a silent policy—one that operates without the knowledge of the individual. It is hard for any prohibitive law to be silent in this way, and in the case of those wishing to end their own lives, it would be plain to them that they were having their autonomy infringed. As a result, even those suffering from reasoning failure would inevitably perceive an infringement of their autonomy. For those not suffering from reasoning failure, there is no route for exempting themselves from the effects of the law; there are therefore likely to be severely harmful effects, in terms of both well-being and perceived and actual autonomy.

However, ending one's life is irrevocable, and, as we saw earlier, this is one of the conditions that potentially indicates large benefits for restrictive paternalistic policies if people are suffering from reasoning failure. The question then is whether the number of people suffering from reasoning failure in this context is also large. How likely is it that people suffer a misjudgment with regard to ending their own lives?

Let us take each of the four categories of reasoning failure in turn. The first category—limited technical ability—does not seem to be a problem here; most people in this situation seem to have little technical difficulty in understanding their situation and the information associated with it. The second category—limited imagination—refers to the difficulty people have in judging their future well-being. We have proposed that this might be most acute when imagining situations a long time in the future, or when the situation is an unusual or unfamiliar one. But here the altered situation is death, or "nothingness." Unless one is of a religious disposition, this must be one of the easiest situations for us to imagine because it simply equates to a dreamless type of sleep, something with which we are all familiar. The absolute absence of any sentience or consciousness makes the comparison with one's current state—that of intolerable pain or distress—one that we are very unlikely to misjudge. Furthermore, the change of state is not one that will occur a long time in the future; on the contrary, people who wish to end their lives wish to *curtail* a long, drawn-out process.

Our third source of reasoning failure was limited willpower. It does seem possible that, in these situations, there might be some kind of bias through visceral decision making, which was included in chapter 5 as a subset of weakness of the will. Here the relevant causal factors might be pain, fatigue, and despair, each of which could induce people to make rash, spur-of-the moment decisions that could go against their better judgment.

However, choosing to end one's life is rarely (if ever) a spur-of-the-moment decision, or something we fall into against our better judgment. Unlike eating kebabs or going to the pub, where we know we really should be eating more healthfully or saving our money for our retirement but fail to do so for the more immediate pleasures of fatty food and a night out drinking, we do not suffer a "temptation" to end our lives. Choosing death is something that most of us would take extremely seriously, and for those suffering terrible illnesses it would have been a consideration they would have had much time to reflect on.

In both the latter two cases of reasoning failure, the more likely error is that we misjudge how our current state of ill-health will progress: either we cannot imagine such suffering getting better even when told this is likely, or we are temporarily tempted to end our lives because it seems an easier option than waiting for our conditions to improve. When the pain had abated we would very likely be grateful that we did not take such an irrevocable decision. If suicide had been chosen in these circumstances, we would miss out on a (future) life worth living. Such possibilities (as well as the more remote possibility of visceral decision making) require safeguards: people should be obliged to receive intensive counseling about the nature of their illness and to reiterate their decision at different times so that independent observers can be sure that the individual is making a calm and deliberate judgment. These safeguards constitute a form of mild libertarian paternalism: choices are not denied, but they must be made with conditions attached.

The final category of reasoning failure is limited objectivity, and here too there seems to be a conspicuous absence of the conditions that would normally lead to misjudgments. Limited objectivity usually occurs when we delude ourselves about our risk of ill-health or other misfortune being lower than the average, or persuade ourselves that our previously held opinions are still correct in the face of contradictory evidence. But here the choice we are taking means that any self-delusion is pointless—we are not going to be alive to enjoy the supposed benefits of such false perceptions.

So how does all this relate to our conditions for a paternalistic intervention to be justified? As noted earlier, everyone in the relevant situation is affected by the prohibition of assisted suicide, so we have to consider only those who have to change their behavior because of it. The benefit to those who suffer from reasoning failure is likely to be considerable—not least because of the irrevocable nature of assisted suicide. On the other hand, the cost to those who do not suffer from reasoning failure is also large: they are condemned to a lifetime of suffering, which for them is a fate—quite literally—worse than death. Since, as we have seen, it is hard to make a case that there will be many individuals in this situation suffering from reasoning failure, the second group—those who suffer costs from the intervention—is likely to be much larger than the first—those who receive benefits from it. Further, for those who suffer from reasoning failure the suggested safeguards will filter at least some of them out. Add in losses due to both the perceived and actual autonomy as a result of the intervention, and the case against it becomes yet stronger.

Overall, unlike in some of the previous cases we have considered, there seems to be little argument for this form of paternalistic intervention. There will, of course, be the need for adequate safeguards to be in place, including measures to ensure that there is not undue family or outside pressure, that information and counseling is supplied so that the individual fully understands the likely course of his illness, and that the decision is reiterated at different times so as to avoid temporary emotional influences. But with such safeguards in place, assisted suicide should not be prohibited.

Conclusion

Any government considering making a paternalistic intervention designed to change individual behavior has to go through at least two important stages. First, it must be established that there is a significant amount of reasoning failure associated with the behavior concerned. In this chapter we have argued that a respectable case for this can be made with respect to smoking and to the decision about how much to save for a pension, but not for assisted suicide. Second, if the judgment is made that there is a significant amount of reasoning failure, then the government has to decide on the form the intervention may take: legal restrictions, negative financial incentives (tax), positive financial incentives (subsidy), or libertarian paternalistic interventions (nudge). In doing that, the government must take account, among other things, the impact of the intervention on well-being and autonomy on different groups of the forms of intervention: a complex task that, as we have illustrated, is far from easy.

The actual outcome of, particularly, the second stage of this process will vary from behavior to behavior and from intervention to intervention, so it is difficult to make any meaningful generalizations concerning it. However, it does seem from much of the discussion concerning this stage—the choice of intervention policy—that the arguments we have been putting forward in this book mitigate against policies involving legal restrictions and in favor of policies that allow individuals a degree of choice. Thus policies involving taxes, subsidies, or nudging and framing devices can be effective in promoting individual well-being, while being less intrusive and hence less damaging of autonomy than bans or other forms of legal restrictions.

9 The Politics of Paternalism

In the preceding chapters we have demonstrated that there is a case for paternalistic interventions by government to address individual reasoning failures. We have also given guidance as to the policy mechanisms that can maximize the benefits of intervention in terms of improving individual well-being, while minimizing the cost in terms of the impact on individual autonomy. However, these contributions on their own are not enough to provide an unanswerable case for paternalistic interventions in every situation of individual reasoning failure. For that would require a demonstration that in the relevant circumstances the government can make better decisions than the individual. The government, after all, is not some abstract entity but is itself a collection of individuals: politicians, civil servants, advisers. Might not these individuals be subject to the very kinds of reasoning failure that we have ascribed to people engaging in self-damaging behavior?

Even if it is possible to demonstrate that the individuals that make up the government are not subject to such failures—or at least are less subject to them, that is still not sufficient to guarantee the success of a paternalistic intervention. For these individuals might use the intervention to pursue their own agendas. Might they be, for instance, rather more concerned with maximizing their own well-being or their own interests than that of the citizens whose well-being or interests they are supposed to be serving? Might they be more self-interested "knaves" than public-spirited "knights" (Le Grand 2006)?

In this chapter we address some of these issues. We begin with a discussion as to whether the government can do better than the individual. We then explore possible ways in which the government could be held to account to ensure that, in its paternalistic interventions aimed at improving the well-being of its citizens, it does actually pursue the "right" agenda.

Can the State Do Better?

A case can be made that the government (or the collection of individuals who make up the government) may not suffer from all the kinds of reasoning failure that, as we specified in chapter 5, can affect individuals' decisions about their own well-being: limited technical ability, limited imagination, limited willpower, and limited objectivity. For these are all personal to the individuals concerned and to their own decisions, and by definition they do not affect people making decisions on behalf of others in exactly the same way.

Indeed the government may have considerable advantages over the individual herself. First, with respect to limited technical ability, the government can dedicate able people or experts to consider certain questions, if necessary over long periods of time. Thus where a decision is subject to particularly complex, technical, or large-scale information difficulties, the government has the resources to employ those best able to devote themselves to the problem full time. For example, in the case of airline safety there may be only a few people who are technically able to assess what would be the outcome of certain standards of safety specification; the rest of us could simply never make more than a guess. Clearly the government official will need to make a judgment that applies to everyone—in this case on the particular level of safety that is deemed minimally acceptable and on the measures needed to ensure that these levels of safety are maintained. This would not be what everyone would choose, given different degrees of risk aversion. But under conditions of complex or overwhelming quantities of information—as suggested by Simon's conception of bounded rationality—it seems reasonable to suppose that, by removing the possibility of significantly mistaken calculation of risk, well-being can be improved by government paternalism.

Where decisions based on probabilities or statistical assessments are concerned, even when the nature of the decision appears to be of no great complexity, people often make erroneous judgments. Again, the information provided to citizens may be "perfect"—they need no extra or qualitatively improved information—but experimental evidence suggests that individuals commonly display inadequate reasoning power to make the correct calculations. Of course, one could argue that the individuals concerned should be aware of their incapacity and seek to "buy advice" on the proper course to take (and this would apply to the airline example above as well). However, often people may not be aware of how limited their reasoning ability is, particularly in relation to apparently simple probabilistic calculations. Furthermore, seeking advice on complex decision making invokes problems of the principal-agent relationship, the agent potentially using his superior understanding to his commercial advantage. When the government undertakes this role, there is perhaps less incentive to exploit the potential consumer.

Second, the government could be argued to have a wider perspective than the individual. This relates to the "limited imagination" category of reasoning failure. In its position of ultimate responsibility for the well-being of its citizens, the government will typically respond when claims are made on it by those in severe hardship. Some of such claims may be the result of some aspect of personal behavior, such as not wearing a seat belt or smoking. The employees in a public health service may be exposed to the consequences of this kind of behavior in a way that many individuals will not be (or not until it is too late). Although public employees have not necessarily *experienced* being in a car crash without a seat belt—no one but the unfortunate crash victim can claim that—their position makes it possible to empathize more accurately with this unfortunate experience than the position of the car driver who has never suffered an accident. They do not suffer from the effects of limited imagination to the same degree that the ordinary citizen does: they observe and deal with actual harmful consequences in real-life situations and can communicate this to policy makers. The government may thus be in a better position to make a judgment on the prudence of the wearing of seat belts than those simply presented with information on abstract possibilities. Put another way, it is in a better position to weigh the costs and benefits (of not wearing a seat belt) than an individual who at any time may see only one side of the picture.

Third, the government could be argued to be more phlegmatic than an individual. This justification relates to the "weakness of will" category of reasoning failure. Unlike individuals, the government is not swayed by immediate gratification (Goodin 1995). The choice between a luxurious holiday now and provision for retirement in the future does not involve a difficulty of temptation for the government. This is not to imply that public officials or politicians are never tempted to abuse or further their own interests. Apart from obvious opportunities for corruption—such as receiving kickbacks in return for the granting of lucrative government contracts—public agencies may suffer from incentives to maximize their budgets for the sake of prestige and kudos, and politicians to maximize their votes, rather than to further the public interest. We discuss this further below. However, the point in this context is that, when they make certain decisions on the citizen's behalf, they do not suffer from the temptation of immediate gratification faced by the citizen herself in relation to that specific decision. The public official may thus be in a position to make a better decision than the individual whenever the good in question involves a significantly delayed payoff—when its benefits accrue at some point in the future, such as contributions to a pension, engaging in healthful behavior, and investing in higher education.

Fourth, the government has an advantage related to the "limited objectivity" failure of reasoning. Indeed that is an advantage that all onlookers or agents typically enjoy, whether academic investigators, employers, professionals, or public employees. Unlike the person making the (potentially) erroneous decision, third parties with no personal interest in the matter can view it objectively. That is, they are not encumbered by the subjectivity that encourages individuals to underestimate their own liability to risk or to misjudge their own fallibility. Subjectivity is of course important in providing a proper motivation for making decisions that accord with one's desires; but here we are concerned with how this subjectivity can occasionally cloud one's judgment. Others may see more clearly what is in our interests exactly because they are not us, just as the football coach is able to see the tactical mistakes of a player who, being bound up in the game, is unaware of his own errors.

So it would seem that the government has several advantages over the individual with respect to many decisions involving reasoning failure, and therefore, by substituting its judgment for that of the individual through a well-targeted intervention, it can raise the individual's well-being. So it *can* do better than the individual; but that does not guarantee that it *will do* better in every case. Are there ways of holding the government to account to ensure that it does only what is right for the individual and does not, for reasons of its own, overreach its authority?

Will the State Do Better?

We have provided a set of justifications for government paternalism, showing how the state can intervene to improve its citizens' well-being, and that, although it can never do so without some impact on individual autonomy, that impact can be minimized. So the government *can* do better. But *will* it do better in practice?

Now if the society concerned were ruled by what might be thought of as a benevolent, infallible dictator—that is, a single, conscious human being who has both the aim of promoting the well-being of the society's citizens and their freedom and the competence to do so effectively—then it might be possible that, armed with the justifications or rationale for paternalism that we have provided, she will always intervene (or take a decision not to intervene) appropriately. But few (no?) societies are actually ruled by competent, benevolent dictators. Indeed, most societies are not ruled by single entities, benevolent or otherwise. Rather, they are governed by a collection of individuals and of organizations of individuals, each with their own agenda, and each interacting with one another in various ways to promote those agendas. Now some of those individuals and organizations will undoubtedly include in their agendas the aims of promoting citizens' well-being and autonomy. One does not have to be overly naive to acknowledge that at times the process of the myriad of personal interactions that lead to policy outcomes will ensure that the aims with which we are concerned (the promotion of citizen's well-being and the preservation of autonomy) come to the fore in determining policy. To take just one example, many countries have successfully introduced a ban on smoking in public places, despite there being relatively little support from economic interest groups for this, and indeed in the face of vociferous opposition from important economic lobbying groups such as the tobacco and hospitality industries.[1]

But at other times, other, more self-interested agendas may dominate the policy-making process. As many critics of government have argued, in democratic societies, politicians will have a strong (indeed, some argue, an overriding) interest in maximizing the votes for them and their party; civil servants often have an interest in increasing their span of control, the number of their subordinates, and the size of their budgets; political advisers will want to keep their jobs; lobbyists will want to further the self-interests of their clients; and so on. These interests will not always conflict with the aims of promoting individual well-being and autonomy—a politician seeking votes, for example, would be foolish to neglect the citizens' concerns for their own well-being and their own autonomy—but on occasion more self-interested concerns will, at best, seriously disrupt the achievement of these aims and at worst, lead to their being lost sight of altogether.

Indeed, some would argue that the very nature of the state itself, as the only legitimate user of coercion, means that, in its decision making it may downplay the importance of, particularly, individual autonomy and hence encourage authoritarianism. They claim that we are in danger of creating a tyranny of do-gooders—a state that governs every aspect of our lives in the name of our own good. In this view, the paternalist concerned with well-being is also a closet authoritarian.

So is there any way of ensuring that the government, in developing "justifiable" paternalistic policies, will primarily consider only its citizens' well-being and autonomy? Can safeguards be put in place that will help prevent it from either slipping down the slope of servicing primarily self-interested political agendas or of promoting an end that may originally have been well-intentioned but that actually results in a suffocating and coercive authoritarianism?

Developing the institutions of democracy is probably the best (or least worst) way of ensuring government good behavior with respect to paternalism. With all its faults, the democratic state incorporates a measure of accountability. The recipient of a government intervention has a means of redress for resisting any paternalism inherent within it. When a democratic

1   In the United Kingdom, although most of the argument over the ban on smoking in public places indeed concerned individual well-being, it was not, overtly at least, concerned with the well-being of smokers (a paternalistic concern) but with the well-being of passive smokers: nonsmokers in the proximity of smokers whose health and comfort might be adversely affected by the smoke (an "externality" concern). But at least there was a concern for someone's well-being.

state enacts laws or introduces policies, there will always be scope for public debate. Furthermore, whether through elections to a representative assembly or through referendums, the citizens subject to a paternalistic policy will have some opportunity to reject it. Debate about the issue will take place quite separately from the operation of the paternalism itself. As we discussed earlier, some policies operate in a silent way—subsidies, for example—and may not be noticed by the individual at the point of their influence. But the enactment of laws is never hidden in open democratic societies where the government must at least seek to justify its actions.

Democratic approval could take the form of what is often termed "tacit consent": that is, the intervention is judged acceptable because no one makes much fuss about it. If such consent were considered to be too tacit, and the approval or disapproval of the policy concerned needed to be more explicit, then, once it had been in place a few years, its continuation could be subject to a vote in the relevant representative chamber, or even subject to a referendum. Indeed the requirement for such a check could be built into the original legislation introducing the policy. A so-called sunset clause could be included in the legislation, stipulating that the policy would expire after a set period unless it were explicitly renewed by a referendum or a vote in the representative assembly.

This separation of the democratic decision to support or reject a policy from how one might feel about a particular intervention as it takes place is important for paternalism. For just as some have argued that the individual voter may not always be trying to maximize his personal gain in elections (Sen 1977), so the separation in time between the democratic decision and the impact of the intervention itself enables voters to record their approval for paternalistic interventions independently of the impact on themselves personally (Goodin 1993; 1995, 145). We noted earlier the idea of second-order preferences underlying the first-order ones, such as the wish not to smoke underlying that decision to light up another cigarette. The time gap between feeling the effects of the intervention and the democratic decision for or against it would give an opportunity for the second-order preferences to be revealed.[2]

Even in the absence of second-order preferences, it is particularly important for paternalistic policies to make use of this democratic time lag because, by its very nature, people will tend to oppose paternalism at the time it takes place. Unless the intervention is completely silent, they will perceive their instant loss of autonomy and, since the well-being gains will often take

---

2   Gerald Dworkin (1988, 15) has made much of the human "capacity to raise the question of whether I will identify with or reject the reasons for which I now act." In other words, people have what Dworkin calls "second-order" preferences about their "first-order" preferences, such as the wish not to smoke just as we light up another cigarette. It is these second-order preferences that could be revealed during a democratic election.

time to arrive and since many will be suffering from limited imagination and find it difficult to conceive of a future state of improved well-being—the status quo bias—they will not be prepared to trade off their loss of autonomy for the gain in their future well-being. But, given time to reflect and review the overall impact of a paternalistic law on their general well-being, people will be in a better position to assess the value of an intervention that may earlier have evoked merely a sense of unwarranted intrusiveness.

So democratic consent of some kind is crucial for the justification of modern paternalism—preferably in the form of some retrospective measure. And, as indicated above, referendums or other forms of direct democracy—whereby citizens effectively bypass the deliberations of a representative national assembly and determine the outcome of a political issue directly—have an appeal as a means of applying the appropriate checks. But referendums do have their own problems—particularly the opportunities they offer for the so-called tyranny of the majority.

Take the following situation.[3] Group A represents taxpayers and voters, and group B the individuals toward whom the paternalistic policy is directed. In the case of direct forms of democracy, the government represents an essentially passive agent operating in between the two. First, consider a situation where no paternalism is at stake: the death penalty. Group A may vote for such a policy that they perceive to be in their interests; legislators would be prevented from obstructing it if the referendum were binding. For some, this is exactly why referendums are important, to prevent the meddling and "antidemocratic" influence of representative democracy; for others, it reflects the more measured and mature approach inherent in a parliamentary system and helps avoid the tyranny of the majority. But it is never questioned that A should at least have their interests taken into account.

But now take a second example: the withdrawal of benefits from people (group B) who refuse the offer of jobs that they are capable of doing. Such a policy may be proposed on the paternalistic grounds that being employed contributes to the mental health of B even if they do not themselves agree and would rather continue living on unemployment benefit. Whether such a paternalistic policy should be adopted would, according to the arguments set out in this book, depend on the evidence that the people in group B suffer from reasoning failure, and the impact such a policy would have on their autonomy.

But under direct forms of democracy, group A will have a determining impact on whether the policy is adopted. And A may not care whether B's mental health is improved, wishing instead simply to ensure that B is prevented from using A's tax revenues to support a life of indolence on the dole. Even if members of group A are not taxpayers, they may nevertheless

---

3 We are grateful to an anonymous reviewer for this suggestion.

wish to see B's "laziness" punished. In both these cases, the motivation is essentially self-regarding on A's part. It may be legitimately self-regarding, but it is not paternalistic—which by definition requires that the good of B is promoted.

In fact there may be a sense that a member of group A does wish to promote the good of B: that is, that she believes it is in the moral interests of the indolent that they should be compelled to work. This would be close to what was termed moral paternalism in chapter 3, itself a form of ends-related paternalism.

So although referendums may have an important role to play in supporting paternalistic policies, it may be that they should be limited to retrospective application when there has been time for experience of the policy by both A and B and mature reflection on it. A paternalistic policy could be proposed and implemented on evidential grounds of the reasoning failure for B, and then subsequently supported or not by a referendum that would also allow for the interests of A to be taken into account. In some cases the interests of both A and B could be served. Indeed the larger the size of group B, the more likely that a referendum will involve a population of voters reflecting and adjudicating on a policy that directly affects them. But if group B is small, we need to be aware that a referendum may well validate a paternalistic policy on the basis of what a majority considers appropriate for a minority, perhaps ends-related or self-regarding, irrespective of the actual good it does them.

Conclusion

We hope to have demonstrated in this chapter that there are circumstances in which the government can do better than the individual in terms of improving the latter's well-being. The government—or the people who make up the government—is unlikely to suffer from the same kinds of reasoning failure as the individual with respect to achieving the latter's own ends and therefore can indeed intervene in ways that promote the individual's well-being better than the individual herself can.

However, the fact that the government *can* do better does not always mean that it *will* do better. The relevant decision makers may make mistakes of their own; or they may have their own interests to pursue that may or may not coincide with the interests of the people they are supposed to be serving. Hence there must be ways in which citizens can hold decision makers to account for their actions to ensure that, in the latter's paternalistic interventions, they do not make errors, overreach themselves, or begin to pursue their own agendas. Although there is no perfect way of holding even democratic governments to account, we have argued that the best—or perhaps the least worst—way of doing so in the case of paternalistic intervention is via a retrospective endorsement of the policy concerned, with either a vote in the representative assembly or a referendum. In either case the endorsement process should take place a few years after the policy has been in place to allow for the electorate to experience the effects of the policy and have time to reflect on it.

10   Nanny State or Helpful Friend?

John Stuart Mill was wrong. In this book we have argued that, contrary to Mill's classic statement on the illegitimacy of government intervention to promote an individual's own good that was quoted at the beginning of chapter 2, there are situations where the government should intervene to save people from the consequences of their own decisions, even if no one else is harmed by those decisions. However, even with justified paternalism, there is an unavoidable trade-off between promoting citizens' well-being and preserving their individual autonomy. Therefore the government's aim should be to develop paternalistic policies that maximize well-being while having a minimal impact on autonomy. The government should act, not as a nagging nanny, but as a helpful friend. In this chapter we summarize the arguments and suggest that they provide a solid foundation for deciding on the appropriateness of government paternalism in general, of different forms of paternalism, and of the various types of paternalistic interventions.

Most of the definitions of paternalism common in the literature are unsatisfactory. For they concentrate on the government, in the name of an individual's own good, paternalistically restricting—or indeed even forbidding—the choices that he or she makes. But interpretations of paternalism defined in this way rule out many forms of government intervention that most would consider paternalistic: subsidies to the arts, which seem to increase, not restrict, the choices available to individuals, and even so-called libertarian paternalistic policies that seem to preserve choice, such as automatic enrollment in pensions or in organ donation programs. It is better to define paternalism in relation to what we have called reasoning failure: a paternalistic intervention is one where the government intends to correct an individual's judgment as to what is the best decision for him or her. Hence we define a government intervention as paternalistic with respect to an individual if it is intended to address a failure of judgment by that individual and if it is intended to further that individual's own good.

But this does not conclude the discussion. For it raises the question as to what constitutes the individual's own good. Here it is useful to distinguish between the *ends* that an individual may have in pursuing her own good and the *means* she uses to achieve those ends. An individual's ends are anything that she wants to achieve by her actions: these are the elements that contribute to her overall well-being. They could be something long term, such as promoting her happiness in old age, or they could be more immediate, such as improving her state of health. The means are the activities she undertakes to promote those ends: her savings, and her current health-related activities and habits, such as (refraining from) smoking. We point out that, while there is no evidence that people make mistakes in deciding on their own ends (indeed it is difficult to see what form such evidence would take), there is a growing volume of evidence from behavioral economics and psychology that even well-informed individuals do make mistakes, or at least misjudgments, over the means for achieving those ends. Collectively we term these misjudgments "reasoning failure" and argue that they arise from four basic sources: limited technical ability, limited imagination or experience, limited willpower, and limited objectivity. In cases where such reasoning failure occurs and where the misjudgments have considerable consequences and can be readily identified, replacing the individual's judgments concerning means by those of the government can be supported on the grounds of increasing well-being.

However, even if we can demonstrate that a particular means-related paternalistic intervention will increase individuals' well-being, this may not be sufficient to justify that intervention. We have argued that there is another important consideration that has to be taken into account: the impact on autonomy. Here the distinction between hard and soft paternalists is important. Hard paternalists are prepared to accept a paternalistic intervention designed to increase an individual's well-being, even if it compromises an individual's autonomy. Soft paternalists, on the other hand, argue that individual autonomy must always be respected, and not traded off for well-being gains. They also argue that it is possible to intervene in others' lives without engaging in such trade-offs because of autonomy failure: the individual's capacity for autonomous decision making is diminished for some reason and therefore is not offended by the intervention. We reviewed the various circumstances in which this autonomy failure takes place and noted the similarities with the various types of reasoning failure we have listed.

We next considered whether the soft paternalistic strategy is successful in avoiding offending autonomy. We argued that it is not. For as long as autonomy has as one of its essential elements the individual's *belief* that he is governing his own life, the object of the intervention will almost always *perceive* his autonomy to be offended. We concluded that soft paternalists are actually not so different from hard paternalists; that both forms of paternalism actually involve trading off well-being improvements against compromises of perceived and actual autonomy; and that, unless one believes that autonomy is a lexicographic right such that no such compromise is ever acceptable, no matter how small the infringement of autonomy or how large the gain in well-being, such trade-offs are inevitable in the realm of practical policy. The aim of policy, however, should be to minimize so far as possible the loss in autonomy, both actual and perceived, while maximizing the gain in well-being.

What are the practical implications of these arguments? Is it possible to identify the areas in practice where some form of paternalistic intervention is most likely to be justifiable? In fact, it is possible to identify categories of consumption or activity that are most likely to be subject to reasoning failures for a large proportion of people because they manifest reasoning failure in most or all of its forms. These are those that

- ⊘ result in a harmful effect that only manifests itself a long time in the future (unhealthy eating, smoking, failing to provide for a pension)
- ⊘ have a very small chance of an immediate catastrophic outcome (driving without a seat belt or riding a motorcycle without a helmet)

These types of activity typically suffer from limited imagination: it is hard to visualize one's future circumstances long into the future, or when the event is very rare. They also are associated with limited willpower—temptation is harder to resist if the benefits from such resistance will not accrue for many years, or if the consequences of a failure to resist seem vanishingly small. And they are linked with limited objectivity—anything risky can be subject to an emotional belief that we are the kind of person that will beat the odds. They may also contain elements of limited technical ability in that a judgment on whether to consume, or to engage in an activity, will involve an accurate assessment of probability, either of an event a long time in the future or of an immediate event with a low probability—something human beings seem quite ill-equipped to do.

If it is accepted that the government is justified in certain circumstances to engage in a paternalist intervention to promote the well-being of its citizens, then how should it do so? There are four basic methods of paternalistic intervention: legal restrictions, positive financial incentives, negative financial incentives, and changes in the choice architecture (libertarian paternalistic or nudge policies). We used two criteria for assessing them: the impact on well-being (the larger the better) and that on autonomy (the smaller the better). We argued that compulsion may score highly on well-being but, since it involves direct coercion, is unlikely to do so on any scale relating to autonomy. Each of the other three is less damaging to autonomy, with libertarian paternalism perhaps the least harmful.

However, there are dangers in legitimating government paternalism in this way. For the government concerned may exceed its authority and undertake paternalistic measures that cannot be justified by the kind of arguments we have been putting forward. This could happen for either of two reasons: the government, or the individuals who constitute the government, may themselves make mistakes in decision making; or, even if they do not make mistakes with their decisions, they may be more concerned with pursuing their own interests than those of the citizens they are supposed to be governing. With respect to the first possibility—that government may make mistakes—while, of course, mistakes will happen, it seems reasonable to argue that they will not be of the same kind that result from the reasoning failure of the individuals affected by the policy measures. For the relevant decision makers have the resources to overcome the technical limitations in processing information that an individual faces in making the relevant decisions, and, because they are obviously distinct from the individual herself, they do not suffer from the other three sources of her reasoning failure: her limited willpower, limited imagination, and limited objectivity. Of course they will have their own reasoning failures that will apply to the decisions that affect themselves; but they will not apply to decisions they make on behalf of others. So, in general, it does not seem unreasonable to assert that the government can do better than the individual in terms of promoting her own well-being by making the appropriate intervention.

What of the danger that those governing the state will promote their own interests rather than those of its citizens? Of course this raises much wider issues than those associated with paternalism. Nonetheless there are concerns specific to paternalistic interventions that, in the name of trying to save individuals from themselves, even democratic governments will in fact be pursuing their own agendas that may or may not include their citizens' well-being and autonomy. So means have to be devised for those affected by the policies concerned to hold the government to account. Here the fact that, in most forms of democratic decision making, whether by representative democracy or by more direct instruments such as referendums, there are gaps between the deliberations over a decision and its implementation offers the opportunity for an important check on paternalistic interventions. For it means that people can review the policy decision at a time that is removed from the point at which they make the immediate decisions concerning the behavior to be affected by the policy; hence they will be less subject to reasoning failure, less personally involved, and, more generally, better placed to make disinterested decisions in the interests of themselves and their fellow citizens.

One way of ensuring that these kinds of checks are enforced is to build what might be termed a sunset clause into paternalistic legislation: that is, the legislation has to be renewed periodically in Parliament, in Congress, or, more generally, by the institutions of representative democracy. This would have a particular advantage in the case of paternalistic interventions because by its very nature people will perceive their instant loss of autonomy and may not be prepared to trade off their loss of autonomy for a gain in future well-being that they find difficult to imagine. But given time to reflect and perhaps to experience at least some of the well-being gains, people will be in a better position to assess the value of the interventions.

The mention of the "value" of the interventions leads us to conclude this book with some more speculative reflections on a rather different kind of political and social problem associated with in paternalism: that of the irritation or resentment that it can create, emotions that often color and indeed contaminate the debates over the nanny state.

We saw in chapter 2 that much of the debate over definitions has been conducted in terms of individual paternalism, and that government paternalism has an important advantage in that it can be subject to democratic control. But there is another important distinction between individual and government paternalism, and that is in the practical way in which the paternalism is implemented. With government paternalism, the involvement of individuals in the paternalism process is limited to policing or monitoring of the regulation, tax, or subsidy. But with individual paternalism—including the actions of professionals or others working for the government—it is the individual himself who makes the paternalistic decision and implements it. With so much of the political debate about paternalism couched in terms of the "nanny state," it is worth analyzing more carefully what "nannying" involves and whether it is as great a problem for government paternalism as is often claimed.

It is individual paternalism that is likely to involve the type of interference that people find most annoying. Imagine a father continually nagging his daughter to give up smoking, or even hiding her cigarettes or throwing them away. Such behavior—however well intentioned—is irritating and captures the essence of what people find objectionable about the idea of paternalism. Now it is quite possible that professionals or other officials working for the government could engage in this kind of nagging, cajoling, or obstructive behavior. Take a government-appointed nurse who continually upbraids a new mother on the importance of breastfeeding, or the local government official who prevents the homeowner from proceeding with a modest development to her house because of some legal technicality. We would contend that it is these types of behavior that are most characteristic of nannying and that lead people to have such disquiet about paternalism.

But does government paternalism actually display these nannying practices? Let us take three of the principal ways in which government paternalism operates: nudges that influence the environment in which choices take place, taxes and subsidies that make goods and services more or less attractive to buy, and legal restrictions that oblige or forbid consumption or behavior. First, we have seen how many of the nudge-type policies are more or less silent, with the individual perhaps now having to make a choice to opt out rather than in, for example, but not being aware that any greater burden has been placed on him. Second, taxes and subsidies merely adjust prices; people are generally used to prices being higher or lower over time, and it is unlikely that price fluctuations are perceived as a conscious intervention to change behavior. Third, legal restrictions, while certainly requiring enforcement, are by no means limited to paternalism. Indeed, the vast majority of laws that prohibit or compel behavior are as a result of nonpaternalistic policies (implementing the harm principle—the criminal law, for example). So, much of the nannying that people perceive is likely to derive from policies directed toward nonpaternalistic ends—such as being forbidden from playing football in a park, or having to obey the speed limit.

Now occasionally it is true that a paternalistic policy may be more intrusive than those just described. A gruesome picture on a cigarette packet, or being forced to make a choice about organ transplants or a pension where none was necessary before, may cause some mild irritation. It is common knowledge that the prices of cigarettes and alcohol are as high as they are because the government wishes to discourage the use of these products, and this too may cause some annoyance. Paternalistic regulations need policing too, whether by the restaurant owner ejecting a recalcitrant smoker, or the police stopping someone without a seat belt. But only in the last two examples is another *individual* intruding and causing the irritation, and even here we typically police ourselves, if only reluctantly. In all the other cases the policy operates, even when not silently, *impersonally*.

The caricature of government paternalism as involving a constant and irritating intrusion in our lives is thus almost always misplaced. Instead, such paternalism usually operates in an impersonal manner—indeed more so than many of the nonpaternalistic rules, laws, and regulations that govern our lives. Policies that, in particular, retain the right to choose, such as taxes, subsidies, and libertarian paternalist policies, constitute a mild and unobtrusive influence on people's behavior. The government can make things better for the individual by such paternalistic interventions; it can be held to account for those interventions; and the interventions do not necessarily make it an infantilizing nanny or an irritating nag. Rather the state— or the government of the state—can help its citizens achieve their own ends, and thereby promote their own well-being and that of the whole society. Not a nanny state—rather, a helpful friend.

Bibliography

Adler, Jonathan. 2002. "Akratic Believing?" *Philosophical Studies* 110 (1): 1–27.

Agulnik, Philip, and Julian Le Grand. 1998. "Tax Relief and Partnership Pensions." *Fiscal Studies* 19: 403–28.

Allender, S., R. Balakrishnan, P. Scarborough, P. Webster, and M. Rayner. 2009. "The Burden of Smoking-Related Ill Health in the UK." *Tobacco Control* 18 (4): 262–67.

Antoñanzas, Fernando, W. Kip Viscusi, Joan Rovira, Francisco J. Braña, Fabiola Portillo, and Iirineu Carvalho. 2000. "Smoking Risks in Spain: Part I—Perception of Risks to the Smoker." *Journal of Risk and Uncertainty* 21 (2/3): 161–86.

Archard, David. 1990a. "Freedom not to be Free: The Case of the Slavery Contract in Mill's *On Liberty*." *Philosophical Quarterly* 40 (161): 453–65.

———. 1990b. "Paternalism Defined." *Analysis* 50 (1): 36–42.

———. 1993. "Self-justifying Paternalism." *Journal of Value Inquiry* 27 (3–4): 341–52.

———. 1994. "For Our Own Good." *Australasian Journal of Philosophy* 72 (3): 283–93.

Aristotle. 1980. *The Nicomachean Ethics*. Translated by David Ross. Oxford World's Classics. Oxford: Oxford University Press.

Arkes, Hal, David Faust, Thomas Guilmette, and Kathleen Hart. 1988. "Eliminating the Hindsight Bias." *Journal of Applied Psychology* 73 (2): 305–7.

Arneson, Richard. 1980. "Mill versus Paternalism." *Ethics* 90 (4): 470–89.

———. 2000. "Perfectionism and Politics." *Ethics* 111 (1): 37–63.

———. 2005. "Joel Feinberg and the Justification of Hard Paternalism." *Legal Theory* 11 (3): 259–84.

Arrow, Kenneth. 1963. "Uncertainty and the Welfare Economics of Medical Care." *American Economic Review* 53 (5): 941–73.

———. 1993. "Excellence and Equity in Higher Education." *Education Economics* 1 (1): 5–12.

Ashcroft, Richard. 2011. "Personal Financial Incentives in Health Promotion: Where Do They Fit in an Ethic of Autonomy?" *Health Expectations* 14 (2): 191–200.

Babcock, Linda, Xianghong Wang, and George Loewenstein. 1996. "Choosing the Wrong Pond: Social Comparisons in Negotiations That Reflect a Self-Serving Bias." *Quarterly Journal of Economics* 111 (1): 1–19.

Barr, Nicholas. 1994. "The Role of Government in a Market Economy." In *Labour Markets and Social Policy in Central and Eastern Europe: the Transition and Beyond*, edited by Nicholas Barr. New York: Oxford University Press.

———. 2004. *The Economics of the Welfare State*. 4th edition. Oxford: Oxford University Press.

Beauchamp, Tom L. 1983. "Medical Paternalism, Voluntariness, and Comprehension." In *Ethical Principles for Social Policy*, edited by John Howie. Carbondale: Southern Illinois University Press.

———. 2004. "Paternalism." In *Encyclopedia of Bioethics*, edited by Stephen G. Post. 3rd edition. New York: Macmillan Reference USA.

Beauchamp, Tom L., and James F. Childress. 2001. *Principles of Biomedical Ethics*. 5th edition. Oxford: Oxford University Press.

Behavioural Insights Team. 2010. *Applying Behavioural Insights to Health*. London: Cabinet Office. https://www.gov.uk/government/publications/applying-behavioural-insight-to-health-behavioural-insights-team-paper.

———. 2011. *Behaviour Change and Energy Use*. London: Cabinet Office. https://www.gov.uk/government/uploads/system/uploads/attachment_data/file/60536/behaviour-change-and-energy-use.pdf.

———. 2012. *Applying Behavioural Insights to Reduce Fraud, Error and Debt*. London: Cabinet Office. https://www.gov.uk/government/publications/fraud-error-and-debt-behavioural-insights-team-paper.

———. 2013. *Applying Behavioural Insights to Charitable Giving*. London: Cabinet Office. https://www.gov.uk/government/publications/applying-behavioural-insights-to-charitable-giving.

Bell, Michael, Eamonn Butler, David Marsland, and Madsen Pirie. 1994. *The End of the Welfare State*. London: Adam Smith Institute.

Berlin, Isaiah. 1958. *Two Concepts of Liberty. An Inaugural Lecture Delivered before the University of Oxford on 31 October 1958*. London: Oxford University Press.

Beshears, John, James J. Choi, David Laibson, and Brigitte Madrian. 2008. "The Impact of Default Options for Retirement Outcomes: Evidence from the United States." In *Lessons from Pension Reforms in the Americas*, edited by Stephen J. Kay and Tapen Sinha. Oxford: Oxford University Press.

Blaug, Mark. 1970. *An Introduction to the Economics of Education*. London: Allen Lane.

———. 1987. *The Economics of Education and the Education of an Economist*. Aldershot: Edward Elgar.

Bovens, Luc. 2009. "The Ethics of *Nudge*." In *Preference Change: Approaches from Philosophy, Economics and Psychology*, edited by Till Grüne-Yanoff and Sven Ove Hansson. Berlin: Springer, Theory and Decision Library A.

Brennan, Geoffrey and Cliff Walsh, eds. 1990. *Rationality, Individualism and Public Policy*. Canberra: Centre for Research on Federal Financial Relations.

Brock, Dan. 1988. "Paternalism and Autonomy: A Review of Feinberg and VanDeVeer." *Ethics* 98 (3): 550–65.

Brock, Gillian, ed. 1998. *Necessary Goods: Our Responsibilities to Meet Others' Needs*. Oxford: Rowman & Littlefield.

Brown, D. G. 1989. "More on Self-Enslavement and Paternalism in Mill." *Utilitas* 1 (1): 144–50.

Buchanan, Allen. 1983. "Medical Paternalism." In *Paternalism*, edited by Rolf Sartorius. Minneapolis: University of Minnesota Press.

Buchanan, Allen, and Dan Brock. 1989. *Deciding for Others: The Ethics of Surrogate Decision Making*. Cambridge: Cambridge University Press.

Buiter, Willem. 2007. "Beware the Perilous Protagonists of Patronising Paternalism: Richard Layard, Julian Le Grand and the New Paternalism." *Financial Times*, October 28. http://blogs.ft.com/maverecon/2007/10/beware-the-perihtml/#axzz2k9cosP5l.

Burrows, Paul. 1993. "Patronising Paternalism." *Oxford Economic Papers* 45 (4): 542–72.

———. 1995. "Analyzing Legal Paternalism." *International Review of Law and Economics* 15 (4): 489–508.

Callahan, Joan C. 1986. "Paternalism and Voluntariness." *Canadian Journal of Philosophy* 16 (2): 199–220.

Callum, Christine, Sean Boyle, and Amanda Sandford. 2010. "Estimating the Cost of Smoking to the NHS in England and the Impact of Declining Prevalence." *Health Economics, Policy and Law* 6 (4): 489–508.

Camerer, Colin F., Samuel Issacharoff, George Loewenstein, Ted O'Donoghue, and Matthew Rabin. 2003. "Regulation for Conservatives: Behavioral Economics and the Case for 'Asymmetric Paternalism.'" *University of Pennsylvania Law Review* 151 (3): 1211–54.

Camerer, Colin F., and George Loewenstein. 2004. "Behavioral Economics: Past, Present, Future." In *Advances in Behavioral Economics*, edited by Colin F. Camerer, George Loewenstein, and Matthew Rabin. Princeton: Princeton University Press.

Camerer, Colin F., George Loewenstein, and Matthew Rabin, eds. 2004. *Advances in Behavioral Economics*. Princeton: Princeton University Press.

Carter, Rosemary. 1977. "Justifying Paternalism." *Canadian Journal of Philosophy* 7 (1): 133–45.

CDC (Centers for Disease Control and Prevention). 2008. "Smoking-Attributable Mortality, Years of Potential Life Lost, and Productivity Losses—United States, 2000–2004." *Morbidity and Mortality Weekly Report* 57 (45): 1226–28.

Chan, Joseph. 2000. "Legitimacy, Unanimity, and Perfectionism." *Philosophy and Public Affairs* 29 (1): 5–42.

Chapman, Gretchen, and Eric Johnson. 2002. "Incorporating the Irrelevant: Anchors in Judgments of Belief and Value." In *Heuristics and Biases: The Psychology of Intuitive Judgment*, edited by Thomas Gilovich, Dale Griffin, and Daniel Kahneman. Cambridge: Cambridge University Press.

Chapman, Simon. 2012. "The Case for a Smoker's License." *PLoSMed* 9 (11): e10001342.doi:10.1371/journal pmed.1001342.

Choi, James J., David Laibson, Brigitte C. Madrian and Andrew Metrick. 2002. "Defined Contribution Pensions: Plan Rules, Participant Choices, and the Path of Least Resistance." In *NBER/Tax Policy & the Economy (Volume 16)*, edited by James Poterba. Cambridge, MA: MIT Press.

Christman, John, and Joel Anderson. 2005. "Introduction." In *Autonomy and the Challenges to Liberalism*, edited by John Christman and Joel Anderson. Cambridge: Cambridge University Press.

Clarke, Simon. 2002. "A Definition of Paternalism." *Critical Review of International Social and Political Philosophy* 5 (1): 81–91.

———. 2003. "Paternalism and Access to Medical Records." *Journal of Information Ethics* 12 (1): 80–91.

———. 2006. "Debate: State Paternalism, Neutrality and Perfectionism." *Journal of Political Philosophy* 14 (1): 111–21.

Cohen, Jonathan. 1981. "Can Human Irrationality Be Experimentally Demonstrated?" *Behavioral and Brain Sciences* 4 (3): 317–70.

Cohn, Elchanan, and Geraint Johnes, eds. 1994. *Recent Developments in the Economics of Education*. Aldershot: Edward Elgar.

Collin, Jeff. 2012. "The Case against a Smoker's License." *PLoSMed* 9 (11): e10001343.doi:10.1371/journal pmed.1001343.

Committee on Higher Education (Robbins Committee). 1963. *Higher Education*. Cmnd. 2154. London: HMSO.

Conly, Sarah. 2013. *Against Autonomy: Justifying Coercive Paternalism*. Cambridge: Cambridge University Press.

Cornes, Richard, and Todd M. Sandler. 1996. *The Theory of Externalities, Public Goods and Club Goods*. Cambridge: Cambridge University Press.

Coulter, Angela. 2002. *The Autonomous Patient: Ending Paternalism in Medical Care*. London: The Stationery Office.

Cudd, Ann E. 1990. "Taking Drugs Seriously: Liberal Paternalism and the Rationality of Preferences." *Public Affairs Quarterly* 4 (1): 17–31.

Culyer, Anthony. 1980. *The Political Economy of Social Policy*. Oxford: Martin Robertson.

Daniels, Norman. 1981. "Health-Care Needs and Distributive Justice." *Philosophy and Public Affairs* 10 (2): 146–79.

———. 1985. *Just Health Care*. Cambridge: Cambridge University Press.

Davis, John K. 2002. "The Concept of Precedent Authority." *Bioethics* 16 (2): 114–33.

de Charms, Richard. 1968. *Personal Causation: The Internal Affective Determinants of Behavior*. New York: Academic Press.

Deci, Edward, and Richard Ryan. 2000. "The 'What' and 'Why' of Goal Pursuits: Human Needs and the Self-determination of Behavior." *Psychological Enquiry* 11 (4): 227–68.

DellaVigna, Stefano. 2009. "Psychology and Economics: Evidence from the Field." *Journal of Economic Literature* 47 (2): 315–72.

DeMarco, Joseph. 2002. "Competence and Paternalism." *Bioethics* 16 (3): 231–45.

De Marneffe, Peter. 2006. "Avoiding Paternalism." *Philosophy and Public Affairs* 34 (1): 68–94.

Deneulin, Séverine. 2002. "Perfectionism, Paternalism and Liberalism in Sen and Nussbaum's Capability Approach." *Review of Political Economy* 14 (4): 497–517.

Department for Work and Pensions (DWP). 2012. *Estimates of the Number of People Facing Inadequate Retirement Incomes*. https://www.gov.uk/government/uploads/system/uploads/attachment_data/file/223015/inadequate_retirement_incomes_july2012.pdf.

Devlin, Lord Patrick. 1965. *The Enforcement of Morals*. Oxford: Oxford University Press.

De Young, Raymond. 1996. "Some Psychological Aspects of Reduced Consumption Behavior: The Role of Intrinsic Satisfaction and Competence Motivation." *Environment and Behavior* 28 (3): 358–409.

Disney, Kate, Julian Le Grand, and Giles Atkinson. 2013. "From Irresponsible Knaves to Responsible Knights for Just 5p: Behavioural Public Policy and the Environment." In *Behavioural Public Policy*, edited by Adam Oliver. Cambridge: Cambridge University Press

Dixon, Nicholas. 2001. "Boxing, Paternalism, and Legal Moralism." *Social Theory and Practice* 27 (2): 323–44.

Donaldson, Cam. 1998. *Why a National Health Service?* London: Institute for Public Policy Research.

Doyal, Len, and Ian Gough. 1991. *A Theory of Human Need*. London: Macmillan.

Dworkin, Gerald. 1972. "Paternalism." *Monist* 56 (1): 64–84.

———. 1981. "Paternalism and Welfare Policy." In *Income Support: Conceptual and Policy Issues*, edited by Peter Brown, Conrad Johnson, and Paul Vernier. Totowa, NJ: Rowman and Littlefield.

———. 1983. "Paternalism: Some Second Thoughts." In *Paternalism*, edited by Rolf Sartorius. Minneapolis: University of Minnesota Press.

———. 1988. *The Theory and Practice of Autonomy*. Cambridge: Cambridge University Press.

———. 2001. "Paternalism." In *Encyclopedia of Ethics*, edited by Lawrence Becker and Charlotte Becker. 2nd edition. London: Routledge.

———. 2005. "Moral Paternalism." *Law and Philosophy* 24 (3): 305–19.

Dworkin, Ronald. 1989. "Liberal Community." *California Law Review* 77 (3): 479–504.

———. 1990. "Foundations of Liberal Equality." In *The Tanner Lectures on Human Values*, Volume 11, edited by Grethe B. Peterson. Salt Lake City: Utah University Press.

———. 2000. *Sovereign Virtue: The Theory and Practice of Equality*. Cambridge, MA: Harvard University Press.

Elster, Jon. 1999. *Alchemies of the Mind: Rationality and the Emotions*. Cambridge: Cambridge University Press.

———. 2000. *Ulysses Unbound: Studies in Rationality, Precommitment, and Constraints*. Cambridge: Cambridge University Press.

Fabre, Cécile. 2006. *Whose Body Is It Anyway? Justice and the Integrity of the Person*. Oxford: Clarendon Press.

Feinberg, Joel. 1971. "Legal Paternalism." *Canadian Journal of Philosophy* 1 (1): 105–24.

———. 1985. *Offense to Others*. Volume 2 of *The Moral Limits to the Criminal Law*. Oxford: Oxford University Press.

———. 1986. *Harm to Self*. Volume 3 of *The Moral Limits to the Criminal Law*. Oxford: Oxford University Press.

———. 1988. *Harmless Wrongdoing*. Volume 4 of *The Moral Limits to the Criminal Law*. Oxford: Oxford University Press.

Feldstein, Martin. 1975. "Wealth Neutrality and Local Choice in Public Education." *American Economic Review* 65 (1): 75–89.

Fischhoff, Baruch. 1975. "Hindsight ≠ Foresight: the Effect of Outcome Knowledge on Judgment Under Uncertainty." *The Journal of Experimental Psychology: Human Perception and Performance* 1 (3): 288–299.

Frankfurt, Harry G. 1971. "Freedom of the Will and the Concept of a Person." *Journal of Philosophy* 68 (1): 5–20.

Frederick, Shane, George Loewenstein, and Ted O'Donoghue. 2002. "Time Discounting and Time Preference: A Critical Review." *Journal of Economic Literature* 150 (2): 351–401.

Freeden, Michael. 1991. *Rights*. Buckingham: Open University Press.

Fuchs, Alan E. 2001. "Autonomy, Slavery, and Mill's Critique of Paternalism." *Ethical Theory and Moral Practice* 4 (3): 231–251.

Garren, David J. 2006. "Paternalism, Part I: Definitional Difficulties." *Philosophical Books* 47 (4): 334–41.

———. 2007. "Paternalism, Part II: Justificatory Gyrations." *Philosophical Books* 48 (1): 50–59.

Gert, Bernard, and Charles M. Culver. 1976. "Paternalistic Behavior." *Philosophy and Public Affairs* 6 (1): 45–57.

Gilovich, Thomas, and Dale Griffin. 2002. "Introduction—Heuristics and Biases: Then and Now." In *Heuristics and Biases: The Psychology of Intuitive Judgment*, edited by Thomas Gilovich, Dale Griffin, and Daniel Kahneman. Cambridge: Cambridge University Press.

Gilovich, Thomas, Dale Griffin, and Daniel Kahneman, eds. 2002. *Heuristics and Biases: The Psychology of Intuitive Judgment*. Cambridge: Cambridge University Press.

Gimbel, Ronald. W., Martin. A. Strosberg, Susan E. Lehrman, Eugenijus Gefenas, and Frank Taft. 2003. "Presumed Consent and Other Predictors of Cadaveric Organ Donation in Europe." *Progress in Transplantation* 13 (1): 17–23.

Glennerster, Howard. 1993. "The Economics of Education: Changing Fortunes." In *Current Issues in the Economics of Welfare*, edited by Nicholas Barr and David Whynes. London: Macmillan.

Glover, Jonathan. 1977. *Causing Death and Saving Lives*. London: Penguin.

Goddard, Eileen. 2006. *Smoking and Drinking among Adults, 2005*. London: Office for National Statistics.

Goodin, Robert E. 1991. "Permissible Paternalism: In Defense of the Nanny State." *Responsive Community* 1 (3): 42–51.

———. 1993. "Democracy, Preferences and Paternalism." *Policy Sciences* 26 (3): 229–47.

———. 1995. *Utilitarianism as a Public Philosophy*. Cambridge: Cambridge University Press.

Goodin, Robert E., and Julian Le Grand. 1987. *Not Only the Poor: The Middle Classes and the Welfare State*. London: Allen and Unwin.

Graham, Andrew, and Gavyn Davies. 1997. *Broadcasting, Society and Policy in the Multimedia Age*. Luton: John Libbey Media.

Gravelle, Hugh, and Ray Rees. 2004. *Microeconomics*. 3rd edition. Harlow: Pearson Education.

Groarke, Louis. 2002. "Paternalism and Egregious Harm: Prader-Willi Syndrome and the Importance of Care." *Public Affairs Quarterly* 16 (3): 203–30.

Gruber, Jonathan, and Sendhil Mullainathan. 2002. *Do Cigarette Taxes Make Smokers Happier?* NBER Working Paper 8872. Cambridge, MA: National Bureau of Economic Research.

Gutmann, Amy. 1980. *Liberal Equality*. Cambridge: Cambridge University Press.

Hart, Herbert. 1963. *Law, Liberty, and Morality*. Oxford: Oxford University Press.

Hausman, Daniel M., and Brynn Welch. 2010. "Debate: To Nudge or Not to Nudge." *The Journal of Political Philosophy* 18 (1): 123–36.

Hayek, Friedrich. 1976. *The Mirage of Social Justice*. Volume 2 of *Law, Legislation and Liberty*. London: Routledge and Kegan Paul.

Häyry, Heta. 1992. "Legal Paternalism and Legal Moralism: Devlin, Hart and Ten." *Ratio Juris* 5 (2): 191–201.

Health and Social Care Information Centre. 2012. *Statistics on Smoking: England, 2012*. Leeds: Health and Social Care Information Centre. https://catalogue.ic.nhs.uk/publications/pub lic-health/smoking/smok-eng-2012/smok-eng-2012-rep.pdf.

Heap, Shaun Hargreaves, Martin Hollis, Bruce Lyons, Robert Sugden, and Albert Weale. 1992. *The Theory of Choice: A Critical Guide*. Oxford: Blackwell.

Hendry, Ross. 1998. *Fair Shares for All? The Development of Needs Based Government Funding in Education, Health and Housing*. London: CASE, London School of Economics.

Hershey, Paul Turner. 1985. "A Definition for Paternalism." *Journal of Medicine and Philosophy* 10 (2): 171–82.

Hill, Thomas E. 1991. *Autonomy and Self-Respect*. Cambridge: Cambridge University Press.

Hobson, Peter. 1984. "Another Look at Paternalism." *Journal of Applied Philosophy* 1 (20): 293–304.

Hodson, John D. 1977. "The Principle of Paternalism." *American Philosophical Quarterly* 14 (1): 61–69.

———. 1981. "Mill, Paternalism, and Slavery." *Analysis* 41 (1): 60–62.

Hurka, Thomas. 1993. *Perfectionism*. New York: Oxford University Press.

———. 2001. "Perfectionism." In *Encyclopedia of Ethics*, edited by Lawrence Becker and Charlotte Becker. 2nd edition. London: Routledge.

Husak, Douglas. 1981. "Paternalism and Autonomy." *Philosophy and Public Affairs* 10 (1): 27–46.

———. 1989. "Recreational Drugs and Paternalism." *Law and Philosophy* 8 (3): 353–81.

———. 2003. "Legal Paternalism." In *The Oxford Handbook of Practical Ethics*, edited by Hugh LaFollette. Oxford: Oxford University Press.

Independent Public Service Pensions Commission. 2011. *Independent Public Service Pensions Commission: Final Report*. London: HM Treasury. http://webarchive.nationalarchives.gov. uk/20130129110402/http://cdn.hm-treasury.gov.uk/hutton_final_100311.pdf.

John, Peter, Sarah Cotterill, Alice Moseley, Liz Richardson, Graham Smith, Gerry Stoker, and Corinne Wales. 2011. *Nudge, Nudge, Think, Think: Experimenting with Ways to Change Civic Behaviour*. London: Bloomsbury Academic.

John, Peter, Graham Smith, and Gerry Stoker. 2009. "Nudge, Nudge, Think, Think: Two Strategies for Changing Civic Behaviour." *Political Quarterly* 80 (3): 361–70.

Johnson, Eric J., and David Goldstein. 2003. "Do Defaults Save Lives?" *Science* 302 (5649): 1338–39.

———. 2004. "Defaults and Donation Decisions." *Transplantation* 78 (12): 1713–16.

Jolls, Christine, Cass R. Sunstein, and Richard H. Thaler. 1998. "A Behavioral Approach to Law and Economics." *Stanford Law Review* 50 (5): 1471–1550.

Jones-Lee, Michael, and Graham Loomes. 2001. "Private Values and Public Policy." In *Conflict and Tradeoffs in Decision Making*, edited by Elke U. Weber, Jonathan Baron, and Graham Loomes. Cambridge: Cambridge University Press.

Kahneman, Daniel. 1994. "New Challenges to the Rationality Assumption." *Journal of Institutional and Theoretical Economics* 150 (1): 18–36.

———. 2000. "Preface." In *Choices, Values, and Frames*, edited by Daniel Kahneman and Amos Tversky. Cambridge: Cambridge University Press.

———. 2011. *Thinking, Fast and Slow*. London: Allen Lane.

Kahneman, Daniel, and Shane Frederick. 2002. "Representativeness Revisited: Attribute Substitution in Intuitive Judgment." In *Heuristics and Biases: The Psychology of Intuitive Judgment*, edited by Thomas Gilovich, Dale Griffin, and Daniel Kahneman. Cambridge: Cambridge University Press.

Kahneman, Daniel, Barbara L. Fredrickson, Charles A. Schreiber, and Donald A. Redelmeier. 1993. "When More Pain Is Preferred to Less: Adding a Better End." *Psychological Science* 4 (6): 401–5.

Kahneman, Daniel, Jack L. Knetsch, and Richard H. Thaler. 2000. "Anomalies: The Endowment Effect, Loss Aversion, and Status Quo Bias." In *Choices, Values, and Frames*, edited by Daniel Kahneman and Amos Tversky. Cambridge: Cambridge University Press.

Kahneman, Daniel, and Amos Tversky. 1973. "On the Psychology of Prediction." *Psychological Review* 80 (4): 237–51.

———. 1979. "Prospect Theory: An Analysis of Decision under Risk." *Econometrica* 47 (2): 263–91.

———, eds. 2000. *Choices, Values, and Frames*. Cambridge: Cambridge University Press.

Kant, Immanuel. (1785) 1981. *Grounding for the Metaphysics of Morals*. Translated by James Ellington. Indianapolis: Hackett.

Kasachkoff, Tziporah. 1994. "Paternalism: Does Gratitude Make It Okay?" *Social Theory and Practice* 20 (1): 1–23.

Kelman, Steven. 1981. "Regulation and Paternalism." *Public Policy* 29 (2): 219–54.

Kleinig, John. 1983. *Paternalism*. Manchester: Manchester University Press.

Komrad, Mark S. 1983. "A Defence of Medical Paternalism: Maximising Patients' Autonomy." *Journal of Medical Ethics* 9 (1): 38–44.

Kronman, Anthony T. 1983. "Paternalism and the Law of Contracts." *Yale Law Journal* 92 (5): 763–98.

Kuflik, Arthur. 1984. "The Inalienability of Autonomy." *Philosophy and Public Affairs* 13 (4): 271–98.

Kultgen, John. 1992. "Consent and the Justification of Paternalism." *Southern Journal of Philosophy* 30 (3): 89–113.

Laibson, David. 1997. "Golden Eggs and Hyperbolic Discounting." *Quarterly Journal of Economics* 112 (2): 443–77.

Le Grand, Julian. 1991. *Equity and Choice*. London: HarperCollins.

———. 2006. *Motivation, Agency, and Public Policy: Of Knights and Knaves, Pawns and Queens*. Oxford: Oxford University Press.

———. 2008. "The Giants of Excess: A Challenge to the Nation's Health." *Journal of the Royal Statistical Society, Series A* 171 (4): 843–56.

———. 2013. "Individual responsibility, health and health care." In *Inequalities in Health*, edited by N. Eyal, S. Hurst, O. Norheim, and D. Wikler. Oxford: Oxford University Press.

Le Grand, Julian, and Bill New. 1999. "Broadcasting and Public Purposes in the New Millennium." In *Public Purposes in Broadcasting: Funding the BBC*, edited by Andrew Graham. Luton: University of Luton Press.

Le Grand, Julian, Carol Propper, and Sarah Smith. 2008. *The Economics of Social Problems*. 4th edition. Houndmills: Palgrave.

Levin, Henry. 1991. "The Economics of Justice in Education." In *Spheres of Justice in Education (American Education Finance Association Yearbook)*, edited by Deborah Verstegen and James Gordon Ward. New York: HarperCollins.

Loewenstein, George. 1996. "Out of Control: Visceral Influences on Behavior." *Organizational Behavior and Human Decision Processes* 65 (3): 272–92.

Loewenstein, George, and Daniel Adler. 1995. "A Bias in the Prediction of Tastes." *Economic Journal* 105 (431): 929–37.

Loewenstein, George, Troyen Brennan, and Kevin G. Volpp. 2007. "Asymmetric Paternalism to Improve Health Behaviors." *Journal of the American Medical Association* 298 (20): 2415–17.

Loewenstein, George, Ted O'Donoghue, and Matthew Rabin. 2003. "Projection Bias in Predicting Future Utility." *Quarterly Journal of Economics* 118 (4): 1209–48.

Lord, Charles G., Lee Ross, and Mark R. Lepper. 1979. "Biased Assimilation and Attitude Polarization: The Effects of Prior Theories on Subsequently Considered Evidence." *Journal of Personality and Social Psychology* 37 (11): 2098–2109.

Madrian, Brigitte, and Dennis Shea. 2001. "The Power of Suggestion: Inertia in 401(k) Participation and Saving Behavior." *Quarterly Journal of Economics* 116 (4): 1149–87.

Malm, H. M. 1995. "Liberalism, Bad Samaritan Law, and Legal Paternalism." *Ethics* 106 (1): 4–31.

Marazziti, D., H. Akiskal, A. Rossi, and G. Cassano. 1999. "Alteration of the Platelet Serotonin Transporter in Romantic Love." *Psychological Medicine* 29 (3): 741–45.

Marshall, T. H. 1950. *Citizenship and Social Class and Other Essays*. Cambridge: Cambridge University Press.

McFadden, Daniel. 1999. "Rationality for Economists?" *Journal of Risk and Uncertainty* 19 (1–3): 73–105.

McMahon, Walter W. 1991. "Relative Returns to Human and Physical Capital in the US and Efficient Investment Strategies." *Economics of Education Review* 10 (4): 283–96.

Meehl, Paul. 1954. *Clinical versus Statistical Prediction: A Theoretical Analysis and a Review of the Evidence*. Minneapolis: University of Minnesota Press.

Mill, John Stuart. (1859) 1974. *On Liberty*. London: Penguin Books.

———. (1863) 1991. *Utilitarianism*. Oxford World's Classics. Oxford: Oxford University Press.

Miller, David. 1992. "Deliberative Democracy and Social Choice." *Political Studies* 40 (Special Issue): 54–67.

Mind. 2006. *The Mental Health Act 1983: An Outline Guide*. Revised edition. London: Mind.

Mitchell, Gregory. 2005. "Libertarian Paternalism Is an Oxymoron." *Northwestern University Law Review* 99 (3): 1245–77.

Munnell, Alicia, Anthony Webb, and Francesca Golub-Sass. 2009. *The National Retirement Risk Index: After the Crash*. Chestnut Hill, MA: Center for Retirement Research, Boston College. http://crr.bc.edu/wp-content/uploads/2009/10/IB_9–22.pdf.

National Committee of Inquiry into Higher Education (Dearing Committee). 1997. *Higher Education in the Learning Society: Report of the National Committee*. London: HMSO.

New, Bill. 1999. "Paternalism and Public Policy." *Economics and Philosophy* 15 (1): 63–83.

New, Bill and Julian Le Grand. 1996. *Rationing in the NHS: Principles and practice*. London: King's Fund.

O'Donoghue, Ted, and Matthew Rabin. 1999a. "Doing It Now or Later." *American Economic Review* 89 (1): 103–24.

———. 1999b. "Procrastination in Preparing for Retirement." In *Behavioral Dimensions of Retirement Economics*, edited by Henry J. Aaron. Washington DC: Brookings Institution Press.

Office for National Statistics. 2012. *Chapter 1—Smoking (General Lifestyle Survey Overview—a Report on the 2011 General Lifestyle Survey)*. http://www.ons.gov.uk/ons/rel/ghs/general-lifestyle-survey/2011/rpt-chapter-1.html#tab-The-prevalence-of-cigarette-smoking.

———. 2013. *Interim Life Tables, England and Wales, 2010–2012*. http://www.ons.gov.uk/ons/dcp171778_329858.pdf.

Oliver, Adam. 2013a. "Introduction." In *Behavioural Public Policy*, edited by Adam Oliver. Cambridge: Cambridge University Press.

———. 2013b. "From Nudging to Budging: Using Behavioural Economics to Inform Public Sector Policy." *Journal of Social Policy* 42 (4): 685–700.

Parfit, Derek. 1984. *Reasons and Persons*. Oxford: Clarendon.

Pensions Commission. 2004. *Pensions: Challenges and Choices. The First Report of the Pensions Commission*. London: The Stationery Office.

———. 2006. *Implementing an Integrated Package of Pension Reforms. The Final Report of the Pensions Commission.* London: The Stationery Office.

Pesendorfer, Wolfgang. 2006. "Behavioral Economics Comes of Age: A Review Essay on *Advances in Behavioral Economics."* *Journal of Economic Literature* 44 (3): 712–21.

Pinker, Steven. 1997. *How the Mind Works.* New York: Norton.

Pope, Thaddeus Mason. 2004. "Counting the Dragon's Teeth and Claws: The Definition of Hard Paternalism." *Georgia State University Law Review* 20 (3): 659–722.

Rabin, Matthew. 2002. "Inference by Believers in the Law of Small Numbers." *Quarterly Journal of Economics* 117 (3): 775–816.

Rabin, Matthew, and Joel L. Schrag. 1999. "First Impressions Matter: A Model of Confirmatory Bias." *Quarterly Journal of Economics* 114 (1): 37–82.

Rainbolt, George W. 1989a. "Prescription Drug Laws: Justified Hard Paternalism." *Bioethics* 3 (1): 45–58.

———. 1989b. "Justified Hard Paternalism: A Response to Ten." *Bioethics* 3 (2): 140–41.

Rapoport, Amnon, and David V. Budescu. 1997. "Randomization in Individual Choice Behavior." *Psychological Review* 104 (3): 603–17.

Rawls, John. 1971. *A Theory of Justice.* Cambridge, MA: Harvard University Press.

Raz, Joseph. 1986. *The Morality of Freedom.* Oxford: Oxford University Press.

Rebonato, Riccardo. 2012. *Taking Liberties: A Critical Examination of Libertarian Paternalism.* Houndmills: Palgrave Macmillan.

Redelmeier, Donald, and Daniel Kahneman. 1996. "Patients' Memories of Painful Medical Treatments: Real-time and Retrospective Evaluations of Two Minimally Invasive Procedures." *Pain* 66 (1): 3–8.

Redelmeier, Donald, Paul Rozin, and Daniel Kahneman. 1993. "Understanding Patients' Decisions: Cognitive and Emotional Perspectives." *Journal of the American Medical Association* 270 (1): 72–76.

Regan, Donald H. 1983. "Paternalism, Freedom, Identity and Commitment." In *Paternalism,* edited by Rolf Sartorius. Minneapolis: University of Minnesota Press.

Richards, Norvin. 1992. "Surrogate Consent." *Public Affairs Quarterly* 6 (2): 227–43.

Rostron, Brian. 2013. "Smoking-Attributable Mortality by Cause in the United States: Revising the CDC's Data and Estimates." *Nicotine & Tobacco Research* 15 (1): 238–46.

Schwarz, Norbert, and Leigh Ann Vaughn. 2002. "The Availability Heuristic Revisited: Ease of Recall and Content of Recall as Distinct Sources of Information." In *Heuristics and Biases: The Psychology of Intuitive Judgment,* edited by Thomas Gilovich, Dale Griffin, and Daniel Kahneman. Cambridge: Cambridge University Press.

Scoccia, Danny. 1990. "Paternalism and Respect for Autonomy." *Ethics* 100 (2): 318–34.

———. 2000. "Moral Paternalism, Virtue, and Autonomy." *Australasian Journal of Philosophy* 78 (1): 53–71.

Secretary of State for Health and the Secretaries of State for Scotland, Wales and Northern Ireland. 1998. *Smoking Kills: A White Paper on Tobacco.* Cmnd. 4177. London: The Stationery Office.

Sen, Amartya. 1970. "The Impossibility of a Paretian Liberal." *Journal of Political Economy* 78 (1): 152–57.

———. 1977. "Rational Fools: A Critique of the Behavioral Foundations of Economic Theory." *Philosophy and Public Affairs* 6 (4): 317–44.

———. 1988. "Freedom of Choice: Concept and Content." *European Economic Review* 32 (2–3): 269–94.

———. 1992. *Inequality Re-examined.* Cambridge, MA: Harvard University Press.

———. 2005. "Why Exactly Is Commitment Important for Rationality?" *Economics and Philosophy* 21 (1): 5–13.

Shafer-Landau, Russ. 2005. "Liberalism and Paternalism." *Legal Theory* 11 (3): 169–91.

Shapiro, Daniel. 1994. "Smoking Tobacco: Irrationality, Addiction and Paternalism." *Public Affairs Quarterly* 8 (2): 187–203.

Sher, George. 1997. *Beyond Neutrality: Perfectionism and Politics.* Cambridge: Cambridge University Press.

Shiffrin, Seana Valentine. 2000. "Paternalism, Unconscionability Doctrine, and Accommodation." *Philosophy and Public Affairs* 29 (3): 205–50.

Shinebourne, Elliot A., and Andrew Bush. 1994. "For Paternalism in the Doctor-Patient Relationship." In *Principles of Health Care Ethics*, edited by Raanan Gillon. London: Wiley.

Simon, Herbert. 1972. "Theories of Bounded Rationality." In *Decision and Organization*, edited by C. B. McGuire and Roy Radner. Amsterdam: North-Holland.

Sneddon, Andrew. 2001. "What's Wrong with Selling Yourself into Slavery? Paternalism and Deep Autonomy." *Revista Hispanoamericana de Filosofía* 33 (98): 97–121.

———. 2006. "Equality, Justice, and Paternalism: Recentreing Debate about Physician-Assisted Suicide." *Journal of Applied Philosophy* 23 (4): 387–404.

Spellecy, Ryan. 2003. "Reviving Ulysses Contracts." *Kennedy Institute of Ethics Journal* 13 (4): 373–92.

Spiecker, Ben, and Jan Steutel. 2002. "Sex between People with 'Mental Retardation': An Ethical Evaluation." *Journal of Moral Education* 31 (2): 155–69.

Stiglitz, Joseph E. 1989. "On the Economic Role of the State." In *The Economic Role of the State*, edited by Arnold Heertje. Oxford: Basil Blackwell.

Strasser, Mark. 1988. "The New Paternalism." *Bioethics* 2 (2): 103–17.

Sugden, Robert. 2009. "On Nudging: A Review of *Nudge: Improving Decisions about Health, Wealth, and Happiness* by Richard H. Thaler and Cass R. Sunstein." *International Journal of the Economics of Business* 16 (3): 365–73.

Sunstein, Cass R. 2002. "Switching the Default Rule." *New York University Law Review* 77 (1): 106–34.

Sunstein, Cass R., and Richard H. Thaler. 2003. "Libertarian Paternalism Is Not an Oxymoron." *The University of Chicago Law Review* 70 (4): 1159–1202.

Taylor, Tamara, Deborah Lader, Aimee Bryant, Laura Keyse, and McDuff Theodore Joloza. 2006. *Smoking-Related Behaviour and Attitudes, 2005.* London: Office for National Statistics.

Ten, C. L. 1971. "Paternalism and Morality." *Ratio* 13 (June): 56–66.

———. 1989. "Paternalism and Levels of Knowledge: A Comment on Rainbolt." *Bioethics* 3 (2): 135–39.

Thaler, Richard H. 1980. "Toward a Positive Theory of Consumer Choice." *Journal of Economic Behavior and Organization* 1 (1): 39–60.

Thaler, Richard H., and Shlomo Benartzi. 2004. "Save More Tomorrow™: Using Behavioral Economics to Increase Employee Saving." *Journal of Political Economy* 112 (S1): 164–87.

Thaler, Richard H., and Cass R. Sunstein. 2008. *Nudge: Improving Decisions about Health, Wealth and Happiness.* New Haven: Yale University Press.

Thompson, Dennis. 1987. *Political Ethics and Public Office.* Cambridge, MA: Harvard University Press.

Tobin, James. 1970. "On Limiting the Domain of Inequality." *Journal of Law and Economics* 13 (2): 263–77.

Tversky, Amos, and Daniel Kahneman. 1974. "Judgment under Uncertainty: Heuristics and Biases." *Science* 185 (4157): 1124–31.

———. 1983. "Extensional versus Intuitive Reasoning: The Conjunction Fallacy in Probability Judgment." *Psychological Review* 90 (4): 293–315.

———. 2000. "Loss Aversion in Riskless Choice: A Reference-dependent Model." In *Choices, Values, and Frames*, edited by Daniel Kahneman and Amos Tversky. Cambridge: Cambridge University Press.

Ullman-Margalit, Edna, and Sidney Morganbesser. 1977. "Picking and Choosing." *Social Research* 44 (4): 757–85.

Vallerand, Robert, and Greg Reid. 1984. "On the Causal Effects of Perceived Competence on Intrinsic Motivation: A Test of Cognitive Evaluation Theory." *Journal of Sport Psychology* 6 (1): 94–102.

VanDeVeer, Donald. 1986. *Paternalistic Intervention: The Moral Bounds of Benevolence*. Princeton: Princeton University Press.

Veatch, Robert M., and Carol M. Spicer. 1994. "Against Paternalism in the Patient-Physician Relationship." In *Principles of Health Care Ethics*, edited by Raanan Gillon. London: Wiley.

Viscusi, W. Kip. 2002–3. "The New Cigarette Paternalism." *Regulation* 25 (4) (Winter 2002–2003): 58–64.

Waldron, Jeremy. 1995. "Money and Complex Equality." In *Pluralism, Justice, and Equality*, edited by David Miller and Michael Walzer. Oxford: Oxford University Press.

Wall, Steven. 1988. *Liberalism, Perfectionism and Restraint*. Cambridge: Cambridge University Press.

Wall, Steven, and George Klosko. 2003. "Introduction." In *Perfectionism and Neutrality: Essays in Liberal Theory*, edited by Steven Wall and George Klosko. Lanham: Rowman and Littlefield.

Walzer, Michael. 1983. *Spheres of Justice: A Defense of Pluralism and Equality*. New York: Basic Books.

Warnock, Mary and Elisabeth Macdonald. 2008. *An Easeful Death—Is There a Case for Assisted Dying?* Oxford: Oxford University Press.

Wasserstrom, Richard A., ed. 1971. *Morality and the Law*. Belmont, CA: Wadsworth.

Weale, Albert. 1978. "Paternalism and Social Policy." *Journal of Social Policy* 7 (2): 157–72.

———. 1983. *Political Theory and Social Policy*. London: Macmillan.

———. 1992. "*Homo economicus, Homo sociologicus.*" In *The Theory of Choice: A Critical Guide*, edited by Shaun Hargreaves Heap, Martin Hollis, Bruce Lyons, Robert Sugden, and Albert Weale. Oxford: Blackwell.

Weinstein, Neil. 1980. "Unrealistic Optimism about Future Life Events." *Journal of Personality and Social Psychology* 39 (5): 806–20.

———. 1996. "Unrealistic Optimism: Present and Future." *Journal of Social and Clinical Psychology* 15 (1): 1–8.

Weinstein, Neil, S. E. Marcus, and R. P. Moser. 2005. "Smokers' Unrealistic Optimism about Their Risk." *Tobacco Control* 14 (1): 55–59.

West, Robin. 1997. "Comment: Rationality, Hedonism, and the Case for Paternalistic Intervention." *Legal Theory* 3 (2): 125–31.

White, Jane. 2008. *Filling America's Empty Nest Eggs: The Crisis Nobody's Talking About*. Retirement Solutions LLC. http://newamerica.net/files/JWhite_whitepaper_401kSecurityAct_1207 .pdf.

White, Stuart. 2004. "The Citizen's Stake and Paternalism." *Politics and Society* 32 (1): 61–78.

Wikler, Daniel. 1979. "Paternalism and the Mildly Retarded." *Philosophy and Public Affairs* 8 (4): 377–92.

Wilkinson, T. M. 2003. "Against Dworkin's Endorsement Constraint." *Utilitas* 15 (2): 175–93.

Williams, Bernard. 1964. "The Idea of Equality." In *Philosophy, Politics and Society: Second Series*, edited by Peter Laslett and Walter G. Runciman. Oxford: Basil Blackwell.

Wolfe, Christopher. 1994. "Liberalism and Paternalism: A Critique of Ronald Dworkin." *Review of Politics* 56 (4): 615–40.

Zamir, Eyal. 1998. "The Efficiency of Paternalism." *Virginia Law Review* 84 (2): 229–86.

Index